Tales of Brooklyn

Stan Fischler

TABLE OF CONTENTS

PHOTO CREDITS

Front and Back Cover photos, photos from the introduction and from chapters "582: Our Castle on Marcy Street," "My Aunt Helen," "Aunt Hattie's Fateful Pursuit of Ice Cream," "The Girl Friends," "Camping Out," "The Day Mom Got Arrested," "They Built a Subway Under My House," "Snow White is My Hockey Coach," "Hungarian Jew and Irish Catholic Become Friends," "Doing the Times Square Trot," "The Drum Lesson," and "Drumming in the Borscht Belt" are courtesy of Stan Fischler from his personal collection

Photo from the chapter "The All-Time Klotz-Fischler Lights-Out Pillow Fight" is courtesy of Paige Grossman

Photos from the chapters "VJ Day and Shrimp with Lobster Sauce," "Vernon Avenue and the Boys on the Block," "Hebrew School, a Trolley Ride, a Blizzard," "Underground and Over-Carpet Hockey," and "Music, Places and Lovely People" are courtesy of Marc Gold

Photo from the chapter "Softball, Hard Feelings and a Blown Pick-off Play" is courtesy of the New York City Dept. of Records

FRONT COVER: Stan Fischler's first time on skates, Vernon Avenue, Brooklyn: 1936

BACK COVER: Stan Fischler on the roof of Ebbets Field: 1956

DEDICATION

My parents, Molly and Ben Fischler, made me what I am today and - as the song goes - I hope you're satisfied.

As Irving Rudd, my pal and Brooklyn Dodgers press agent (1950-57) liked to say, "We were poor but we were having so much fun, we didn't know we were poor."

That pretty much fit The Fischlers of 582 Marcy Avenue. My folks never had a car; my dad labored in a smelly putty factory and my mom's kitchen was smaller than that on a Pullman car. This book has the photo to prove it.

Yet, we got by - another good tune, "I'll Get By" - because I had them. And a Grandma Etel and a Grandpa Simon (*Sziga* in Hungarian), plus the very underrated Aunt Helen, who was like a big sister to me.

We never had a car because we didn't need one. The GG Subway literally ran under 582 Marcy; the Myrtle Avenue El was a half block away. And we were surrounded by trolleys: the Myrtle Avenue, Tompkins Avenue, Nostrand Avenue and Lorimer Street lines, all only a block away.

There wasn't a playground for six blocks, but who needed one? We had Vernon Avenue between Marcy and Nostrand. Except for the occasional car rolling down the dead-end street, we played punchball, stickball, the ever-popular ring-a-levio, hide-and-seek, stoopball, triangle, and box-ball - all in the street, or "gutter" as we liked to call it.

Nor was there a community center in the nabe. Who needed one? All important matters - especially baseball arguments - were dealt with in Al and Shirley's candy store on the corner of Nostrand and Vernon. Instead of champagne, for a couple of pennies you could get a two-cents plain and if you had a nickel, one solid egg creme. (With no egg, no cream and with cream misspelled. You'll note that I've spelled it correctly in the chapters that follow.)

With their meager income, my parents gave me all I needed and dear Uncle Ben provided the Lionel electric train set I coveted. Dad built me a terrific hockey game that enabled me to play right hand against the left and Mom did wonders with lamb chops and letter writing which, I believe, inspires my key-pounding to this day.

Life at 582 was full of stories and a variety of characters. One was Aunt Hattie, "from Albany," who often visited us and who loved ice cream more than anyone I knew - or know. During the record-breaking blizzard of late December 1947, Aunt Hattie was visiting and semi-panicked when she discovered we were out of ice cream. She then dispatched me on an expedition to bring back the Breyer's.

After an hour of plowing my way past shuttered stores, I found a candy store, struggled home and presented the ice cream to Aunt Hattie. Because of the surprise ending to the adventure, I enjoyed telling it to pals from time to time.

One of those times was when I worked with my dear pal, Glenn (Chico) Resch, during a New Jersey Devils road trip. For some reason, Glenn found Aunt Hattie and my ice cream expedition very amusing. But the beauty part was that, over the years, he'd ask me to repeat the tale, and I obliged.

Finally, for some strange reason, two years ago, Chico asked me to write the "Aunt Hattie And The Ice Cream" story and send it to him and his lovely wife, Diane.

They liked it. Then, Glenn uttered the deathless words: "Why don't you write more of those Brooklyn stories from 'way back when'?"

Hmmm, I thought, why not? So I wrote another and sent it to him; and it, too, got a thumbs-up from Diane and Chico. And, by the third one, I was enjoying the tales and the writing.

By the twentieth, my wonderful literary agent, Doug Whiteman, said "Write ten more and we'll have a book."

I wrote fifteen more and we do have a book. But - and this is a big BUT - not without the support of pals who, in one way or another, provided encouragement. Big time.

Self-publishing costs dough-re-me and Doug was front and center, with a generous donation of time, editing and the needed shekels.

Still, there were more costs to cover. Marc Gold, who for decades has been like my kid brother, delivered side-by-side with my former intern and great pal, Sreesha Vaman. They put us over the top, and Chico added the cherry.

Special thanks to Hillel Kuttler: Without your diligence, enthusiasm, professionalism and caring about this project, the book would never have materialized in its present form. Thanks – a thousand times thanks for all you've done. Or, to put it the 582 way, you are the quintessential pal's pal.

Other good friends came through with key support. Huge thanks to Nancy Schuckman, her pal Raseh Nagi, Abe (Vernon Avenue) Yurkofsky and Cousin Joan Anderman. Plus a host of others -- and you know who you are. THANKS!

Oh, yeah, The Dedication.

Howie Sparer was my best friend and never-ending source of encouragement until his passing - far too young - in 1963. Howie was as big a part of my young life as anyone while being one of the nicest lads ever to grace this earth.

To my parents and the memory of Howie Sparer, these BROOKLYN TALES are dedicated.

And, of course, this collection is dedicated to my sons, Ben and Simon, who got a taste of Brooklyn and for whom this was written along with Ezra, Odel, Ariel, Niko and Avigail, my beloved grandchildren. It will give them an idea how *zeda* and *abba* was at their age.

FOREWORD

An Ode To Shirley

The stories you will read here about my upbringing and early-adult life in Brooklyn, N.Y. -- while inspired by my friend and ex-NHL goaltender, Glenn Resch -- were told long before he urged me to write them. In fact, my telling of them dates back to 1967, when I had the good fortune to meet Shirley Walton, date her, become engaged to "Toots" and marry her in 1968.

By that time she not only had heard my "The Original" Aunt Hattie ice cream story, but met Mrs. Sheier at her Albany home. Shirley was a dedicated listener, and on our trips driving to Chateau Fischler in the Catskills, she learned how Howie Sparer and I nearly kidnapped a Brooklyn trolley car in Sea Gate, how I chased Stuie Karger into a 1934 Cadillac -- Stu survived -- during a game of Ring-a-levio in 1943 and what Vernon Avenue was like as a home for chums playing punchball, stoopball, two-hand touch football and other street games.

By the time our two boys, Simon and Ben, were old enough to read, Toots had heard just about every one of these Brooklyn Tales, and so had the boys. Way back then, Shirley suggested that I write down my adventures as a lad who went to the Kismet Theater every Saturday matinee, how I befriended an Irish-Catholic hockey nut named Jim Hernon from Woodside, Queens, and how I -- thanks to Jim -- became a loyal member of the Woodside Whippets in the Queens YMCA Roller Hockey League, whose president was Frank Tempone.

At the time she urged me to write, I begged off on the grounds that I was too busy with hockey, parenting and what not. As usually was the case, Toots was right. I should have started writing these tales a long time ago. My only regret is that Shirley never got to see them in print, but she always was an intent, inspiring listener.

Which is why this collection is dedicated to Toots and why -- in between writing chapters -- I penned the following essay, *Hockey's Female Pioneer: Shirley Walton Fischler*.

INTRODUCTION

HOCKEY'S FEMALE PIONEER

Shirley Walton Fischler

At a time when more women than ever are succeeding in all aspects of the hockey world, I respectfully suggest a brief pause to remember a female hockey pioneer, long forgotten.

That would be my late wife, Shirley Walton Fischler.

I'm reminded of Shirley for a couple of reasons not the least of which is that she would have recently celebrated her 80th birthday. (She died of cancer six years ago.) For the record, we were married for 48 years.

Women who have succeeded in high hockey places such as Cammi Granato, Jessica Berman, Kathryn Tappen, Shannon Hogan and AJ Mleczko just to name a few, would have loved Shirley because she did what no other woman had done.

Success stories that include Kendall Coyne-Schofeld, Theresa Feaster, Alexandra Mandrycky and Meghan Chayka are others who would have admired Shirley's breakthrough bid.

Simply put, she broke the press box's gender barrier almost a half-century ago. Her campaign for female journalistic equality began at the start of the 1970s and finally succeeded in 1972.

Stan and Shirley at home

But why did it remain a virtual secret when it could have been a big story?

"Shirley's problem," one close friend observed, "was that she needed a good press agent. She wasn't looking for attention -- just equality."

But, "Toots," as she was known to family and friends, wasn't one for thumping her tub. Matter of fact, she shunned publicity. The limelight, she insisted, was for others.

Ironically all of this was happening while she was hosting a weekly one-hour radio program, *"Young Side,"* for the American Broadcasting Company (ABC), one of the three largest networks in the U.S.

She also was an accomplished hockey writer who was refused access to the Madison Square Garden press box simply because she was a woman.

She had been assigned to cover a Rangers-Maple Leafs playoff series for a leading Canadian daily newspaper, the Kingston, Ontario Whig-Standard. But it wasn't as easy as that.

Individual Rangers press tickets clearly stated, "Women not permitted in the press box." It was there in writing for every single game.

Stan and Shirley playing table hockey

When she attempted to cover the first Leafs-Rangers game at MSG during those playoffs, she was politely denied entry. This despite the fact she already had a long list of hockey writing credits.

She was co-editor-columnist of *Action Sports Hockey* magazine. She had co-authored hockey books and also was writing assorted features for the *Toronto Daily Star* newspaper, then Canada's most popular journal.

Shirley believed she had every right to sit with the gentlemen journalists and once chronicled her saga in a magazine story. It went this way:

"My moment of glory-infamy started in 1970 when I naively applied for 'Associate' membership in the Professional Hockey Writers' Association (then called the NHL Writers' Association).

"I had been writing hockey for two years on a regular basis and according to the constitution of the organization, I qualified for membership. I knew that the PHWA has something to say about who got into press boxes.

"I applied to the PHWA president of the New York chapter and was told that women could not belong to the organization because that would give me access to the press box and they didn't want that.

"I was also told that part of the problem was 'The dressing room.' Well, guess what? I didn't want to be in the sweaty, liniment-smelling dressing room with a horde of exhausted athletes and reporters."

A meticulous researcher, Shirley read the fine print of the PHWA constitution and found the secret words -- "an organization for men."

But the PHWA quickly changed the word "men" to "persons" and found still another way to erect a no-female curtain around membership.

Shirley: "The PHWA did away with 'Associate' members which was my qualification for the organization. Even free-lance members were no longer qualified. That eliminated my husband, Stan, from membership."

The easy way out was to forget about it, but that would be ducking this segregation problem. No way would Shirley do that.

When Bob Owen, publisher of the prestigious Kingston Whig-Standard, hired her to cover the '71 playoffs in New York, she took her Olivetti typewriter up to the MSG press box.

The press box steward politely told her she could not enter. As it happened former Yankees pitcher-turned-broadcaster Jim Bouton was right behind Shirley and said he would be her witness if and when it came to trial.

Meanwhile, she had to sit in a regular cramped side arena seat with her typewriter on her lap and stat sheet under her right buttock. She filed her story and then decided enough of this nonsense was enough.

"I'm going to take this to the New York City agency that handles these matters," she told me.

A woman named Eleanor Holmes Norton ran the city's Human Rights Commission and ordered a formal hearing. But not before Shirley felt the wrath of the opposition.

Shirley: "I was called a 'crybaby,' a 'troublemaker,' and a 'publicity hound,' just to name a few of the mildest expletives."

Rangers general manager Emile (The Cat) Francis and his publicist were polite but went along with the opposition. Only one journalist took Shirley's side -- Neil Offen, a young *New York Post* reporter.

Offen wrote a column supporting Shirley's bid for press box entry. After hearing both sides of the issue, Eleanor Holmes Norton decided in Shirley's favor and she finally was admitted to the media section.

Stan and Shirley with The Cup at the Islanders' victory party after the club had won its fourth consecutive title

I still have the official confirmation papers before me, dated November 16, 1972. One is from MSG's rep, John C. Diller, and the other from the Human Rights Commission's Joy Meyers.

Still, it was tough on my wife. "I had to face all the male writers who had been calling me names -- or worse, trying to ignore me for two years," she remembered. "I still had to prove I was the professional I said I was."

That was accomplished with her game stories, features and attendance at her first post-game media scrum led by g.m. Francis. The "showdown" took place when Francis entered the press room.

Shirley: "I was positive that he'd pretend I didn't exist."

The Cat instantly noticed her and said, "Hi-ya, Shirley," in the pleasantest tones. "How's it going? How've ya been?"

Emile made her feel warm and welcomed and known. And when the press conference was over, she walked out with notes in hand and her professional face cool and composed.

"As I walked past some of the (male) reporters," she recalled, "one of the men leaned to another and whispered loudly: 'Who's that, one of the player's wives?'"

Shirley not only shrugged it off, she returned to the typewriter -- later computer -- and continued to reel off "Firsts" that went completely unnoticed. To wit:

* Shirley and Yours Truly became the first husband and wife team to work together on hockey television. The season was 1973-74; an entire season of New England Whalers games for Boston TV.

* Shirley was the last journalist to interview Hall of Fame goalie Terry Sawchuk before he died. Her interview appeared in the *Toronto Daily Star*.

Terry Sawchuk: 'can never come back from this'

By SHIRLEY WALTON
Special to The Star

* She was the architect of the Macmillan *Hockey Encyclopedia*, which remains the best research volume in the sport.

* She wrote more hockey books than any of the PHWA writers who banned her from membership.

The list goes on and, by now, you get the point.

Shirley Walton Fischler was a courageous leader in the women's battle for equality and opportunity in hockey's journalistic world.

It's time that this "secret" gets some attention and recognition!

PART ONE
My Brooklyn

582 -- OUR CASTLE ON MARCY AVENUE, THEN AND NOW

If -- in the year 1939 -- you were standing across the street from 582 Marcy Avenue in Williamsburg, Brooklyn, you wouldn't find anything particularly impressive about that three-story brownstone.

It looked a lot like 584, where the hated Grubers lived. Grandma Etel Friedman believed the Grubers deserved the all-time Brooklyn Antipathy Award simply because they were Litvaks (Lithuanian Jews) and not Hungarian Jews like Etel.

Our sister brownstone, 586, at the corner of Vernon Avenue, was a bit classier than 582. It featured bushels of neatly-trimmed shrubbery and a tiny front garden, but most of all, the ultra-gorgeous Florence Myers.

My grandfather, Simon Friedman, owned 582. (He couldn't care less about the Litvaks next door.) Gram and Gramp lived downstairs and had a bedroom on the second floor in the back.

Their high-ceilinged bedroom included a panoramic view of the backyard and the huge, royal-blue (Toronto) Maple Leaf which I painted on the far brick wall because I loved the Leafs. (It did not win critical acclaim.)

Also, the oversized Leaf was surrounded by two large hockey sticks and a puck. The unauthorized art work was completed while everyone else was out of town on vacation. (I deftly hid from view on their return.)

The second floor also had another bedroom; this belonging to my Aunt Helen -- my mom's kid sister. Aunt Helen -- alias "Hale" -- was a spinster, which, in a way, was nice for me. I, therefore, had an "older sister."

On the top floor was Chez Fischler, where my parents moved at the very height of The Great Depression. To say that our apartment was small would be insulting to the word *tiny*.

When we moved to 582, our minuscule abode didn't even have a kitchen. And if you didn't own an electron microscope you might have had trouble finding the bathroom, virtually hidden near the staircase. (But it worked.)

Who cared? Not me. The roof didn't leak, the subway station was down the block and we finally found someone who magically could turn a hallway into a kitchen. Some would call him a magician. I called him Uncle Sam.

Uncle Sam Pelton converted the corridor into a kitchen. He barricaded one end, installed a sink, then a skinny refrigerator and finally a skinnier gas stove. Poof! Just like that we had a tiny kitchen that worked.

Molly Fischler in the tiny kitchen of 582 Marcy

My guess is that 582 was built in the late 19th century, when heat was produced via a coal stove in the cellar. But wise Grampa was no friend of bitumen and replaced coal with gas heat, a Marcy Avenue first!

For my money, the best part of 582 was the backyard. Compact? Yes, but curiously refreshing nonetheless. And the most arresting curiosity was the large, green growth sprouting on the left.

Just to simplify forestry terminology, we called it a "tree" but that's like calling a donkey a horse. That leafy green growth was best described by our unofficial botanist, Aunt Helen, as "an overgrown bush." So be it.

Thing was, our tree-bush was tall as a small oak, provided umbrella-like shade and boasted a Currier & Ives look after a solid snowstorm. When all's said and done, a bush wouldn't call it a bush, nor a tree call it a tree.

At age ten, I tried to turn the backyard into a mini-Ebbets Field; in other words, a wrist-watch-sized ball field. The teams were divided by two: me against Howie Sparer. He pitched, I hit. Then, I pitched and he hit.

Half the hits were four-baggers since the ball often landed in the backyard of 584 Marcy. By the time either one of us could vault the wood fence, retrieve the ball and vault again, the other guy enjoyed an inside-the-park homer.

Cousin Joan Friedman -- seven years younger than me -- found exciting 582 sport on the hall staircase leading to my grandparents' bedroom.

"There was a smooth banister next to the stairs," Joan recalled, "and I made a practice of sliding down it from the second to the first floor. This was a big thrill for a girl like me who lived in an apartment house."

Cuz Joan made the mistake of saying that 582 had a "basement" where she also played games. Basement? No. Cellar? Yes, because it more resembled an 18th Century English coal mine than a finished basement.

That said, Larry Shildkret and I once turned the facsimile coal mine into a ball hockey rink. That experiment lasted ten minutes, enough time for Grandma Etel's S.O.S. (She feared poisonous dust fumes from below.)

The only sane game we played at 582 involved the one-story downstairs bathroom extension that fronted on the backyard. It was called Off The Roof, and only required a used tennis ball and the palms of two hands.

Cousin Joan: "We'd toss the ball up onto the one-story roof and then had to guess where it would roll down. The 'game' aspect depended on how many times you could catch the ball out of ten throws."

Speaking of sporting relatives, the good "sport" of 582 was my athletic Aunt Helen. She skied when no one else skied. Also, she ice skated on racing blades, played tennis at Prospect Park and loved hiking.

I never went skiing with Aunt Helen, but when spring arrived, she'd take me along on jaunts to Bear Mountain with her pals in the New York Hiking Club. (That's when Hale, as she was known, was most like a big sister to me.)

No question, Grandma Etel was the Queen Victoria of 582. Uncle John Cooke -- an orphan who was raised by Etel -- nicknamed her "Fif," as in *Mademoiselle Fifi*, via the novel by Guy De Maupassant.

As queen of 582, Fif had written her own Constitution. Article One demanded that there be no smoking of "stinky" cigars. The rule was aimed at Grandpa Simon, alias Cziga. (That's Hungarian for Simon.)

Since Grandpa Simon smoked his "stinky" cigars all day at his putty factory, no problem. When he arrived home, Cziga beat Fif's no-cigar-smoking rule with an adroit, neighborhood end run.

Grandpa Simon would remove the cellophane wrapping from a fresh Phillies cigar, light up and then walk around the neighborhood for a half-hour, blowing smoke like a freight yard switching a locomotive.

When he returned to 582, Gramp would take what was left of the cigar and hide it in the mailbox. On his next walk, he'd grab the unused cigar, light up, head for Vernon Avenue and do one more choo-choo-train imitation.

To the family, 582 was known as Grand Central Station. Among relatives and friends, it was a place to convene, shoot the breeze, eat and to the great pleasure of Uncle Ed, have a good snooze.

The guaranteed night when 582 bulged with relatives was Erev Pesach, the evening before Passover. For this holiday, Cziga orchestrated services with Maxwell House Coffee *haggadahs* for all worshippers.

Not that it was a totally serious occasion. Uncle Ben, who always made a point of sitting opposite me, would flash one of his assortment of funny faces and I, in turn, would work very hard not to laugh; and always fail.

Guaranteed at every Seder was the fight card, starring all daughters-in-laws armed with their feuds. Most of the verbal battles -- no punches ever were tossed -- took place in the kitchen within earshot of the dinner table.

The U.S. Army would have described the content of 582 feuds as "Chicken Shit."

Cousin Joan: "My mother (Aunt Lucie) was criticized for using the non-kosher soap for washing the dishes. On the way home, she would complain about the mens' undershirts showing from an open collar. In other words, they weren't wearing ties!"

As for 582's neighborhood make-up, unofficially it was four-fifths white -- Jews, Italians, Irish -- and one-fifth black. The blacks were mostly confined to dilapidated tenements around the corner under the Myrtle Avenue el.

There were no neighborhood changes until the post-World War II years. The word "mugging" was unknown and therefore unspoken. But that would change starting in 1947.

At that time, wrecking balls invaded the turf north of Myrtle Avenue and soon the low-income Marcy Houses -- alias "Projects" -- emerged. By 1950, white flight had reached its peak.

Fear moved in and our neighbors moved out. The Sparers relocated to fancy Flatbush and the Birnbaums to Long Island. We stayed put until 582 Marcy had become the second-to-last white family residence in sight.

I personally felt the change for the worse one night during a casual five-block walk to Lewis Avenue and back. In the midst of my walk, the stroll turned to a jog. I was worried about being mugged. Period!

The nabe got worse after Grandpa Simon died and Aunt Helen suffered a fatal brain tumor. Eventually Fif was moved to the Coney Island Hebrew Home for the Aged. Fif issued this complaint of the facility: "Too many Litvaks!"

My parents relocated to a Mitchell-Lama middle-income co-op across from Pratt Institute and 582 was put up for sale. The once handsome, well-kept three-story brownstone pulled in five grand. (Repeat: FIVE GRAND!)

By that time, I was newspapering at the *New York Journal-American* and had moved into a Manhattan apartment on East 19th Street and First Avenue with my pal, Dave Perlmutter.

I grudgingly returned to 582 only twice more. In 1981, my friend, Bob Stampleman, a Montrealer, requested a tour of Williamsburg, so I took him to our former castle on Marcy Avenue.

Alas, there was no 582!

The corner house, 586, also was non-existent. The Grubers' brownstone, 584, had been reduced to a 15-foot pile of rubble. As for our former castle, there were just hints of a brownstone house having been there.

Actually, it looked as if a bomb had scored a direct hit, leaving only the left and right walls intact. On closer examination, I could see through to the backyard and -- there it was -- a faded royal blue Maple Leaf on the garage wall!

As we drove away, all I could think of was bandleader Count Basie's vocalist, Jimmy Rushing, warbling "What Has Become Of The You And Me That Used To Be?"

My second and last *Tour de Marcy* took place a few years ago after my pal Glenn "Chico" Resch urged me to take him to the old nabe. A Canadian from Regina, Saskatchewan, Resch was curious about The Burg.

I parked at the corner of Marcy and Myrtle and walked with him to where 582 used to be. The bombed-out crater was gone. In its place was a handsome, almost-finished, three-story, streamlined edifice with a sign out front, New Condo For Sale – yet another signal of Williamsburg's gentrification.

After briefly checking out the new 582, Resch noticed a black lady with two kids standing at the corner of Marcy and Vernon. He walked over and asked if she lived in the neighborhood.

"Yes," she replied. "I'm on the next block -- Willoughby."

"Do you like this area?" Chico went on.

"I love it," she countered with a slight hint of doubt, "but I gotta leave soon."

"How come -- if you like it so much -- you're gonna go bye-bye?"

"Can't afford it anymore!" she shot back. With that, the lady grabbed her kids and crossed Vernon en route to overpriced Willoughby.

Resch and I returned to the car and headed back to Manhattan.

"So," he asked me, "whaddya thinking?"

After a short pause, I was reminded of a novel by one of North Carolina's most famous authors.

"Ya wanna know something, my fine-feathered friend?" I concluded. "Thomas Wolfe was right. You *can't* go home again."

(P.S. I never did and never will!)

The back wall, complete with maple leafs, at 582 Marcy

MY AUNT HELEN -- OR BIG SISTER -- OR BOTH; TAKE YOUR PICK

She was my mother's kid sister, but not by much. Only a couple of years separated them.

She was my big sister, so to speak, although we were separated by a lot of years.

Helen Friedman, alias "Hale," lived on the second floor of 582 Marcy, one floor below us. Like everyone else in the family, she hung out in the downstairs living room -- or kitchen, if she wanted dinner.

I got to like my Aunt Helen at an early age and for a lot of reasons – mostly because she was nice to me 99 44/100 of the time.

Only once time did Hale let me down. Likewise, I disappointed her once, big-time.

Like my Mom and Aunt Hattie up in Albany, Helen was an athlete. When I was seven years old in 1939, I discovered two long slats of wood hidden behind the cellar door. Turns out that they were skis. Long before most folks took to the sport, Hale was riding New York Central's Ski Train on Sundays up to Phoenicia, New York, two hours away.

The mountain – and I use the word very loosely – outside the Catskills village boasted the first rope tow in New York State. Aunt Helen rode the rails there almost every winter weekend until sadly, around 1946, The Central discontinued its Ski Train.

When Hale wasn't skiing, she'd don her ice-racing blades and hustle over to the Brooklyn Ice Palace on Atlantic Avenue near Bedford Avenue and hope that Olympic gold-medal speed skater Irving Jaffee would ask her to do a pairs-only skate.

"All the girls wanted to skate with Irving," Aunt Helen would say. "He was a good-looking guy, Jewish and an Olympic champ. I would love to have gone out on a date with Irving Jaffee."

But that never happened.

As far as I could tell, not many guys dated Hale, and I never could figure out why. Granted, she wasn't as pretty as Molly Fischler, my mom – nor as convivial as their sister, Aunt Hattie.

Yet Hale was attractive in a pleasant sort of way. She had a nice body, good legs and a warm, if not beautiful, face - *punim*, as we would say in Yiddish.

I didn't worry too much about Aunt Helen's love life, except once. She was an avid member of the New York Hiking Club and began dating a fellow member named Lyman Barry.

One night while I was hanging out on the first floor, Lyman came a-courtin'. I vividly remember having a feeling that maybe this guy actually would marry Hale. But he never showed up at the house again and that was that.

In her role as my big sister, Aunt Helen would take me places and do fun things, like invite me to her workplace. That was a big deal for me because of the work and the place.

This was 1942, the war was on and my aunt was working at what we called "a defense job" or "war work."

Hale was nothing like the ubiquitous Rosie The Riveter. Her contribution to the war effort was accomplished in a small plant on Bergen Street, a few blocks south of Court on the fringe of downtown Brooklyn.

The factory produced goggles for the U.S. Army, Navy and Coast Guard. A neat guy named Harry Biegeleisen was her boss, and on my occasional visits, Mr. B would gift me with a pair of goggles of my choice.

Harry Biegeleisen, Inc., conveniently was located just a block from a very unusual subway station labeled Court Street. It happened to be the terminal of a "Shuttle" subway service in Brooklyn -- the curious HH Local.

Originally, the HH line was to be part of the Second Avenue subway planned in 1928 to run from Manhattan as a super-express all the way out to Brooklyn's Coney Island.

Two stations in Brooklyn actually were built for the HH: the aforementioned Court Street and Hoyt-Schermerhorn, which encompassed no less than six tracks, two of which were reserved for the HH.

But The Great Depression wasted the blueprints for the Second Avenue line. Now, in 1942, all the HH had to show for itself was the shuttle connecting Hoyt-Schermerhorn and Court, a line on which I traveled with Hale to Harry Biegeleisen's.

For little old me the HH was like a private, underground limo. Hardly anybody ever rode the HH because it operated virtually parallel to the existing GG Brooklyn-Queens crosstown local.

But I loved the HH for its Toonerville-type run. Often alone on the HH, I'd muse about what an evening with Hale would be like this time.

Once she finished work, we'd stroll along Court Street, enjoying each other's company. But one such stroll remains riveted in my mind, I guess because of the timing and the weather -- it was snowing -- and Hale.

It was two weeks before Christmas, and although Court Street wasn't known for its attractive stores, one establishment caught my eye because it wasn't what it was supposed to be: an auto-supply shop.

Pyramid Auto's show window didn't feature tires or auto batteries. Instead of car jacks there was a Lionel electric train chugging past such table games as Big Business and Parcheesi. To say the least, I was riveted.

It was like the department store window in Jean Shepherd's *Christmas Story*. And like Ralphie, I was very happy to merely gawk and appreciate the display for what it was: a toy department in an auto-parts store.

"Isn't it neat?" I remarked to Aunt Helen. She nodded agreement, although I could tell that Hale wasn't as appreciative of the O-gauge freight set that was circling the window as I was.

My favorite days with Aunt Helen were Sundays from 1940 until war's end. This was good, outdoor stuff, far from the madding city crowd.

As a loyal member of the New York Hiking Club, she would be up early and head off to such exotic places as Bear Mountain State Park and Harriman State Park, where the air was clean and there were trails everywhere.

A hike with Hale was good stuff because her companions were fun people and they had no problems having a kid traipse along with them. One of my best trips with them involved what hikers called a trail-clearing expedition. The NYHC group that day crossed a pair of peaks on the Timp-Torne Trail.

Aunt Helen and I would ride the Cortlandt Street ferry from lower Manhattan across the Hudson River to Weehawken, New Jersey, where the New York Central's West Shore Line had its terminal.

In the early 1940s, the NYC ran regular trains up to the Catskills. It was a colorful ride at water level along the Hudson in old passenger coaches pulled by a steam engine. I could have stayed on that train all day.

We'd get off at Tompkins Cove station and then walk a mile to the Timp-Torne trailhead. Our job was to cover the trail and clear the debris that clogged its path. It was pleasant, rewarding and good exercise.

The capper came at about 4:30 p.m. when the trail's blue-and-white markers led to Bear Mountain Inn. All things considered, the warm, hospitable inn was about as pleasant a landing strip as one could seek at the end of a hike.

After a hearty, well-deserved dinner, we hustled down to the Bear Mountain train station. You could almost hear the tune -- "Waitin' For

The Train To Come In" -- as it whistled 'round the bend overlooking the broad Hudson.

Steam locomotives always knocked me for a loop, and this was no exception. I was weary but never happier as the old Central West Shore chugged its way to Weehawken.

On another Sunday, we'd do our hiking somewhere near Millburn, New Jersey, or up in Westchester County, New York, not far from Ardsley, home of the best ice cream parlor this side of the DeKalb Avenue Sugar Bowl in my home borough.

Those were the good days with Aunt Helen. The bad one should have been a good one, but I botched it big-time.

Suffice it to say, I meant well when I invited Hale to be my guest at a hockey game at Madison Square Garden. I figured it would be a token of my appreciation for all the neat things she'd done for me.

This was a Sunday afternoon double-header at The Garden, and now we were immersed in the second game, involving the Eastern Hockey League's N.Y. Rovers. Suddenly, a goal was scored that excited me.

To enhance my cheering in those days, I armed myself with a large cowbell which was well-attached to my right hand; ready to be rung at a second's notice.

As soon as the red light flashed, signaling a goal, I jumped from my seat like a nut case and proceeded to ring the cowbell in triumph. Well, actually, that's what I had in mind.

My intentions were good, but my aim was bad. As I finished my leap, the cowbell scored a direct hit on Aunt Helen's jaw. Had the scene been in a Three Stooges movie, I'd have been on the floor pounding in laughter.

But my Aunt Helen was hurt – not go-to-the-hospital hurt but not far from it, either. Hale took the beating like the trooper she was but it also marked the beginning and end of her hockey-watching career.

Helen knew a lot about first aid and already had passed two courses during World War II. One was as a nurse's aide, and the other as our neighborhood's air raid warden.

Her warden's equipment was impressive, especially since she was gifted with a military-style uniform and a white, steel helmet. I was so impressed that I was tempted to salute her every morning.

Of all the lessons Hale taught me, the best was the art of roughing it in the great outdoors with her hiking club. It didn't matter to me whether we hiked in a torrential downpour or a hot summer's day; I loved it.

Best of all was the time she got permission from her fellow NYHC campers to bring me along for an overnight at the club's cabin adjoining Budd Lake, New Jersey.

Bunking with the campers was a big deal for a kid like me, and I cherished every second of it -- until I discovered that the hiker's bunk lacked what we in Brooklyn called a "John" or in England, a "water closet."

It was in rugged, mostly uninhabited Budd Lake that I was introduced to that monument to nostril-clearing, the outhouse. Or, as Hale liked to say, "No rush; no flush!"

I got used to using the outhouse for one very good reason, again to quote Hale: "When ya gotta go, ya gotta go." I even got to appreciate the outhouse, which, smelly as it was, never dimmed my love for Aunt Helen.

By the time I was old enough to drive, Hale strategically bailed me out of trouble when my 1939 Chevy's clutch failed on the Henry Hudson Parkway during a trip back to New York City from the Catskills.

I needed fifty bucks to get a new clutch installed, and I was short 49 bills to pay for the work. I sent an S.O.S. to Aunt Helen, who quickly gave me the balance and promised not to tell my mom or dad.

Hale fulfilled the key part of the rescue operation. The new clutch worked fine, except she spilled the beans and told my folks.

It wasn't as bad an act as Benedict Arnold's. In fact, the more I thought about it, the more I concluded that what Hale did was perfectly natural – actually the right thing to do under the circumstances.

It was what big sisters were supposed to do. Besides, knowing Aunt Helen, I'm sure that she believed her conscience was clear.

We stayed pals well into my early years at Brooklyn College. I carried on the hike tradition -- only now with my BC pals -- and went to an occasional movie with Auntie H either at Loew's Kameo or the Savoy on Bedford.

During the summer of 1952, while I was playing drums in a dance band at the Western View Hotel in Monticello, New York, I received a letter from home that Aunt Helen wasn't well. It didn't sound good.

About two weeks before our Catskill gig had ended, I got word from home that Hale had died of a brain tumor at a Brooklyn hospital. "She went so fast," Mom said. "Maybe it was better that way."

Not to me it wasn't. Not "better" at all. Not if I couldn't give Hale a hug and a kiss and thank her so much for the hikes, the laughs, even the outhouse and for not bitching when I nearly broke her jaw at a hockey game.

When the drumming gig was over and I finally got home, Hale's loss hit home as I walked past her bedroom.

I had lost my big sister, and I needed a tune to soothe my hurt. It came right away, as did the recollection of that long-ago interlude at the Bear Mountain railway station: "Waitin' For The Train To Come In."

It came and went.

So did my beloved Hale.

Aunt Helen in her nurse's aide uniform at 582 Marcy

THE CANDY STORE

No single edifice was more "Brooklyn" than the candy store.

In my corner of Williamsburg, we had three near my house at 582 Marcy Avenue. One was Al and Shirley's on Nostrand Avenue at the corner of Vernon Avenue, where Vernon dead-ends. That was our favorite. Al and Shirley were a cool couple, and they made the best egg creams in the borough.

The second was Goldstein's on Marcy very close to Willoughby, run by an older and grumpy guy. I mention it because most of the time the fellas tried not to go there – except for one day and an unforgettable "find" on Mr. Goldstein's shelf.

The third was a candy store-plus that operated under a fancy-schmancy category: luncheonette. This one happened to be named Goldie's Emporium, which was not to be confused with the Palace of Versailles or the Taj Mahal. The Goldstein of Goldie's Emporium was no relation to Mister Goldstein from Marcy and Willoughby. The Goldie of Goldie's Emporium was the dean of malted-milk makers, Morris Goldstein. "Call me Moe," he'd say. Moe Goldstein was *the* man.

Moe was famous for a very good reason. Moe was the first guy in The Burg to drive a new 1949 Hudson four-door sedan. It was streamlined on top of streamlined. (But that's for a later automotive column starring my 1939 Chevy.)

Moe also was automatically a funny guy because how could anyone named Moe not be a funny guy? (The Three Stooges' star was funnier as a Moe than, say, a Julius.)

Getting back to Al and Shirley's, it's worth noting that it doubled as a neighborhood communications center. Still mired in the Great Depression, many families on Vernon Avenue could not afford a telephone.

But Al and Shirley's had a pay phone, and everyone on the block knew it. So, if you didn't have a phone, no problem. Your aunt or cousin or best buddy simply called Al and Shirley's, and Al took care of the rest.

There almost always was a kid hanging out in the store. Al would have the kid fetch the callee; in return, the kid-messenger would get a penny or, on a good day, maybe even a nickel from the person he summoned.

One day Gilbert Birnbaum was hanging out when a call came in. Al told him to get the guy at 28 Vernon, which he dutifully did. When the chap was done, he put a coin in Gillie's palm and the poor kid nearly *plotzed*.

After the guy left, Gillie turned to Al and said, "Al, this guy gave me a quarter. A quarter!" Al smiled. "I forgot to tell you, Gillie, he's the new bookie on the block, and his phone ain't in yet!"

Al and Shirley's had four rotating stools at the counter, plus a large candy display case next to them, past which was a library of brand-new comic books: Action Comics, with Superman; and Detective Comics, with the erstwhile man about town, Bruce Wayne, alias Batman (co-starring snotnose Robin and the Batmobile, which was no match for Moe Goldstein's Hudson).

For as little as a penny, you could get a nice-sized, unwrapped Hooton chocolate bar gifted with a nut or two. For a nickel, there was Pepsi-Cola (12 full ounces, that's a lot; twice as much for a nickel, too, Pepsi-Cola is the drink for you.) For the same price, Coca-Cola gave you only a lousy six ounces. The heck with that!

Shirley would gladly sell you a glass of seltzer, a cheap thirst-quencher known as the Two Cents Plain, or a chocolate ice cream soda for a dime. And for no cents at all, Al and Shirley's, like all candy stores, doubled as a community center, mostly for kids like me, who'd play games like Initials with each other.

"Who's D.M. on the Dodgers?" I'd ask.

"Who?" a chum would reply.

"Ducky Medwick."

"Wrong; his real name is Joe."

By contrast, Goldstein's candy store on Marcy, rubbing shoulders with Willoughby, was less inviting than Al and Shirley's. It had one distinct advantage, though: It was closer to my home. Plus, Mister G had a shelf with a few games such as Chinese Checkers along with pink Spalding rubber balls – better known as a Spaldeen – best used for the most popular nabe game of punchball.

Here's why Goldstein's had a purpose in the young lives of Howie Sparer and me. By 1943, Uncle Sam was in the midst of a long war. That meant there was a rubber shortage in the country, including The Burg, and, therefore, a Spaldeen shortage as well. Big-time; you couldn't find a reasonable facsimile of a Spaldeen if you did a handstand while singing the Spike Jones version of "Da Fuhrer's Face."

So, here are Howie and Fish walking home from the New Hebrew School on Stockton and Tompkins. On this warm afternoon, we were closest to old man Goldstein's, so why not drop in? So we did. We each ordered a Two Cents Plain and gazed at the shelves behind the counter.

There were Chinese checkers, backgammon and, and, and … what the –

Suddenly, Howie grabbed my arm, pointed to an orange-colored sphere on the second shelf and whispered, "Is that really a Spaldeen up there? Can't be."

"Sure looks like one; let's ask Mr. Goldstein."

We pointed out the item that piqued our curiosity, and Mister G dutifully pulled it off the shelf, gave it a necessary dusting, as it may have been molding there for decades, and placed it on the counter.

Neither Howie nor I could believe that this much-coveted ball still was available at that point in the war. Surely it was a fake, something made out of what they were calling synthetic rubber. Disgusting stuff.

Howie fingered it like a diamond dealer checking out a wedding ring and then gave it the true test: two bounces on the floor. Holy, Moly! It bounced like a Spaldeen was supposed to bounce.

He handed it over to me for the necessary second opinion. Two bounces, felt good. But we knew that wasn't enough. We knew Goldstein wouldn't lie about it, but we had to ask the fateful question: Is this a real Spaldeen?

Mister G, whose accent was miles beyond Brooklynese, turned apoplectic. He clearly was insulted beyond reason. "Is it real?" he shouted. That was roughly equivalent to wondering if the Statue of Liberty in New York Harbor was a cardboard copy of the real thing.

Subduing his anger, Goldstein looked us both in the eyes and delivered the line that has remained with me for years as only Mr. G could in his own dialect.

"Boy-ess, dis iss da real Meech-Chhoy! (Translated from Brooklynese: This is the real McCoy!)

Taking Mister G at his word, we bought the priceless ball for a dime and got three good punchball years out of it. McCoy or Meech-Chhoy, it was real.

Not that every candy-store owner was completely on the level. Which brings us a bit further down Marcy, near Penn Street, and Goldie's fabulous Emporium.

We likened the Emporium's front window display to the Egyptian exhibit at the Metropolitan Museum of Art. But instead of mummies, there were two toothpick models; one of the Empire State Building and the other of the Eiffel Tower. It was whispered all the way to the Williamsburg Bridge that nowhere else but in the Emporium's window would you find toothpicks put to such exquisite use. (By the way, it turns out the picks were only on loan from Moe.)

Maestro Moe of Goldie's Emporium was an important purveyor of food because he added a lunch menu apart from drinks and ice cream, which was how his candy store became a luncheonette. You could get a B-T down with mayo or a tuna on rye; maybe even scrambled eggs over.

But the *piece de résistance* was Moe's malted. *The* best. Why? For the pure and simple reason that Moe made his malteds in the secret style. Normally, for a genuine malted, you pour milk in the gleaming silver container, then none other than Fox's U-Bet chocolate syrup, then Horlick's malt powder and, finally, *supposedly,* ice cream. (But not this time.)

One July 4th, I worked at Goldie's behind the counter and was let in on the secret malted formula. Milk, yes! Fox's U-Bet, yes! Horlick's malt, of course! Then comes the "secret" ingredient. Shhhhhh! Don't you dare tell.

You grab the ice cream scoop and, with a flair, open the ice cream lid and wave the scoop *over* the ice cream. No touching the delectable stuff down below, please. And then you squeeze the empty scoop into the gleaming container as if it's ice cream. *Sacre bleu,* it's only air. (Shhh. Mum's the word. Loose lips sink Goldie's.)

Then, to the Sunbeam malted machine and, poof, just like that -- with folks who knew their malteds best -- the Burg's winner comes pouring into your glass and you can't do anything but savor it. Don't ask questions; just savor.

Moe's son, Jack, has been one of my buddies since we were Brooklyn College freshmen. He worked the Emporium nightly after classes. I recently asked Jack about the malted madness, and he reaffirmed the secret recipe -- no ice cream, please -- but also confirmed a long-held rumor.

One of Moe's regular customers was a teacher, who would visit the Emporium most evenings. Her favorite item was – what else? – a chocolate malted. Of course, Moe would follow directions listed above and then would place the delectable looking potion on the counter.

The teacher would take a sip and then unfailingly ask Moe if he wouldn't mind putting a bit more malt in the drink; she felt that that extra added attraction would make it *perfecto royale.* Of course, Goldie never would refuse such a rudimentary request.

Following is what Jack told me.

"There was a container on the back bar with the label MALT on it. However, that container was empty. No matter. He would take the cover off the container and put his spoon in the empty container, then shake his empty spoon into the malted mixer before mixing it."

The beauty part came next. She'd take a sip and profusely thank Moe (No Seconds On The Malt) Goldstein. "This is so much better!"

And now you know how culinary history was made, for in his little Emporium on Marcy Avenue, near Penn, Moe Goldstein re-invented a malted milk into a shake!

A typical 1930s-era Brooklyn candy store

AUNT HATTIE'S FATEFUL PURSUIT OF ICE CREAM

The two official dishes at our Williamsburg home were my Grandma Etel's Hungarian goulash for dinner and ice cream for dessert.*

*At 582 Marcy, the "dessert" hours could run from 4 a.m. to 3 a.m. early the next morning. The ice cream of choice was Breyer's chocolate, preferably in bulk.

Once every four months, there was an extra added attraction since Molly Fischler, my mother, would take a crack at doing a Breyer's imitation in her tiny kitchen.

Mom's experimental desserts were hampered by her skinny, 1936 Electrolux refrigerator and limited ingredients. Good try, Mom, but the product extracted from her ice tray was not really ice cream as we know it today. Not even close.

It was more like a blend of weak Jell-O and frozen Fox's U-Bet. Of course, Dad and I were so pleased with Molly Fischler's noble attempt that we cheered every spoonful, hoping for a more realistic taste three months hence.

By far, the family's most avid ice cream connoisseur was my mother's kid sister, Aunt Hattie (Sheier), who lived in Albany, New York.

Hattie envied us Brooklynites because in Albany the only ice cream available was made by one Capital District dairy. It was called Norman's Kill ice cream and, I promise, you wouldn't kill for it.

By contrast, in Brooklyn, we could choose from top stuff -- Breyer's, Sealtest, Borden's and Horton's. There was one other ice cream company that -- for the moment -- will go without mention because of the subject's sensitivity.

The good news from Hattie's viewpoint was that she frequently could visit her Brooklyn family, where *real* (Breyer's) ice cream was stashed in the first and third floor refrigerators.

Plus, Aunt Hattie had a second ice cream silo available in the distant -- but reachable after a subway expedition -- Gravesend section of our beloved borough. There she could devour Breyer's by the gallon, and for free!

Hattie's sister-in-law, Kate Friedman, ran a candy store in Gravesend, not far from Coney Island. It was so far from Williamsburg we called it Yenivelt, meaning "the other world." Hattie couldn't care less; she would find a way to get there.

Until December 27, 1947, Hattie never was deprived of ice cream on any of her regular Brooklyn tours. But on that fateful date, her route to Kate's candy store was blocked, likely for days.

An all-time record blizzard was burying Brooklyn to the point that the borough looked like an outpost in the Yukon Territories. There was absolutely no movement of cars, trucks, trolleys, pedestrians or even stray dogs.

And the snow kept coming while the ice cream wells on both the first and third floors at 582 Marcy had gone dry. This called for prompt action, and I was summoned for the vital, ice cream-saving mission.

"Stanley," Aunt Hattie implored, "here's five dollars. Go get a quart of chocolate. If they have it in bulk, make it half chocolate and half butter pecan."

No problem. At age 15, I loved a challenge, I adored snow and I knew a Hattie S.O.S. when it sounded. She wasn't kidding around. Then again, neither was I. After all, I loved Breyer's chocolate almost as much as Aunt Hattie.

On went my hooded Mackinaw, rubber galoshes, plaid scarf, and out I trundled to blizzardy Marcy Avenue. True to the mounds of snow, not a creature was stirring -- nor a vehicle.

I ploughed north toward the Williamsburg Bridge. Past Stockton Street, Floyd, Park, Hopkins, Flushing, then Lorimer. Suddenly, I looked up at this bleaker-than-bleak scene and *it* dawned on me.

I had walked a whole snow-forsaken mile and nothing -- but *nothing* -- was open. No candy stores, no groceries, no dry cleaners, no kosher delis. Nothing. By the time I got to the Williamsburg Bridge I was oh-for-everything.

The joy had turned to oy! (As in *oy vey*, woe is me – now what do I do?) Glumly, I envisioned myself, well-soaked in snow, returning to 582 empty-handed. How could I face Aunt Hattie and explain the chocolate shutout?

Desperately, I took a right turn under the BMT Broadway el and, as a last resort, I decided to walk as far as the Loew's Broadway Theater. If I had no luck, I'd take a right at Vernon and walk home un-ice-creamed and humiliated.

Then, it happened.

Up ahead, where Flushing met Broadway, I noticed a light in a lone store. Yes! Yes! It was a candy store and it was open. I gleefully handed the man my soaking-wet $5 bill, got the coveted quart, joyfully spun around -- and out.

Triumphantly, I turned right onto Vernon and schlepped west toward Marcy. By now the fun had gone. I was exhausted beyond belief but was spurred on by the quart of chocolate ice cream and the vision of a triumphant welcome from Hattie.

I barely made it across the Marcy tundra, tumbled into 582 and directly stumbled to the kitchen, where I deposited the wet-to-the-gills brown paper bag on the kitchen table.

Retreating to the vestibule, I pulled off my galoshes, snow-drenched Mackinaw and gloves. From the kitchen, a strange noise -- definitely not a roar of approval -- drifted down the hall as I pulled off my soaked socks.

As I approached the kitchen, I could hear Aunt Hattie peeling the last rips of wet brown paper off the bag. She took one look at the quart of chocolate ice cream and then stared disapprovingly at me. Her eyes blazed fury.

Were it not for the blizzard still blowing outside, my aunt's wailing response would have been heard all the way to Kate Friedman's closed candy store in distant Gravesend: "YOU MEAN YOU GOT REIDS?!!"

Then, a pause as Aunt Hattie searched for the kitchen's garbage can. With an angry toss, she pitched a knuckler quart of Reid's ice cream into the gaping receptacle. And that was that.

My sense of shock was beyond tears. How could she do such a dastardly thing after the blizzard I had so successfully endured?

Then, the answer gradually entered by brain. Aunt Hattie was a genuine ice cream savant. Reid's was to ice cream what Thunderbird was to wine. This was the consummate, tasteless insult to her sense of taste.

But still -- I repeat, but still -- for the last 73 years, I have debated with myself on how a jury of ice cream mavens would have ruled on Hattie's abject rejection of Reid's: guilty or not guilty?

A good seven decades later, I finally completed the thought process and can reveal that the verdict on Hattie Friedman Sheier of Albany, New York, is in: NOT GUILTY!

The jury would rule that Aunt Hattie, the connoisseur, merely was being true to her strict ice cream values. There was nothing phony about my aunt when it came to the important things in life.

This was serious stuff. After all, what Breyer's lover in her right mind would dare eat that Reid's crap?

Certainly not a Friedman nor a Fischler! Nor, in this landmark ice cream case, Hattie Sheier, the family's ultimate arbiter of ice cream tasting.

Blizzard or no blizzard.

Aunt Hattie with Uncle Paul at their Albany house

THREE BARBER SHOPS,
NO WAITING!

There was absolutely no logical reason to have three barbershops within two blocks of my house, at 582 Marcy Avenue, between Myrtle and Vernon. But there they were -- Dave's, Johnny's and Buscemi.

Remarkably, two out of the trio were embedded in one block, Nostrand between Vernon and Myrtle. Both were operated by Italian gentlemen who turned out to be as different as the Serengeti from the Sahara.

Barber One, Johnny Mastro-Marino, apparently was unaware that a certain implement, a broom, had been invented three to five centuries earlier.

Maestro Mastro-Marino had a notion that if he left enough cut hair on the floor, the thousands of black, brown, blond and grey locks would unite overnight and sweep themselves out onto the Nostrand Avenue sidewalk.

Didn't work!

You might wonder why I would bother patronizing such a messy place. The answer: loyalty. Mastro-Marino was the father of my P.S. 54 classmate, John Mastro-Marino, Jr.

I figured that I owed Johnny Jr. a few clips at his father's joint just for friendship's sake, not to mention getting a good feel for what the African plains were like -- that is, if filled with cut hair.

On the other hand, my father liked his barbershop clean. So, he'd walk a few more steps along Nostrand for Buscemi's, a guaranteed *Good Housekeeping*-award winner, if such a prize existed for a hair-cutting joint.

Meticulous in his own right, Ben Fischler liked a spanking clean barber shop that smelled good, looked good and never betrayed a single hair on the floor for more than one minute.

Signor Buscemi was so classy -- not to mention super-handsome -- that he wouldn't think of calling his establishment a mere barber shop. That explains why the neatly-scrolled sign in front proclaimed: TONSORIAL PARLOR.

I looked it up: tonsorial parlor is a barber shop. What made Buscemi's TP so arresting was its look and bacterial count. It was as pristine as an operating room.

Like his shop, Buscemi's hair was whiter-than-white. He wore it neatly curled in the back in a manner that suggested that only Mrs. Buscemi could have worked it over so well before he left for work.

Distinctly different from Mastro-Marino and Buscemi, my barber was Jewish. Yeah, a Kosher hair-cutter named Dave Cherry did his clipping on Marcy near Willoughby, diagonally across from my house. Cherry opened for business early in 1947, around the time that crew cuts had come into vogue. I wanted one badly because my favorite Toronto Maple Leafs right wing, Howie Meeker, had one.

"Can you give me a crew cut?" I asked Dave Cherry.

"*Nu,*" my Jewish barber shot back, "*vu is* a crew cut?"

Anticipating Cherry's ignorance of the latest hair styles, I pulled out an 8-by-10 glossy photo of Howie Meeker with a crew cut; his hair was flatter than a landing strip. Cherry sized up the photo for ten seconds and went to work.

I loved my Jewish barber with his Yiddish accent and ability to deliver a crew cut, but my Kosher-cutter betrayed one weakness. Like Mastro-Marino's aversion to a broom, Cherry refused to use a hairbrush to remove loose neck hairs.

Instead of a brush, Cherry briefly turned his mouth into a wind tunnel and *blew* off the hairs. Ordinarily, that wouldn't be an issue, except that my favorite barber wasn't called the King of Halitosis for nothing.

To put it mildly, Cherry redefined bad breath, and that created both a problem and a game.

It meant that I had to be vigilant in the barber's chair. The trick was anticipating Cherry's hair blowing by holding my breath for ten seconds in advance, then exhaling ten seconds after -- by which time Dave's breath attack disappeared.

All things considered, Cherry's assault on my nasal passages was a minor barbershop episode compared to the tragic tale that followed. It featured my Brooklyn College buddy Jack Goldstein, who had avoided crew cuts for years.

Finally, one day in 1951, I convinced Jack that the girls would love him all the more if he had a crew cut. He thought that was a good idea and, after classes on Flatbush Avenue, we detected an inviting sign.

"SIX BARBERS, NO WAITING!" it read. In we went. We found an empty barber chair for Jack and a waiting barber. "Give my friend a nice crew cut," I said, "and I'll tell you when it's just right."

I took a seat, opened a copy of *Life* magazine and, within minutes, fell asleep faster than fast asleep. When I awakened, Egad! Sir Goldstein's head could have passed for a shiny bowling ball at Flatbush Lanes.

Naturally, I thought that this would be the laugh riot of the half-century -- until we arrived at Jack's house. The usually affable Mrs. Goldstein took one look at her son, who now resembled the last of Custer's well-scalped survivors.

Gathering what remaining strength she had at her command, Mrs. G. blurted, "Jackie, what happened to you?"

He deftly and honestly fingered me for doing an imitation of Rip Van Winkle when her Yonkel was getting de-haired.

When Jack finished his hair-by-hair, play-by-play, what could I, the culprit, possibly do but exit Stage Right. Or, in this case, Stage Wrong.

While doing so, Jack's mom indicated that I would not be welcome in her abode from Rosh Hashanah to Decoration Day. And if I happened to drop into their downstairs establishment, Goldie's Emporium, guaranteed, the chocolate malteds would not include ice cream.

I considered that a fair punishment for my hirsute crime. At least, she didn't deny me any ice cream sodas.

Funny, but as I penitently faded out of sight, I could swear that I heard something roughly equivalent to the following dialogue:

Mrs. G.: "Jackie, did you at least tip the barber?"

Jack: "Yes, mom, I did."

Mrs. G.: "Then you *really* got clipped!"

WORLD WAR II, WILLIAMSBURG AND ME

I should have been at the Polo Grounds in Harlem on the afternoon of December 7, 1941. I dearly wanted to be there for many reasons.

The New York Giants football team was hosting the Brooklyn Dodgers football team and it was Tuffy Leemans Day, to boot.

My dad had promised to take me to my first National Football League game on that fateful day, but my trip was vetoed by a determined case of the measles.

Dad gave my ticket to my Uncle Sid. Meanwhile, I stretched out on our green living room couch and listened to the football broadcast on the radio.

Like any respectable Brooklynite, I rooted for the Dodgers, who, like any respectable Brooklyn team, was the underdog. But not today!

It was a heck of a game, with our heroic Brooklyn quarterback, Ace Parker, leading the Brooks to a 21-7 upset victory.

Forget about the Giants' Tuffy Leemans, a terrific fullback in his own right. Brooklyn's own, Pug Manders, scored three touchdowns, rendering Leemans a forgotten man.

Not forgotten was a halftime announcement that came over our living room Victor radio. The Japanese had bombed Pearl Harbor.

Pearl Harbor? Who knew from Pearl Harbor?

It was a faraway place on a strange-sounding group of islands called Hawaii. It soon would not seem that far away, and we would rapidly know all about Pearl Harbor, even nine-year-old me sitting on a green couch.

Just like that, World War II intruded in my living room and my life. In no time at all, my P.S. 54 class had memorized the words to "Remember Pearl Harbor."

Everybody was playing Kate Smith's rendition of "God Bless America," and very soon Al and Shirley's candy store on the corner of Nostrand and Vernon reserved its front window for photos of our servicemen.

Not that I had been unaware that there was a war on before the Japanese bombs blasted our battleships, virtually destroyed Hickam Air Field and killed thousands of American GIs.

War danger was nothing new to my dad, who had enlisted in the U.S. Navy when Uncle Sam entered the War to End All Wars in 1917. He'd served on the minelayer U.S.S. *San Francisco*, which patrolled the North Sea.

That was tough stuff, especially for a guy who couldn't swim. But Dad survived and brought with him a mine squadron yearbook with pictures of all the ships in his group plus action shots. I still have it and show it to my grandchildren.

I knew that the Nazis had blitzed the Brits and that Hitler was well on his way toward running roughshod over all of Europe. Once 1942 arrived, every kid in P.S. 54 knew there was a war on.

We were so into it that we learned every word of every song from every branch of the armed forces. Songs like "Anchors Aweigh" and "The Caissons Go Rolling Along" right up to the "Song of the Seabees."

Every family had ration books whether you were buying sugar, butter or gasoline. And heaven forbid you should ask for more than you deserved. Once, buying a pound of butter, I was hit with the seditious put-down, "Don't you know there's a war on?"

How could a kid of ten, as I was in 1942, not know?

My favorite toy company, Lionel, best known for producing electric trains, joined the war effort by making arms in its New Jersey factory. To keep the electric-train spirit going, Lionel had the colossal gall -- or is it effrontery -- to sell a *cardboard* train set. *Oy vey!*

Car-watchers like myself were frustrated beyond all reason. Only a handful of 1942 models were made, as GM, Chrysler and Ford retooled to manufacture Sherman tanks while the Willys-Overland Motors company built jeeps for the Army.

Although it wasn't on the P.S. 54 reading list, newspapers were a must for us to follow the fighting. Believe me, 1942 was not a good year for the Allies. Nor was it a good year for professional sports.

One by one, star athletes joined the armed forces while President Roosevelt pronounced big-league baseball important for morale. Ditto in Canada, where Prime Minister Mackenzie King said that the National Hockey League should remain open for the duration.

Virtually every team was able to stay in business, except in the National Football League, where the Philadelphia Eagles and Pittsburgh Steelers merged to become -- I kid you not -- the Phil-Pitt Steagles.

In some sporting ways, World War II offered a sweet use for our adversity. For me, the best was formation of the Curtis Bay Yard, Baltimore-based Coast Guard Cutters ice hockey team.

This unusual hockey team's roster was a composite of NHL players and minor-league pros who had enlisted in the Coast Guard. Starting with the 1942-43 season -- and through 1943-44 -- they played in the Eastern Amateur Hockey League.

That, of course, was a delight for me, since they'd be facing off against the New York Rovers at the old Madison Square Garden several times during the season. The Cutters not only were very good, they were extremely colorful.

On Sunday afternoons, they'd show up at MSG accompanied by a 30-piece marching band, which filled one end of the Garden. When the Cutters scored, the band would swing into "Semper Paratus," the Coast Guard's marching song.

Art Coulter, who captained the Rangers' 1940 Stanley Cup champs; Johnny Mariucci, the Chicago Blackhawks' toughie; and Manny Cotlow, a rough-hewn Jewish defenseman, were among my favorites.

The Cutters presented a problem for me. On the one hand, I fervently rooted for Uncle Sam to win the war. But on the other hand, the war's end would mean no more Coast Guard hockey team for me to enjoy.

But by March 1944, some of the Cutters were called to active duty in the South Pacific. By the end of their second season, the hockey club folded, since all the players had gone overseas.

In a perverse sort of way, wartime restrictions like gas rationing were good for us kids. That meant there were few cars on Vernon Avenue, which, in turn, meant that the street became our full-time playground.

We could enjoy a whole game of punchball, or association football* or stickball and not have to worry about cars interrupting our games.

*Also known as touch football, the mildest form of the grid game that could be played in the street without (much) harm. Usually played two on two or three on three.

I remember one morning when we gathered for a punchball game and discovered a Pontiac parked in front of 29 Vernon right on top of first base.

No sweat. Since nobody locked autos in those days, Murray (Red) Matlin opened the car door, released the emergency brake and six of us pushed the sedan five yards down the block. Then the game began!

Once my Uncle Joe, Uncle John and my mom's cousin, Irving Lee, were inducted into the armed forces, I took a more intense interest in various aspects of the war.

What intrigued me most was the U.S. Naval Air Force (precursor to the U.S. Air Force), which I'd check out in person starting with the summer of 1942.

As it happened, during July and August, my parents would take me to Riis Park, a beach in the area of Queens called the Rockaways, every Sunday. This was a treat not so much for the swimming but for the bus ride and plane-spotting.

To reach Riis Park from Flatbush, our green bus rolled past Floyd Bennett Field, a naval air station. We could see everything from Grumman F4F Wildcats to Consolidated PBY Catalina flying boats and even -- by 1944 -- Vought F4U Corsairs.

I got myself a copy of a Penguin Books' *Plane Spotter's Guide*, which included every conceivable warplane on both the Allies and Axis sides. I studied that book, so I felt I could handle being an anti-aircraft gunner.

Then, I discovered a card game with a color picture of a warplane on each card. Turned out that it also was a fun game to play. That, happily, intrigued my buddy Norman Karger as much as yours truly.

Norman and I would almost daily play the game in my backyard on summer afternoons. To this day, I look back on that deck of airplane cards -- and the afternoons with Norm -- as some of the most pleasant moments of my life.

There was nothing pleasant about the war, however. Not a day went by without my checking windows of families with servicemen. A flag with a blue star in the window meant that some family had a man in uniform. A gold star meant that he was killed in action. There was more than one gold star on Vernon Avenue.

Signs of the war were everywhere. A half-block away, a section of Vernon Avenue's sidewalk was reserved for metal collection. Old pots, pans, rolled-up cigarette silver and, well, anything metal was tossed on the pile.

Once a week, the Sanitation Department truck would haul it away. We were told that the metal was turned into vital military materiel: bullets, tanks and whatnot. Sounded legit to me.

My Uncle Joe wound up in the Seabees, the navy's construction battalion, posted on the island of Attu in the Aleutians. No fun there. Uncle John got a break and wound up in the U.S. Maritime Service's office in Sheepshead Bay, Brooklyn.

Cousin Irving Lee was the family scholar, a renowned expert in general semantics and an author as well. Cousin Irving was a major in the Army Air Corps. Among other things, he wrote survival manuals for downed pilots.

My mom and Cousin Irving were good pals, and when he was stationed on Waverly Place in Greenwich Village we went to visit. A tall, handsome man and a great guy, Cousin Irving dazzled me in his Army uniform.

Among my keenest memories of the war years of 1941-45 was the total spirit of patriotism that enveloped the country and how it permeated our lives. I don't remember a minute when I ever doubted we would win the war.

We felt that winning spirit everywhere, especially in songs such as "We Did It Before (And We Can Do It Again)." Or such local tunes as "Buy Your Bonds In Brooklyn -- We Got A Quota To Fill." There was scary stuff, like "Comin' In On A Wing And A Prayer," not to mention funny stuff, especially Spike Jones's rendition of "Der Fuhrer's Face."

Who could forget Irving Berlin's "I Left My Heart At The Stage Door Canteen," the Andrews Sisters belting out "Don't Sit Under The Apple Tree (With Anyone Else But Me)" or Bing Crosby's "(There'll Be A) Hot Time In The Town of Berlin"?

Hollywood fortified the winning spirit with such classics as *Wake Island, Casablanca*; the ever-popular Abbott and Costello gems, *Buck Privates* and *In the Navy*; and Bob Hope, starring in *Caught in the Draft*.

We loved the Brits for their indomitable spirit, epitomized by Prime Minister Winston Churchill. And we despised France for quitting the war in 27 days.

The Holocaust remained mostly a mystery until after the war, although my grandma's relatives in Slovakia stopped writing in 1942. Sometime later we received a fateful letter from the Red Cross that they no longer could be found,

By 1944 every nabe hangout -- especially the Sugar Bowl on Willoughby and Tompkins -- had photo spreads of every GI within a seven-block radius and then some.

It wasn't until around April 1945 that we felt victory was in the bag. The Nazis bowed out in May. Three months later, it was V.J. Day – and that was that. Virtually every block in our neighborhood had a celebration of some kind and, eventually, the boys began coming home. These were marvelously happy times. We had won the war!

Naturally, there were laughs. My favorite nabe tale was about Sy Kass. He enlisted in 1942, but before taking off for the Navy, he left a pair of shoes with Ralph Mercante, who ran the boot shop on Nostrand near Willoughby.

Seaman-to-be Kass put the shoe ticket in his pocket, hung his civvy clothes in a closet and went off to war.

Sy returned in 1945, donned a civilian suit and found a ticket in a pocket. It was for the Oxfords he had left with Ralph, the shoemaker, in 1942. Sy walked over to Ralph's shop and got a big welcome-home hug.

After giving Ralphie the check for his shoes, Kass was dumbfounded when his favorite shoemaker said, "Sy, I'll have them for you in three days."

Williamsburg street scene, 1930s

A CONEY BONANZA

In the summer of 1945, Coney Island was the entertainment center of the world.

Okay, okay. Not the whole, wide world but at least the world of Howie Sparer and me.

On one day, two 13-year-olds could go to Steeplechase, known as The Funny Place; ride the vastly underrated Wonder Wheel; invade the penny arcade; ride the bumper cars; and have hot dogs and fries at Nathan's.

That's just for starters.

The Bobsled was the "sleeper" thrill ride, imported from the 1939-40 World's Fair and hidden in The Bowery midway behind Skee-Ball. For added attractions, we had the beach, the *shvitz* (steam baths) and Tirza's Wine Bath. Tirza did a near striptease while bathing in the cheapest kosher wine, but who was going to fuss about that? Certainly not us!

Our day at Coney was well-planned. We always started with Skee-Ball for two reasons: It required a kind of billiard skill, and you could win coupons which led to prizes. For a nickel, you got five wooden balls that were to be rolled up a ramp that contained three levels marked 10, 20, and 30, and a center hole worth 100.

Early in my Coney career, I developed a winning Skee-Ball technique. Roll the ball off the side of the ramp, and it had a good chance to land in the center hole. Out of the five balls I threw on this day, I nailed the center hole three times, a personal record.

The Skee-Ball boss checked out my numbers and handed me five coupons. That seemed like a neat little bonanza until I checked out the gift list and realized that all I got for my skill was a lousy rabbit's foot.

No sweat. It was a gorgeous summer day, enhanced by the aroma of popcorn, boiled corn and ever-popular hot dogs. Howie looked up and down Surf Avenue and pointed to the north side of the street.

"Let's do the carousel," he insisted.

Who could resist the Surf Avenue merry-go-round? This was a mini-landmark that featured a ring distributor. Once the carousel got into full swing, you could lean over from the outside horse and catch a ring.

It was a bit chancy since the "lean" could have led to a plummet right off the moving carousel. But at age 13, who even thought about such a dangerous ring grab? You grabbed -- and hoped.

Every once in a while, we'd catch a gold ring, good for one free ride. But not on this day, so we proceeded to the bumper cars. This was a perennial favorite for several reasons:

1. Driving a car: We didn't need a driver's license to get behind the wheel. Plus, there were no rules of the road. You just drove and hoped you didn't get rear-ended more than a dozen times.

2. Acceptable aggression: Since there were no cops to worry about, you drove like a hit-everyone maniac or went after anyone who had the temerity to whack your car in the ass.

It was especially fun to pursue female drivers because, hey, a gal you blindsided could turn out to be better than a blind date.

The bumper cars never ceased to be fun. On this particular drive-in we hit plenty of vehicles, but none had a gal who was a hit with us. Hey, it happens.

Back on Surf Avenue, Howie came up with the idea I'd been waiting for. "Let's do the Steeplechase," he said.

In 1944, the Steeplechase was Coney's best self-contained amusement area, the other good one being Luna Park. For half a buck, you got a big, round ticket that listed every ride, game or athletic event available.

By far, the most popular was Steeplechase's namesake, only we simply called it "The Horses."

You climbed aboard one of four carousel-type horses mounted on a raised track that circled the entire acreage, and that was a lot. The idea was for one of the four horses to win the race. You never knew in advance who would come in first.

But the real kick was the uniqueness of the horses. There was no ride quite like it in the world as we knew it. And it was damn exciting. Granted, we were strapped in, but once the horses got going, the speed was scary and the turns -- *oy vey* -- turned knuckles very white and hearts very thumpy.

Winning the race invariably was less important than reaching the finish line still on your mount. Howie won the race and we both were still alive, hence it was a very good ride and a terrific parlay.

Some of the Steeplechase features were athletically challenging and all were inside the gigantic arena. One was a sliding pond about three stories high and very steep. When you got into position to slide, you were sorry.

Since I never was crazy about heights, it took me about three minutes of self-hypnosis to finally push off. What helped was that my buddy already was down at the bottom with no signs of wear and tear.

So, off I went, spending about half the trip down trying to find some sort of braking system in my legs or -- at worst -- arms. By the time I figured it all out, I was at the bottom. That's when I finally opened my eyes!

Another cockamamie, gravity-challenging experience consisted of a very high, long, many-curved tube in which you slid on your back. That was the easy part, unless you had a migraine. When you reached the bottom, that's where the real trouble began. You got deposited in a maze of large spinning disks that passed you from one to another until you finally got dumped off to the side.

The reason why I only tried this annoying ride once in my life was that the spinning disks not only made me dizzy, but each time I moved from one disk to another, my arm got pinched in the transfer and I was wounded at the end.

There was only one way to feel better after that ordeal, and I offered the prescription to Howie: "Let's get the hell outta here and go to Nathan's," otherwise known – as it still is – as Nathan's Famous.

Located diagonally across from the BMT subway's Stillwell Avenue terminal, Nathan's in 1944 needed neither seafood nor a corn counter, both of which were added a decade later. The deal was simple: You got by far the best hot dog in the world and the best French fries, preferably with salt added. No more, no less.

To say that the French fries were as succulent and tasty as a good filet mignon would be the understatement of the half-century. They were better. As for the hot dogs, they fulfilled every rave notice.

By the way, Nathan's had a Nathan. His name was Nathan Handwerker. The Nathan of Nathan's was like a culinary cheerleader. He would walk around the establishment telling his help, "Give 'em and let 'em eat!"

Which they did. Crowds almost five-deep was proof positive, even around midnight.

The hot dog-French fries menu did not end at Nathan's. Just about five yards away on Surf Avenue was my third-favorite food treat -- frozen custard. You gave the man in the white uniform a nickel and he then produced a non-sugar cone. He moved to the dispensing machine, pulled the lever and kept turning the cone as the chocolate custard poured out.

What never stopped amazing me was the fact that the dispensing guy always piled twice as much custard on the cone as I expected. The custard, by the way, tasted as good as ice cream.

"I got a buck left in my pocket," I advised my partner. "What's next on the agenda?"

"Let's try the Boardwalk and see what's what."

The "what" that was "what" turned out to be Faber's Poker.

Mind you, neither Howie nor I were particularly fond of playing cards, especially poker, so there was no attraction there. Plus, we had no idea what Faber's Poker was all about.

"Maybe we should ask Mister Faber how his game works," I told Howie.

"Yeah, try and find him. Easier to find Mister Nathan's at Nathan's."

We walked in to see two rows of what they called pokerino. Each game had a series of holes in which a rubber ball would fit. For a nickel, you got five balls and hoped for the best.

Since neither Howie nor I knew what the heck we were doing, we sat down next to each other, put a nickel in the hole and out rolled five rubber balls.

Once the ball was released, it bounced around the holes a couple of times and then settled in one that corresponded to the ace, king, queen, jack or joker.

To our astonishment, when we finished our five rolls, an attendant walked over and presented us with a couple of coupons each. Then we checked the coupon-gift list and discovered that pokerino was a far cry from Skee-Ball.

With a couple of coupons, you could get something a lot more worthwhile than a good-luck rabbit's foot. But why be greedy? We still had plenty of nickels, which meant it was time for Round Two.

Bingo! Beginner's luck was turning into *luck*. The second time around, we each annexed another pair of coupons. And that meant more good prizes.

By the time we ran out of nickels, we still had not run out of luck. But it was time to cash in because Faber had some awfully tempting prizes.

Since I was taking the BMT Brighton Express home after this, I had to justify the last buck I spent at Faber's Poker.

"I'm gonna make my mother happy with my prizes," I told Howie, trying to justify our being at a poker joint.

Studying the various levels of gifts -- of course with Mom in mind -- I cashed in my coupons for the following gems destined to make her pleased and love me all the more.

1. A magic sugar dispenser. This genius invention was a glass container with a red cone at the top that amazingly poured one teaspoonful of sugar with every turn of the glass. I thought: This will absolutely knock my mom out with joy.

2, A giant juice container. Every kitchen needs one. Fill the glass dispenser with up to a gallon of orange juice, bring to the breakfast table and pour. Can't miss being a hit.

3. A salt-and-pepper set. In case our old ones somehow get lost, these will be held in reserve. It will lessen Mom's anxiety about losing the ones on the dining room table.

Flushed with success, I bade Howie good-bye -- he was going in the other direction to Sea Gate -- and made my way to the Stillwell Avenue BMT terminal.

The goodies were safely nestled in a brown paper bag, which I guarded like a fullback nursing a pigskin on an end run. This, however, was a challenge, since it was rush hour at Coney, with hordes pouring through the turnstiles.

I should mention that no ride on the BMT Express was acceptable unless I got to the front window first, peering out at the tracks like the motorman I wanted to be.

Since the Stillwell terminal was, naturally, at the start of the trip, I had a good chance to get the window, and I did. But the people kept filling the subway car, and soon I began to feel squeezed by the standing-room crowd.

"At all costs," I told myself, "I must protect the glassware in the bags, or else. No way I can come home without all three items intact."

That said, I curled my body around the bag while simultaneously ensuring that I had sole occupancy at the front window. But the best tests were yet to come.

Another bunch of Coney visitors got on at the Eighth Street el station, then at Ocean Parkway and then at Brighton Beach. "If I survive them," I said, still talking to myself, "it'll be clear sailing."

My positioning was excellent and my motivation at its highest level. The bag with my mom's gifts survived the crowd and now I triumphantly -- proudly as well -- climbed the two flights to our apartment.

"Mom," I enthusiastically blurted, "guess what I got for you. I won prizes at Faber's Poker."

Of course Ma Fischler had no clue what this meant, so I began my Santa Claus routine by pulling out the salt-and-pepper set. I placed them on the kitchen table, hoping for even a small hug and a kiss.

Mom pointed to the dining room table. "But I already have a salt and pepper set," she said. "What do I need with another?"

Strike one.

"How about this?" I responded. Out came the extra-large juice dispenser. Mom gave it a disdainful look, reached into the kitchen cabinet and pulled down a reasonable facsimile.

"Why do you think I don't use this one?" she said. "It's too big. There's only three of us, and your father doesn't drink juice, anyhow."

Strike two.

My confidence already shattered, I still counted on the magic sugar item to be my rallying hit.

Reaching into the bag, I was the magician pulling the rabbit out of the hat. Before Mom could say a word, I explained.

"Ma, you see this cone?" I said, turning it open and then pointing to the trick item. "You turn it upside-down and you get a teaspoon of sugar. Isn't that something? Ha, Ma? Ha, Ma?"

Mom just happened to have a cup of coffee on the kitchen table with a sugar bowl and tablespoon on the side.

"See this?" she said, carefully extracting sugar with a spoon and shoveling it into the coffee. "I like this better."

That marked the first and last time I graced the tables at Faber's Poker.

The world-famous Cyclone, Coney Island

THE ALL-TIME KLOTZ-FISCHLER LIGHTS-OUT PILLOW FIGHT

I had one "aunt" who really wasn't my aunt.

Her name was Selma Klotz, better known to me as Aunt Selma.

Selma and her husband, Nat, were the parents of Lewis -- alias Lew -- Klotz. Aunt Selma and Uncle Nat also were best friends with my parents, Ben and Molly Fischler.

Family history indicated that at one time Nat dated Molly and Ben dated Selma, but I never got that *bubbmeintsa** straight, so it remains in the realm of family semi-fiction.

*Yiddish for a grandmother's tale

In any event, the Klotzes and Fischlers were so close that it was inevitable that their two male offsprings -- me and Lewis -- would become pals.

As a matter of fact, I believe that the Stan-Lew friendship goes so far back that Joe Kodak was still selling Baby Brownies for a buck at the time.

So close were the Fischlers and Klotzes that the first time I knew that there was a Selma Klotz, she was introduced to me as Aunt Selma. Who was I to argue?

I found Aunt Selma a likeable lady even though she occasionally set off the Richter scale by screaming bloody murder at Lewis. Still, there was a lot to like about Aunt Selma.

For starters, I liked the briskness about her gait, and she was a good-looker in a pleasant, Flatbush sort of way. (Mind you, the Klotz estate actually was south of Flatbush and north of Sheepshead Bay. I called it Klotzville.)

I wouldn't go so far as to say that Brooklyn's East 22nd Street between Avenue S and Avenue T was rural, but in modern 1941, East 22nd was as unpaved as the turf outside OK Corral in *High Noon*.

(Alas, the "World of Tomorrow," as labeled by the 1939-1940 New York World's Fair, had not yet arrived at Ye Olde E.22d).

Sherman tanks would have enjoyed training along East 22nd. As to utilizing Union Hardware roller skates, not! Bicycles, maybe, but only with balloon tires.

For me, the best part of visiting Aunt Selma, Uncle Nat and Cousin Lewis was the voyage. We went by trolley, of course. At that time, Brooklyn was the Streetcar Capital of the World.

(The Brooklyn Dodgers baseball team got its name because Brooklynites spent half their lives dodging trolleys. The team's full name was Brooklyn Trolley Dodgers, later shortened to Dodgers for tightened newspaper-headline purposes.)

In 1941, my tastes ran to trolley cars of any model, age or speed. As it happened, for me to reach Chez Klotz, I had to ride not one but two streetcar lines, an extraordinary treat if ever there was one. First, I'd take the Nostrand Line to Bergen Street, get off, then walk a block to Bedford, where the Ocean Avenue Line began its run.

The Nostrand, which I rode plenty, was pretty normal as trolleys go. The Peter Witt-designed streetcars were built in 1922 and still were very efficient and serviceable when I rode them. What made the Ocean Avenue version of the Peter Witt so special was its powerful, dynamic motor, which enabled the old Peter Witts to outrace brand-new Chevys and Pontiacs driving alongside.

The Ocean line didn't do much sprinting until it reached Farragut Road and curved left on Ocean Avenue. Then the race was on, and the souped-up Peter Witt -- to my delight -- usually won. The trick was that Ocean Avenue was given to enormously long streets, which meant that the trolleys really could make like the 20th Century Limited from, say, Avenue M to Avenue N, and then N to Quentin Road. (Flatbush was too sophisticated in those days to have an Avenue Q.)

It took 40 glorious minutes for me to reach my destination; which happened to be Avenue S, then a five-minute walk to East 22nd, followed by a right turn. Halfway down the block, there it was: La Casa Klotz.

Apart from my surprise at viewing an unpaved Brooklyn street, I was stunned by the size of the homes, much bigger than those on Vernon Avenue.

The street also was dotted with what we didn't have much of in Williamsburg -- automobiles of assorted varieties, including a Willys-Overland, from the same firm that began building jeeps for the U.S. Army.

Lew's home was two stories high -- already impressive -- and, even though I had never visited Iowa, I fantasized that Lew's abode looked like a farmhouse 30 miles or so from Des Moines.

Parked right in front of *Chateau Klotz* was an almost-new 1941 Ford sedan. It belonged to glove salesman Nat Klotz, who drove that speedster all over New York State peddling his handware. I loved that Ford!

Now, that may not have been a big deal to you, but Fords then had a reputation for having big, powerful motors that -- in my mind at least -- enabled them to outrace Plymouths, Hudsons and, yes, even a General Motors LaSalle.

Always excited when I visited Aunt Selma, I pressed the buzzer, and there she was, wearing a big smile, delivering a hug and announcing that chocolate milk, cookies and Lewis awaited me at the dinner table.

So far, so good. Lewie and I devoured our goodies, found silly things to laugh about and enjoyed the great outdoors, as much as kids could on unpaved East 22nd.

We then went back to the house, where Uncle Nat pored over the *World-Telegram* newspaper and did some sports schmoozing with me. I truly was honored chatting with him because Mr. Klotz was Dad's best friend.

In fact, Dad was so fond of Nat that he reserved his most affectionate – and very rarely used -- compliment for him. "That man is a prince," Dad would say, and it would be said with the utmost regal feeling of warmth.

After dinner, Uncle Nat and Aunt Selma announced that they were off to see *Gone With The Wind*, and that Lewis and I should behave ourselves and get to bed before it was too late, whatever that meant.

The only words we heard were, "We're going to the movies." The rest, about maintaining revolutionary decorum, was like a paid, political announcement to our effectively closed ears.

Once they were out of the house, we knocked off a couple of Chinese checkers games and then figured it was time for some indoor exercise. And what could be better than a one-on-one pillow fight?

For the ring, we chose the relatively small guest room -- where I'd wind up sleeping. This was a mistake. Not a big mistake, mind you, but a colossal one.

We chose our pillows, counted to three and whacked away with maniacal gusto. According to my unofficial whack-by-whack count, Round One was a pretty even affair.

We had a brief pause for station identification and then prepared for Round Two on the bed, which we mounted to continue the fray.

After absorbing one of Lew's crisp blows to my cranium, I drew my pillow back for the counterattack and -- in a pillow-fight sense -- went for the fences.

Except that there were no fences in the guest room. There was, at mid-ring, a cute, little, unobtrusive reading lamp, conveniently attached to the wall.

POW! I swung hard, hoping for the K.O. blow. I did connect, but not with Lewis.

My pillow arced down hard on the neat, tiny reading lamp, sending it across the room, good for at least a double, maybe even three bases, except we weren't doing a Dodgers thing.

But that's not all. Accompanying the lamp, like a tail on a big jet, was a chunk of wall. As the suddenly-winged plaster soared to the other side of the room, it left a gaping hole the size of a regulation basketball.

Our pillow fight suddenly was suspended. Lewis and I immediately convened a high-level conference. The topics for the night included: What do we do with the flying lamp? How do we cover the hole in the wall?

The unanswered questions were simply followed by more logical queries: Was there a hardware store open that sold plaster of Paris? If so, we could plaster the hole that now began looking like the entrance to the Lincoln Tunnel. Where was Thomas Edison to help us get the lamp back functioning?

Alas, the answers came in the form of the obvious equation: hopeless-to-the-radical-50.

We also concluded that there was no alibiing a pillow fight. Once Aunt Selma saw the cave we had constructed in her wall, she'd surely be fuming and also was wise enough not to conclude that there had been a brief Martian incursion.

Ergo: we were screwed, left, right and sideways.

Our one flicker of hope remained with Uncle Nat, who had a knack for cooling Aunt Vesuvius.

Eventually, they returned. We had no choice but to lead them to the guest room and point out where the blitz had hit.

"Who did this?" screamed Aunt Selma, reaching the normally unreachable C above high C.

Before either of us could take the blame, Uncle Nat, barely muting a giggle, intruded, almost.

Aunt Selma turned on him. "So, you think this is funny, Nat?" she said.

Well, since he already did, Uncle Nat returned his wife's volley with the perfect squelch, saying: "Send the boys to bed. I'll fix it tomorrow."

Breakfast the next morning was more somber than usual. But when Aunt Selma delivered the pancakes and maple syrup, she couldn't contain herself.

"Well," she harrumphed, "I hope you boys had a good time last night." She paused, then added: "I know that my wall certainly didn't."

She seemed to like her own semi-cute line and appeared to be waiting for something roughly equivalent to a round of applause.

But all Cousin Lewis and I could muster was a temporary case of lockjaw.

Just then, the Supreme Court justice rendered her own answer, and the case against naughty Stan and Lewis was dismissed.

Aunt Selma burst out laughing!

Aunt Selma

THE GIRL FRIENDS, ROUND 1

Miss America did not live across 582 Marcy Avenue from me. Nor did Betty Grable nor her gorgeous colleague, Rita Hayworth.

They didn't have to live in my Brooklyn, circa 1938.

That's because Marilyn Pinzin did, and right across Marcy at Number 583.

I can't say that I even came close to "loving" Marilyn Pinzin. At age six, who knew from Cupid? But I must admit that there was *something* about her thighs that moved my inner spirit. Shall we say, "The thighs had it"?

Put it this way, it would have been a helluva note for me to call Marilyn my girlfriend. We were too young. "Gal pal," maybe. We were only six, going on nine.

But there was this one encounter with Marilyn that had to be rated Bingo! All I can report is that on that afternoon in Chez Pinzen, something unusual happened. Accidentally or otherwise, the lovely Miss P -- whether she knew it or not -- had a significant, lightning moment of sex appeal.

Of course, I had no idea what that curiously refreshing feeling was all about until we engaged in an impromptu wrestling match on her living room floor.

During this brief encounter, our legs (accidentally, I presume) intertwined when suddenly -- I dare say, happily -- I felt a surge of "something" happening down in the Southland, between my thighs. Call it a "thigh of relief," if you will.

Since I was nowhere near an electrical outlet and batteries were not included in my knickers, the "something" had everything to do with the sexpot of 583 Marcy, the suddenly voluptuous Marilyn Pinzen. (No Barbie doll, she!)

But as fast as that *something* happened, it was over. Mrs. Pinzen ordered Marilyn to dinner and I crossed Marcy somewhere between ecstatic and confused but with an idea that I had discovered a new form of electricity.

I just needed one more experiment, one more wrestling card with Marilyn. Then the two of us would share the Nobel Prize for discovering thigh electricity. Even from their graves, Edison and Marconi would be proud.

That hope ended within days when a Seven Santini Brothers moving van pulled up in front of the Pinzen *chateau*. I didn't even have a chance to warble a chorus of "Bye Bye Baby" to my almost-sexpot-almost-girlfriend, Marilyn.

She and her family had disappeared. Address unknown.

What I desperately needed now was a new wrestling partner, another Miss Pilzen. At last, in the seventh grade of P.S. 54, in spring 1945, the lithe form of Teresa Gallo crossed my crosshairs. She out-Pilzened Marilyn.

Teresa was a blazingly natural redhead if ever there was one. Her arsenal included a pair of legs that would've caused Marlene Dietrich to faint in envy. And you wouldn't believe how good she was at schoolyard dodgeball!

Thanks to our home-room teacher, Mrs. Morton, Teresa was conveniently located right down the row from me. And since there were no demerits for just peering across the row, I had a semester's worth of freebie looks at Red Gallo.

But I wanted more than the odd peek. After much brainstorming, I came up with a plan – not as sure as D-Day, but a strategy nonetheless. I would invade Spencer Street.

Red Gallo lived on Spencer, a mere seven blocks from my house. And I had transportation: a brand-new Roadmaster bike, guaranteed to win me points. I could even give her a handlebars ride to the pizza joint on DeKalb.

On a Saturday morning, I'd pedal over to Villa Gallo and ride my spanking red Roadmaster back and forth until the one and only redhead strolled out of her house.

Seeing me, Teresa would say something like, "Stanley, what are you doing here?"

I'd say, "Just happened to come by on my way to a drum lesson." Then, we'd strike up a conversation. After that? Who knew, but it would be worth the try.

The sunny Saturday arrived. I hopped on my Roadmaster, peeled over to Spencer and pedaled back and forth in front of Teresa's house for an hour or so, occasionally peeking through the windows for a sign of flaming red hair.

I got a lot of mileage, double the frustration, but no Teresa. The short ride home felt very long, for some reason. It got even longer the next month.

Classes resumed at P.S. 54 in September, and there still was no Teresa. I soon discovered that she moved to some distant place called Lake Ronkonkoma in Long Island's Suffolk County. If you think I was heartbroken, you should have seen my thighs!

Fortunately, they would be revived in 1946, at Eastern District High School, my next educational destination. E.D.H.S. offered me algebra, trigonometry, English studies and a bevy of *nofkies*, i.e., beautiful possibilities in technicolor.

Best of all was Marilyn Wurtzel, a buxom blond who played second trombone to my first trombone in the Eastern High band. I sat immediately to Marilyn's left.

From purely a strategic standpoint, I was in a good place. My trombone slide and right elbow were dangerously close to Marilyn, whose reputation was known school-wide.

By mutual acclaim, Marilyn was known as The Sweater Girl of E.D. High, and nobody was closer to that sweater than yours truly. Every time I pulled my trombone slide from the C position, my right elbow caught a feel of the Wurtzel sweater. Since merry Marilyn never beefed about my breast-brushing, I figured she kind of liked it.

When it came to futures with Marilyn, I knew there was nothing. She already was dating guys who drove Studebakers, while I was limited to a front-row seat on the Nostrand Avenue trolley.

However, the good news was that my slide-on-sweater routine was enough to keep me happy with Marilyn, although I never could get my trombone slide as far down as thigh level. Close, but no cigar – and certainly no thigh.

Fortunately, there were other potential beauties on the E.D. scorecard. Namely, Fulvia De Felice. This was one Italian sweetheart whose beauty matched her musical name. As good luck would have it, our drama teacher chose me to play Romeo to Fulvia's Juliet. I felt like Mickey Rooney wooing Judy Garland in MGM's *Andy Hardy* series.

As we began rehearsing *Romeo and Juliet*, I eagerly anticipated the kissing scene as the start of something big between us. What a chance for Fulvia to be fulsome.

As we drew closer and closer, my insides did cartwheels and I began singing -- to myself, of course -- *I Don't Want To Set The World On Fire*. The song title's lyrics continued: "I Just Want To Start A Flame In Your Heart."

Wait! What's going on? My Juliet is giving me her cheek, not lips. That's not how Shakespeare wrote it. I had forgotten that Miss De Felice was a devout Catholic. For fabulous Fulvia, even giving me cheek was borderline X-Rated.

Then along came Elaine Eiglarsh, who was very close to being "it." I met Elaine at a high school basketball game. My pal, Gilbert Greenberg, pointed her out. Elaine's gold-and-white cheerleading garb was *ooh, la, la.*

"I'll introduce you," Gil promised. So he did, and so we hit it off: first with dual chocolate ice cream sodas at The Sugar Bowl, then with a walk in Tompkins Park. Was this really *it?*

Elaine's face was heavenly beautiful -- a la Alice Faye -- and she laughed at all my jokes, even this oldie:

"Why did the chicken cross the road?"

"That was no chicken; that was my wife!"

But there was a bit of a problem. I was a leg man, always was. Elaine's legs were not in the Red Gallo class. No hubba-hubba-hubba for them. No wolf-whistle for the Eiglarsh gams. Sorry.

Then I came to my senses. What a neat chick, I realized. What a smile. What vim, vigor and vitality. And she laughed at my jokes. For a few fun weeks, Elaine became my first genuine A-Number-One, Yankee-Doodle-Ipsy-Pipsy girlfriend.

The deal was good. She lived only three blocks down Marcy, between Pulaski and DeKalb, an easy walk. The Sugar Bowl was two blocks away. We could sink nickels in the jukebox playing Goodman, Miller and Crosby all afternoon.

Elaine liked Tommy Dorsey's "Marie," with Sinatra singing. She shared my love of the Andrews Sisters' "Rum and Coca-Cola." Frankly, I liked Elaine Eiglarsh a whole, helluva lot. And then, something went wrong.

I wish I could tell you how we broke up or why we broke up or anything relative to our split. To this day, I can't figure it, other than it made me sad. Very sad.

What I do remember was that the final break-up happened on a rainy day, and I was alone at home on the third floor of 582.

I don't know how Hollywood's Otto Preminger would have choreographed this scene, but, in retrospect, it did have a touch of -- shall we say -- melancholy. As in the song "My Melancholy Baby."

What I do know is that I pulled a 12-inch -- not the usual 10-inch -- record out of my album and placed it on my new Zenith phonograph's turntable. Accidentally or coincidentally, the tune was Bunny Berigan's "I Can't Get Started With You." Bunny -- superbly and sorrowfully -- did the vocal and then blew his trumpet better than he ever did in his life.

The downpour outside on Marcy provided the perfect background for the love song, and Bunny, of course, did the rest. I still can hear him warbling the winsome words:

You're so supreme, lyrics I write of you/Scheme, just for the sight of you.

Dream, both day and night of *you*/What good does it do?

I must have played it through four times, not weeping, just thinking about what might have been between me and the lovely, sprightly Elaine.

The rain stopped, and so did Bunny. Within six hours, I had forgotten about Elaine Eiglarsh, the belle of Marcy Avenue.

Remarkably, happy days *were* here again. That night, April 16, 1949, my beloved Toronto Maple Leafs defeated the Detroit Red Wings, 3-1, to sweep the final and win their third straight Stanley Cup in a four-game sweep of the Final Round. No team ever had won three straight Cups in a row.

I was ecstatic beyond all reason. I went to The Sugar Bowl and ordered two egg creams. I slowly downed them both, toasting my Toronto heroes Turk Broda, Bill Ezinicki and Teeder Kennedy. My team; my Leafs! Yeah!!!

After downing the second egg cream, I walked over to the jukebox, jingling nickels in my palm. By the time the glowing Wurlitzer had played Bing Crosby and the Andrews Sisters singing "Don't Fence Me In," the question – Who needed Elaine Eiglarsh when I had my winning Maple Leafs? – was answered.

So was this one: Who needed a lamenting Bunny Berigan when I could play Benny Goodman's "Sing, Sing, Sing" on the Sugar Bowl juke box?

Nothing against sweet Elaine, but I still could smile because I had my Leafs to keep me warm.

In that spring of 1949 -- just in time and in overtime -- hockey conquered love.

Stan (l) with Anthony Greco and Marilyn Pinzin, Stan's first "girlfriend"

VJ DAY AND SHRIMP WITH
LOBSTER SAUCE

How do you celebrate a surrender?

The French and Germans used railway cars in 1918 and 1940, respectively, but in 1945's-Brooklyn, we only had trolley cars.

Since a streetcar was no place to hail V-J (Victory Over Japan) Day, we did it in other ways. My celebration started at the Miami Beach of Brooklyn -- Sea Gate by the Sea.

This was a villa inside The Gate, which was located at the very western tip of Coney Island. The family of my best friend, Howie Sparer, rented the house, and I happened to be a guest on that fateful summer day, August 15, 1945.

Howie's folks -- Sally and Sidney -- had made dough in the food business and Villa Sparer, overlooking the Atlantic, was a result of their churning out endless jars of Gold Crest mayonnaise in their plant on DeKalb Avenue, corner of Marcy.

The amiable Sparers represented Brooklyn Jewish royalty. Exhibit A was their Sea Gate villa. Exhibit B was Sally's 1937 four-door, eight-cylinder Packard. The company's slogan was "Ask the man who owns one." Or ask the lady. Sally loved it. She truly was a regal driver who treated her vehicle as if it just came off the Packard production line.

The Sparers spawned a fun-loving, unpretentious family that included Howie's big brother Gerson (alias Gershy) and bigger sister

Norma, a rare beauty who resembled the leggy Varga Girls featured every month in *Esquire* magazine.

On that historic morning, Howie and I were messing around in the Atlantic surf and sunning ourselves on Sea Gate beach. Since there were no bathing beauties around to ogle, we discussed two very important questions:

- Could the once-lowly St. Louis Browns win their second straight American League pennant despite having a center fielder, Pete Gray, who had only one arm?

- Would the lousy war be over today maybe, or tomorrow, or next week at the latest? The atomic bombs already had been dropped on Hiroshima and Nagasaki. We were getting closer -- and impatient.

Suddenly, barely audible over the crashing waves, Sally Sparer was calling us back to the house. There was a rare sense of urgency in her voice; Sally was a cool kitten of a lady, a middle-aged beauty. Clearly, a knock-out.

When we reached the villa's porch, Sally was barely able to contain her grin. "WE WON THE WAR!" shouted Sally. "IT'S ALL OVER!"

We were gleeful beyond words. "The boys will be coming home again," Howie blurted. "I can't wait to see the big parade."

"Yeah," I noted on an equally vital matter, "and Lionel will be making electric trains again; no more of the cardboard crap."

Always on top of current events, Howie brought up a more immediate topic, asking "How do we celebrate V-J Day?"

Sally knew. "It's like doing a bar mitzvah," she said, "only we're not going to shul [synagogue]. The party will be here this afternoon, and, boys -- get out of the way -- I have to start preparing."

That meant grabbing the telephone and calling the *mishpochuh*: relatives and close friends. Details of the surrender and other military matters could wait until the last glass of Dr. Brown's Cel-Ray Tonic was quaffed many hours later.

By mid-afternoon, Villa Sparer was bulging with aunts, uncles, cousins, neighbors and -- wait a minute -- a GI. He was a real soldier, wearing a smart, khaki uniform and adorned with something even prettier, the gorgeous Norma.

The soldier boy was tall, mustached Morris Gold who -- at least to my Hollywood-oriented eyes -- looked an awful lot like a Jewish Clark Gable.

Although I didn't spend more than a dozen seconds checking out the lovebirds, Norma and Morris seemed more tightly coupled than a pair of subway cars on the Brighton Line. I can't recall if Moe stole a kiss or not, but he should have.

By 6 p.m. the celebration had peaked. The Nova lox was gone, three cubes of potato salad sat longingly on a platter and a dozen bottles of Manischewitz wine were ready for the round file.

It was then that Sally pulled me and Howie aside and whispered, "Boys, now we're going to have our own celebration. Come with me."

Dutifully, we followed Sally to the 1937 Packard, not knowing what was in store but with a sense that good things were ahead. Sally started her limo and declared, "First, we'll go eat Chinks and then I'll take you kids to Coney."

Until that evening, "Chinks" only meant one thing to me. Once a week, I'd walk a couple of blocks from my house at 582 Marcy to Tompkins Avenue and Pulaski for my weekly, solo meal at our local Chinese eatery, Yee Ping Hing.

For half a buck, I'd order egg-drop soup, chicken chow mein and an almond cookie to accompany the free tea. For years, my order stayed the same, with no change except maybe a ball of ice cream for dessert instead of the almond cookie.

Sally parked on Brighton Beach Avenue under the BMT el and escorted us to a Chinese restaurant that could have been named Not Yee Ping Hing. Sally handed each of us a menu. "Pick what you want, boys."

Wow! I'd never seen things like this before. General Chow's chicken. (Which war did this general win to have a chicken dish named after him?) Right underneath the military man's listing was shrimp with lobster sauce.

I asked myself, "Do I stick with what I know so well, chicken chow mein, or dare I go to the unknown but enticing shrimp with lobster sauce?" Tough, tough call.

The waiter arrived, I flipped a coin in my head; it came out tails. With a slight hesitation, I ventured into the unknown and finally blurted: "Shrimp with lobster sauce."

The waiter smiled, jotted down the orders and began walking to the kitchen. Suddenly, I had second thoughts. Do I really want this exotic item? But it was too late; he disappeared into the kitchen.

Minutes later, the waiter arrived with my order, and I did a triple-take. The dual blend of the aural and visual was almost too much for my nasal nerves and my eyes to behold. It looked too good to eat.

This remarkable concoction made my Yee Ping Hing chow mein seem like cold, burnt toast by comparison. I couldn't tell at first which I liked better: the sight of the little rowboat shrimps at anchor or the yellow sea of lobster sauce.

Finally, I dug in and instantly knew that this would be the best meal of my life, even better than Quaker Puffed Rice Sparkies with heavy cream.

"How do you like it?" asked Sally, noticing that I looked like a greenhorn having my first stateside meal. And, in a culinary sense, I was, as I timidly replied, "It's terrific."

Truth is, I couldn't tell whether I preferred the shrimp or the lobster sauce. And it left me with the feeling that there were a few dozen other items on that menu that would top chicken chow mein at Yee Ping Hing.

After dinner, Sally hustled us off to Coney, where there were an embarrassment of celebratory riches. Do we start with the penny arcade, the bobsled ride, bumper cars or that monument to bowling skill, Skee-Ball?

We chose the latter because prizes were easy to get if you put up enough points with the five balls for a nickel. A certain amount of dexterity was involved in rolling the wooden ball into the center of the four holes.

Since Sally gave us an unlimited amount of nickels, each of us came away with such valuable prizes as salt-and-pepper shakers and a stuffed monkey.

V-J celebrants had Coney packed from Surf Avenue to the Boardwalk on this momentous occasion. The sky was clear, a breeze wafted in from the Atlantic and all seemed right with the world -- until Howie blurted the fateful line: "Why don't we try the roller coaster?"

That was a shocker. Up until then, Howie and I had limited our Coney rides to such standards as the Steeplechase horses, the Surf Avenue carousel with gold rings and the ever-popular bumper cars.

As far as we were concerned, the roller coaster was in the too-scary-for-words realm. But this was V-J night, and it was time to throw caution to the zephyrs. We agreed to do it. But which of the many roller coasters should we go on?

The Cyclone was out of the question. Way too scary. The Thunderbolt was too many blocks away. Across Surf Avenue from the Cyclone was the L.A. Thompson Scenic Railway, a roller coaster by any other name. Built in 1884, it was the forerunner of the best coasters in Coney.

I was nervous about our impetuous "yes," but there was no backing off now. Sally already had bought us tickets. Next thing we knew, we were on line.

The L.A. Thompson Scenic Railway was different from all the other Coney roller coasters. The Cyclone *et. al.* -- were situated on the board-walk side of Surf Avenue, but the L.A. Thompson Scenic Railway was not. It sat on the north side of Surf, directly under the double-deck elevated tracks of the assorted BMT lines that terminated a few blocks away at Stillwell Avenue.

"Here it comes!" Howie shouted as the four-car coaster braked to a stop and the riders climbed out. I studied their faces to see if any had fainted or burst into tears during the ride, but there were no visible clues.

We were seated in the middle of the train. With a lurch, off it rolled, first under the darkened steelwork of the el and then, to the rhythm of clanking chains, we were being pulled up the big hill.

I studied the landscape and was overwhelmed by the cool sea breeze combined with my angst over the first plunge. Now we were at the peak, and the view looking down the tracks inspired a lively question: "Do we live through this adventure?"

The cars' three-second descent provided the most intense thrill I had experienced in my thirteen years on Planet Earth. But this was only the beginning.

Down, up, down -- all in semi-darkness -- gave the Thompson an added attraction. It also provided the last half of the ride with the security that comes with knowing that the final stop lay just ahead.

Ecstatic beyond belief, we decided on a second ride, but Sally pulled the watch on us and we triumphantly returned to the limo.

"What a great way to celebrate V-J Day," I blurted to Sally as she brought the Packard into the Sea Gate driveway. "Thanks for everything."

Morris Gold, the GI, and Norma Sparer, the raving Sparer beauty, were somewhere else celebrating V-J Day in a more romantic manner.

Matter of fact, their V-J Day celebration was so romantic that they wound up getting married.

Howie and I couldn't top that, but we did promise to celebrate our own creation -- V-C Day, for victory and courage. We had vowed to be daring beyond all belief and ride the Cyclone – and ride it we did. And lived to tell the tale.

Our celebration equaled in intensity our joy on V-J Day -- but with one missing delicacy: shrimp in lobster sauce.

Howie Sparer and his mom, Sally, c. 1940

KISSING THE BOOKENDS
GOODBYE AT P.S. 54

One of the best classes at P.S. 54, at Hart Street at the corner of Nostrand Avenue, was simply called "shop," orchestrated by Mister Montague, whose first name we never figured out.

How could you beat it? You went to Mr. Montague's carpentry room a few times a week and you came out with a free, always-practical gift, guaranteed to please your parents.

Of course you had to work for it, whether you were crafting a silent waiter (armed with a tall ash tray), a tray that served drinks or, best of all, bookends. What could possibly be more useful than a pair of shop-made bookends?

After all, every kid in P.S. 54 (circa 1944) read books, and nobody wanted the volumes to fall on their faces. That's where the bookends came into play; they kept *Submarine Sailors* and *The Kid from Tomkinsville* straight up.

Mr. Montague was the man behind all of our construction projects. That meant discipline was the order of the day in shop. The penalties went this way: Do something to piss off Mr. Montague, and you got a demerit -- maybe two!

A demerit could be a major league concern for anyone in shop. A few Ds, and you've got your parents on the case. Get five of them, and the worst thing in the world at P.S. 54 would happen: *You would get left back!*

Nothing -- and I do mean *nothing* – could be worse than being left back at P.S. 54. Students feared it, parents feared it, but not Mr. Montague, whose ultra-scary technique was clever -- at times downright sinister.

It went like this:

A. Kid fools around.

B. Montague catches him

C. Kid thinks Mr. Montague is going to yell at him.

D. Nay, he lowers his voice to just short of a whisper: a frightening fake-out.

If Hollywood ever made a movie about Mr. Montague, he would have been played by Jimmy Cagney. He looked like Cagney, talked like Cagney and like Jimmy in *White Heat*, he took no crap from anybody. Perhaps, shopmate Ralph Hubbard never saw that film, but he sure got melted by Montague one morning.

Ralphie was a funny black guy who lived in a tenement on Myrtle Avenue, around the corner from me. In time, Hubbard would become a Korean War hero, but for the moment, he was merely our hero in shop.

Why? Because he defied Mr. Montague. He fooled around, got a few well-muffled laughs from me and Neil Brown and -- whoops – Montague's superb radar caught Ralphie in midfoolery.

A hush fell over the shop classroom as Mr. Montague's eyes turned into searchlights, with poor Ralphie Hubbard in the crosshairs. The voice turned soft but firm while young Hubbard wanted very much to be somewhere in Tahiti.

Then came the lowered voice: "Mis-ter, Hubbard." Then, a pause, as Montague held up his right hand before beginning the count, using three fingers on his right hand.

"Mis-ter Hubbard, D-D-D," Montague said, his fingers rising with each number. "One, two, three."

Yikes! Hubbard had pulled off a demerit hat trick, previously unheard of in P.S. 54's long history of demerits. Having unofficially set a new school record, Ralphie momentarily turned white, then vowed to shut up for the rest of the semester.

(By cancelling his shop comic act for the duration, Ralphie avoided further demerits and was duly applauded by Mr. Montague with a promotion to the sixth grade like the rest of the boys.)

I should add that Ralphie was only one of a three-lad act that enjoyed japes as much as we did working on our bookends. Neil Brown and yours truly comprised the other two-thirds. Unlike Ralphie, we made no nice-guy promises.

Somehow, Brownie and I avoided demerits until two weeks were left to the school year and our bookends were 90 percent completed. We even had our initials inscribed on the upright ends, and only awaited the final shellacking.

It was, so to speak, the last of the eighth inning, and Neil and I figured the bookends were in the bag. Looked like game-over -- we win -- and then IT happened. Montague caught us fooling around while sandpapering our bookends.

First, Mr. M's voice dropped a few decibels to ensure that he had scared the living shit out of us.

"Mis-ter Brown, and Mis-ter Fischler," he said, "will you please bring your book-ends up to the front of the room and give them to me."

US: (Trembling, head to foot.) "Yes, Mister Montague."

Montague: "Now, I want you each to give your bookends a great, big kiss."

US: (More Trembling): "Yes, Mister Montague." Then we each kissed our bookends.

Montague: "Do you know why you are kissing your bookends?"

US: "No, Mister Montague."

Montague: "You have just kissed the bookends goodbye. They are going to the nuns at St. Mary's Church on Clinton Avenue. Now take your seats."

Stunned to the very core, Brownie and I stumbled back to our tables, wanting to weep but knowing that weeping was out of the question. Shop sportsmanship ruled that you take your demerits as they come; grin and bear it.

At last, the end-of-class bell rang. As penitent Neil and I headed to the door, Montague waved a come-to-my-desk hand to his prisoners.

"Boys, did you learn a lesson today -- and if so what is it?" he asked.

"Not to fool around in shop, Mr. Montague," we answered.

"Exactly. That's what I wanted to hear. Now, here are your bookends. Take good care of them."

We did.

My bookends are now 75 years old and still doing their job: holding up some of my favorite books: *Boys of Summer, Even The Browns, The Hockey Encyclopedia* and *If You Can't Beat 'Em In The Alley.*

The sign of shellac is gone, but the S.F. initials are intact, along with memories of my very fond -- and scary -- moments with Mr. Montague.

I don't know what happened to Mr. Montague. Ralphie once told me that our shopmaster had lost a son in World War II.

I still have my bookends, and the nuns at St. Mary's Church don't. Once in a while, I look over at my bookends, and I have a feeling I know what Mr. M would think: that, at age 89, I'm still fooling around. Of course, he'd be right.

The back side of PS 54 in recent years

GOING DOWNTOWN

"We're going downtown!"

Those three words didn't mean "I love you," but they were music to my 10-year-old ears in 1942.

Uttered either by my mom or Grandma Etel, the utterance meant that they would take me shopping downtown on Fulton Street.

It also meant that there was a 7-1 chance I'd wind up buying something for myself. Anything. Didn't matter if it was a cheap toy (unlikely) or a glass of papaya juice (bet on it) at the hot dog stand next to A&S.

Of course, every Brooklynite of any age knew that A&S meant the Abraham & Straus department store, the Macy's of Brooklyn, The Palace of Purchase, The Titan of Toy Departments.

Every self-respecting Brooklyn lad loved A&S because it featured the best toy department of Fulton Street's Big Three, the others being loser Loeser's and non-entity Namm's, just a couple of blocks from A&S.

In those pre-historic days, the way to measure the absolute quality of a toy department was by the size of its Lionel electric-train display. The tracks said it all.

The toy departments at Namm's and Loeser's didn't have a fighting chance. By far, A&S boasted the most Lionel track miles and featured train lines you wouldn't find elsewhere.

Across the aisle from the three-track Lionel lines were the more realistic two-track American Flyer sets. For the truly economy-minded, A&S added the cheap, fragile but still interesting Marx boxed train line.

But neither Mom nor Gram – as I called Grandma Etel -- could care less about Lionels, American Flyers, Marx's or anything else in the toy department for that matter. That was a fact of life I never could fathom.

The adults shopped for what I regarded as useless things -- like clothes, a new lamp or a pop-up toaster. I was brought along as a spectator who might -- just *might* -- cash in on the Fulton expedition.

As always, getting there was half the fun. We'd take the GG Crosstown local to the Hoyt-Schermerhorn station, which conveniently was adjacent to Loeser's basement. (It actually had a fancy showroom *inside* the subway station.)

Proximity meant that Loeser's was our first stop. That's where Gram bought knitting wool for the dozens of sleeveless sweaters she annually crocheted for me – as if a half-dozen were not enough.

We always bypassed Namm's. One day, I asked why. "Who needs Namm's," Mom explained, "when A&S is next door?"

Even the A&S architecture topped its competition. The tall department store was new and Art Deco all the way. It looked like a retail version of the Empire State Building and promised something for everyone.

That "something" included what my buddy, Howie Sparer, called The Annual Downtown Delight. I labeled it That Great, Great Come-and -get-it Day. Either way, it was a winner for two of the wartime years, 1942 and '43.

For two Decembers, our thoughtful and sensible mothers, Molly Fischler and Sally Sparer, made good on their unwritten pact. Call it The Mothers' Treaty.

Two weeks before Christmas, Sally would hustle me and Howie down to the A&S toy department. A week later, my mom repeated the drill. Each of us was allowed to pick one gift: a grand total of two gifts for two years.

In 1942, I chose Trap A Tank, a perfect wartime game. You turned a crank and three little tanks would move through tank traps. The first tank to the finish line won. (The toy lasted just short of a month.)

A year later, my choice was a hockey game made by the Gotham Toy Company. Ah, this was a gift with substance. It featured a metallic rink with a goalie at each end.

The goalies could swing around 180 degrees and whack a steel ball at great speed, back and forth, until someone dispatched the steel ball behind the goalie and down the chute. He shoots! He scores!

It was an exciting game except for the wear and tear on the poor tin goalies and the mechanism. Gotham had built it to last, and so it did -- for two weeks of vicious, intense whacking. Then, *TILT!* The springs broke.

All that could be salvaged were two goalies and a steel ball. In fairness, it was good enough for carpet hockey (which you will learn more about later in these Tales), using the two tin goalies as forwards and defensemen and, of course, ball-stopping.

Apart from game-purchasing, the second-best reason to hit downtown Brooklyn was for the movie theaters along Fulton Street, Brooklyn's version of Times Square.

You started with the Paramount, followed by Fabian Fox, Loew's Orpheum, Majestic, RKO Albee, Duffield and Loew's Metropolitan. The Met even had a second marquee entrance on Schermerhorn Street.

It was my tough, Hungarian, Grandma Etel who always took me downtown to the flicks. One scary -- to me at least -- occasion, she got involved in a battle of nerves at the Met that was more melodramatic than the day's flick.

The one-round bout began when an usher met us at the top of the aisle, flashlight beaming. As we marched along, he suddenly applied the brakes, turned to Gram and blared, "No seating in the front dozen rows."

The poor guy couldn't have realized that he had just shot a volley across Gram's regal Hungarian bow. She looked him in the eye and paused without saying a word. I instantly knew what she was thinking: "*Dumbkopf,* you're trying to tell me, a proud Hungarian, that I can't go down to the front half. Are you a *schlemiel* or what?"

With that, Gram barreled past the poor chap as if he were a cigar-store Indian and found two sweetheart seats in the front section, while the befuddled usher disappeared into the darkness, KO'd by Gram.

I was stunned by her *chutzpah*. When we got home for dinner, I told my dad about the frightening (to me) incident and added: "How could Gram get away with doing something like that?"

Father replied: "She's a Hungarian, right? They can do things that only Hunkies can do. For instance, a Hungarian is the only person who can go through a revolving door behind you and come out ahead of you. Get it?"

I asked Dad if I could pull off a coup, the way Gram did at the Met.

"No way," Pop concluded, "you're only half a Hunkie!"

By 1944, neither Howie nor I needed any parent nor grandparent to take us downtown. At age 12, we were old enough to do the A&S commando assault solo, so we did.

It was May '44, with a year more of the war to go. Songwriters continued composing tunes related to the conflict. Even department stores like A&S featured what they called song pluggers: an on-site singer or musician who promoted a song's sheet music.

The A&S song plugger was near the rug department, where my Uncle Sid sold carpets. We gave him a quick hello and walked over to a crowd surrounding a guy on a stage, tinkling a grand piano.

He was playing brand-new tunes and selling the sheet music, which included both words and music. "Let's hang out and listen," Howie suggested, and we did – and were we ever glad we did.

The pianist knocked off and sang a couple of inconsequential tunes before swinging into a melody of bandleader Les Brown that neither Howie nor I ever had heard before. When he started warbling, the words went like this:

Gonna take a sentimental journey

Gonna set my heart at ease

Gonna make a sentimental journey

To renew old memories …

I never thought my heart could be so yearny

Now why did I decide to roam?

I'm gonna take that sentimental journey

Sentimental journey home.

We knew instantly, instinctively, that this song, "Sentimental Journey," would be a hit. The beauteous star, Doris Day, soon would make it so.

Each of us purchased the sheet music for "Sentimental Journey" and, having memorized the music, we read through more lyrics -- and began singing and reading and singing some more:

Seven, that's the time we leave, at seven.

I'll be waitin' up for heaven,

Countin' every mile of railroad track

That takes me back.

I never thought my heart could be so yearny

Now why did I decide to roam?

I'm gonna take a sentimental journey

Sentimental journey home.

We certainly didn't know that this would turn out to be the last trip to downtown Brooklyn that two best friends ever would make together.

Leaving A&S, turning right on Fulton toward the RKO Albee, we hummed "Sentimental Journey" for what would be our final *sentimental journey* home.

Alas, going downtown never would be the same after that.

Abraham and Straus, Fulton St. in the 1930s

VERNON AVENUE AND THE
BOYS ON THE BLOCK

There was a lot to like about Vernon Avenue, between Marcy and Nostrand, in Brooklyn, but there also was a nagging, geographic problem.

Those of us who lived there were eternally puzzled. We didn't know the proper name of our nabe.

Some of us thought we were in Williamsburg. My family certainly did, and had evidence to prove it. How could it not be The Burg if the *Upper Williamsburg* Jewish Center was only a couple of blocks away?

Others claimed that Vernon Avenue actually was situated in Bedford-Stuyvesant. Those naysayers claimed that Myrtle Avenue was the boundary line and, therefore, 582 Marcy missed being in the Burg by half a block.

The fact is we were in a No-Neighborhood's-Land. Not that it was such a big deal, just that it was confusing. Geographic schizophrenia was the ailment from which we suffered, assuming you call that "suffering."

"What neighborhood do you live in?" my Cousin Judd once asked me, knowing full well that his address -- 469 Miller Avenue, off Sutter -- was at the epicenter of Brooklyn's East New York neighborhood.

My answer was as muddling as the fact. "I'm either in Williamsburg or Bedford-Stuyvesant," I said, knowing that that wouldn't please him.

"Make up your mind," he shot back.

But I couldn't, and anyway, it didn't really matter

What mattered was that those of us who lived on or around Vernon loved it for what it was: a long, cozy block where the tree that grew in Brooklyn might well have been.

Vernon's virtues were many, starting with its blend of Italians, Poles, Jews, at least one Greek family, Irish – you name it, and we had it.

Except there were no blacks on Vernon. They were around the corner in tenements on Myrtle Avenue. One of my best friends from P.S. 54, Ralph Hubbard, lived there in an apartment under the el with his mom and older brother.

Although nobody on Vernon Avenue would think of it in sociological terms, the long block between Nostrand and Marcy unofficially and unobtrusively was divided in half.

The eastern half -- closer to Marcy -- was quiet and almost suburban-like. Nothing much happened there except in Mr. Kimmel's backyard, where he hosted more live tortoises than Turtle Bay. I happened to have seen them, since my Aunt Lottie originally was a Kimmel before she became a Friedman. Lottie would allow me occasional tortoise tours.

That joyride ended when I accidentally tripped over one that appeared to be in training for a hare race. I very nearly crushed its shell. (Do tortoises get concussions? Should turtle helmets be mandatory?)

Across the street, the Cacasi family played a short and dismaying part in my life. Signor Cacasi got pissed off at me and my buddy Norman Karger when we asked permission to string telegraph wire through his backyard.

The Fischler-Karger plan to put Western Union and Postal Telegraph out of business was aborted with a no-no-no in both Italian and English by Signor Cacasi.

Nobody played any ball or other games in the eastern half of Vernon. In fact, the only big story there took place when Gilbert Birnbaum, my classmate and the second fastest kid on the block, dolefully announced that his family was moving away from Vernon.

Such startling news shook our gang to the very core, since none of us ever knew of anyone who would move away from Vernon. It made absolutely no sense at all. Hence, action was necessary and a posse was formed.

That included yours truly, Howie Sparer, Jay Koslo and Neil Brown. The day we got the news, all four of us invaded Birnbaum's house once the day's classes ended at P.S. 54.

As we climbed the stairs to Gillie's third-floor apartment, Mrs. Birnbaum shouted down, "What do you boys want?"

"We want to see Gillie," young Sparer shouted back. By that time we were at the third floor, which was overrun with so many large cardboard cartons that we had to squeeze our way through. Suddenly, Gil appeared, tears in his eyes.

Losing a close pal such as Gilbert Birnbaum perplexed our quartet, so Jay launched one more foray into the world of Vernon logic. He pleaded with Mrs. B, "Why can't Gillie stay here?"

"Sorry, boys, we're moving to Queens. Say goodbye. The movers have arrived."

With that, we conducted a solemn, tearful, orderly retreat out into the fresh Williamsburg air. We turned left and soon sniffed the ambience of Vernon's western half, or the "Wild West" as we called it.

Just past Jake the Bookie's home on Vernon's border, we found the action, as always, intense. Each segment was like an outdoor arena. The macadam opposite Vernon's biggest tree was reserved for punchball.

Likewise, stickball -- the rare times we played it -- had its "field" in front of Richie Mishkin's almost-mansion. Just short of the Nostrand corner, there invariably was a stoopball game or boxball or maybe even triangle.

In between was room for association football, two-hand touch, ring-a-levio, hide-and-go-seek and Johnny-on-the-Pony. We made Vernon our play street because there wasn't a genuine city playground around for at least eight blocks.

My oldest pal from Vernon was Abe Yurkofsky, who became a doctor. Now 90, Abe recently explained why Vernon was so much fun for him.

"As an only child. I treasured the fact that there was always someone around," Abe remembered. "Stepping outside brought me a world of friends and acquaintances. We spent our daylight hours outdoors, with a friend always available."

With the exception of a few, isolated creeps, there were no really bad guys nor gangs in the immediate vicinity. We only heard about the terrifying Rhumba Rascals and the Navy Yard warriors, but they were far, far away.

Of the big guys -- anyone two or three years older than me -- there was a curious fellow on the block named Joseph Settembrinini. Nobody called him by either "Joe" or "Set." He was and always will be called "Devil." As far as I knew, Devil never had another name. He was Devil. Period.

Devil was scary, so I made it my business to stay a healthy fourteen or so yards away from him when I knew Devil was around. It was more out of respect for his nickname than any hurt he ever did to me or my friends. The other big guys were okay fellows.

Abe, Richie Mishkin, Jerry Katzman -- son of the kosher butcher -- and Alex Ogman, better known as "Voonie," occasionally would join us in games.

Or, more to the point, allow us to participate with them.

Another of the big guys, Murray Matlin, appropriately nicknamed Red, played with us more than the others. He was likeable and generally rated as the best punchball player and fastest runner on Vernon. For some reason, Red always ran with his hands at his sides.

The local store owners were mostly pals. Jack, the fruit and vegetable man on the corner of Vernon and Marcy, was a swell guy. Ditto for Leibel, another kosher butcher, who shared the back of the store with Jack.

Al and Shirley ran their candy store, on Nostrand and Vernon, like it was a community center – which, in fact, it was. Al and Shirley's sugar bowl* was highly regarded for

*Brooklynese for candy store

excellent egg creams and the hard-to-find Frank's Orange Soda, 12 ounces and made in Philadelphia. And only a nickel!

Frank's robust, glass bottles of orange soda could be found lodged between huge pieces of ice in the humongous, red-steel Coke container in front of the comic book library, the latter considered a rich source of learning for all the lads.

By far, Vernon's most controversial vendor -- later to be unanimously voted Most Disliked -- was Dominic Gerardi. He was a cunning man with a booming voice who sold Italian ices out of a horse cart from May through September.

As Dominic's nag executed a right turn, swinging the ice wagon onto Vernon from Marcy, Gerardi's call of the wild could be heard all the way to Canarsie: "Lemona, chocolata, pineapple, a-cherry," over and over and over again.

That commercial announcement was followed by Dominic waving a large bell six times, just in case we didn't hear his calls of the ice flavors the first, second or eighth times.

Gerardi's colorful ice wagon made its Vernon Avenue premiere during the summer of 1942, and was held over by popular demand in 1943, 1944 and 1945 – what we called Our War Years.

Dominic sold two sizes of ice. For a penny, you got the economy white cup; for a nickel, you obtained what my Aunt Hattie liked to call the *gazunta* portion, with the container three times the size of penny ice.

(Family Note: My mother forbade me to eat either the penny or five cents version on the grounds that "Dominic makes the ices in his cellar." It was a great, uncertified scientific discovery that had to be true, since Mom said so.)

Sometime during the summer of 1944, Dominic delivered a promise that tempted every kid on the block and quite a few adults as well.

"Whena da war is over," he promised, "everadabody gets free ices." Then just to underline his point. "FREE ICES!"

In May 1945, V-E Day signified that the war in Europe had ended. But that didn't count with Dominic, who diligently maintained his penny and nickel prices until, as he put it, "Da war was a-really over."

V-J Day, Japan's surrender, officially ending World War II, took place on August 15th, 1945. It was to be the great-great-come-and-get-it-ices-day that we eagerly awaited. To all on Vernon, the sound of Dominic's promise of free ices happily echoed in our ears.

Then, *it* happened. Or, rather it *didn't* happen.

According to Vernon Avenue's Historic Society, the sweet Dominic sounds of "lemona, chocolata, pineapple and a-cherry" last were heard on Vernon Avenue on August 14, 1945.

Starting the next day and forevermore, there never again was a Dominic, a Dominic horse or a Dominic wagon. August 15 was eventually celebrated as No Find Dominic Day.

Never again. No clip-clop of his horse. No clang, clang, clang of his large bell. Instead of free ices, we got what Howie called "the square root of *chai-cock*." *Gornisht*, translated from Yiddish: nothing. Zippo.

For all intents and purposes, Dominic Gerardi's disappearing act would have made The Great Houdini deliver a low bow followed by a standing ovation.

No matter. Who needed free ices when there was a daily visit by the Bungalow Bar man, driving his brown-and-white ice cream-filled Chevy?

Every kid knew that if you bought a BB ice cream pop -- any flavor -- and the stick had *Bungalow Bar* stamped on its side, you got a freebie chocolate pop the next time around.

According to my records, Catherine Tripodi, Howie Sparer, and Murray (Red) Matlin were the lucky BB winners over a three-year period. (I struck out on three pitches.)

According to my personal observation, the golden age of Vernon Avenue began immediately after the war and lasted about five years.

The biggest deal was that the boys came home. Our GIs, whose uniformed photos adorned the big window of Al and Shirley's candy store, began drifting back, all conquering heroes for my dough.

Well, not all of the Vernon boys in khaki returned. Unfortunately -- sadly --we had a few homes with gold stars hanging by the windows. For the Gold Star moms on Vernon, war *was* hell.

Typical of the returnees was my Uncle Joe -- Mom's kid brother -- who flew home from the Aleutian Islands, where he was stationed with the Navy Seabees.

Other GI relatives we welcomed included Joe Donenberg, who served with the field artillery in Germany; Uncle John Cooke, out of the U.S. Maritime Service; and Cousin Irving Lee, a major in Army Intelligence.

Vernon's golden age was marked by the arrival of new cars -- Studebaker was the first to have an ultra-modern design – refrigerators and electric trains. In that five-year postwar period, the Yankees won two more World Series titles. Not to mention Jackie Robinson and Larry Doby in 1947 breaking baseball's color barrier in the National League and American Leagues, respectively.

Still, storm clouds were gathering over Vernon. First, it was the Sparer family's decision to move from 1-5 Vernon to 602 Montgomery Street in classy Crown Heights. Their exit didn't necessarily suggest a trend, but it pissed me off no end, since Howie was my best friend.

Alas, the Sparers' quiet departure – an ominous trend-setter, to be sure – proved to be the first indication of the massive departure of white families, a phenomenon that came to be known as "white flight." And as the 1940s gave way to the 1950s, the Veteres, the Greenblatts, the Myers, the Browns, and the Podolskis all went bye-bye to Long Island suburbs like Shirley and Ronkonkoma.

And then there were almost none of us left – just the Friedmans and Fischlers at 582 Marcy; and, down the block, Rosie Surdo with her son and daughter. (Even they eventually retreated all the way to sunny Bay Ridge.)

One day in 1955, the sweetheart of Marcy Avenue -- my grandpa's three-story brownstone, number 582 -- was sold for $5,000, mere Monopoly money.

Grandpa died, Grandma moved into Coney Island's Brooklyn Hebrew Home and Hospital for the Aged, and my folks found a nice, new Mitchell-Lama apartment called Willoughby Walk, across DeKalb Avenue from Pratt Institute.

By then, I was newspapering with the *New York Journal-American* and sharing a Manhattan apartment at 309A East 19th Street with my buddy Dave Perlmutter. Every so often, I'd yearn for another look at Marcy and Vernon.

I finally checked out 582 one afternoon in the early 1970s. All I could find was the building's foundation. The remainder had been reduced to rubble. Too traumatized to go on, I drove off without checking Vernon.

A decade passed. One day, for some strange reason, I decided to bike over to The Burg and, once and for all, see what good, old Vernon Avenue was all about in this new era. Nervously, I pedaled south on Marcy and finally made the right turn onto Vernon.

Alas, there wasn't much to see. Mr. Kimmel and his backyard turtle farm were long gone. So was Signor Cacasi, who foolishly had rejected the Karger-Fischler Trans-Vernon Telegraph Line. Even the once-busy, exciting western end of Vernon was empty. No punchball, no Al and Shirley's for an egg cream. Nothing.

I pedaled past Voonie Ogman's brownstone at No. 16 Vernon and Richie Mishkin's large, two-family house across the street that looked more like a mini-mansion.

My classmate Marilyn Smolen had lived at No. 12 alongside Abe Yurofsky at No. 8. The Karger boys -- Teddy, Norman and Stu -- were in the four-story, no-elevator apartment at 7-11. But, no more.

At the corner of Nostrand, 1-5 Vernon was still there, but no Howie, Gershy or Norma Sparer, surrounding their Stromberg-Carlson radio listening to *The Kate Smith Hour* with their parents Sally and Sidney.

I had seen enough of Vernon's new nothingness. I turned my GT Avalanche back toward Manhattan, secure in the knowledge that the old nabe now also could be equated with the square root of *chai-cock*.

Thus ended my love affair with Vernon Avenue, never to be rekindled.

Yeah, I still harbor magnificent memories from The Great Depression and those war years. Some may wonder why folks like me and Abe Yurkofsky wax poetic about those happy days on Vernon Avenue.

"We were poor," my pal Irving Rudd once explained, "but we didn't know it 'cause we were having too much fun!"

Voonie, Richie, Howie, Norman and Stu would second that motion.

Me, too!

The Sparer family, 1941
Back, l to r: Norma, Sidney, Sally, Gershy
Front: Howie

PART TWO
Going Beyond
Brooklyn

WHO REALLY DISCOVERED STATEN ISLAND?

Far be it from me to give you a history lesson, but there's a time and a place for everything – and now's the time to set the historic and geographic record straight.

Once and for all, the municipal authorities should give credit where credit is due: to Howard Sparer and Stanley Fischler because we, not some guy named Verrazano, really "discovered" Staten Island.

I kid you not. Our discovery of this lovely island across New York Harbor from our native Brooklyn was made in July 1943. I'll leave it at that because once you consider the facts of our lightly financed (about two bucks) expedition, you'll know the truth.

For starters, finding Staten Island was no easy task. Neither pal Howie nor I owned a map, a compass or a *Michelin Guide*. What we did have -- just barely -- was street smarts, Brooklyn-style.

We also had two bicycles, which we rented from a shop on Franklin Avenue across from Ebbets Field. All we had to do was leave a buck deposit and that was that.

Now that we had our one-speed, fat-tired, old two-wheelers, the next question was simple enough: Where to go? The answer was plain enough: I dunno.

That settled, we began pedaling along the outer rim of Prospect Park until we reached Ocean Parkway, the grandest of grand Brooklyn boulevards. (Eastern Parkway is runner-up.)

The beauty part of Ocean Parkway in 1943 was not only its array of massive oak trees or its two service lanes. As extra added attractions, the parkway boasted a bridle path and a bicycle lane all the way to Coney Island. But Howie and I had no interest in Coney; we'd been there, done that. We were explorers. We had to get off the beaten path and explore.

After five minutes of bicycling along Ocean Parkway, we encountered a funny-looking street that came off at an unusual angle. It was strange enough to be checked out, which we did.

Egad! It wasn't just a plain, old street. It was another parkway, only disguised as a street. Its name was – and still is -- Fort Hamilton Parkway.

"I never heard of this," shouted Howie.

"Neither have I," I shouted back. "Let's try it."

And so we did. Even without a bike path, a bridle path or even service roads, Fort Hamilton Parkway had its own special appeal. It was unchartered territory, but fascinating nonetheless.

Matter of fact, we liked Fort Hamilton Parkway so much that we pedaled and pedaled until it came to an end. To put it another way, FHP stopped at the water's edge. Turned out, we had come all the way to New York Bay.

Now what?

We sure as heck weren't going to turn around and go back, but we did have to turn left or right. We turned left, rolling along the waterside, when suddenly we were greeted by a big sign with an arrow. *Take the Electric Ferry*, it read.

"Is this a joke?" blurted Howie. "How can a ferry be electric?"

What could I say to that other than, "Let's find out."

And we did. It happened to be none other than the 69th Street ferry. It was conspicuously small as ferries go, but it did have one big thing about it. Splashed on both the port and starboard sides of the vessel were huge letters reading ELECTRIC FERRY.

Don't ask me where the electricity for the ferry came from, but I fully expected to find a sign by the engine room that read, *Batteries Not Included.*

As it happened, this electric ferry was designed primarily for cars and trucks. Pedestrians were allowed on, but there was no sitting room or lounge. There was, however, plenty of room for our two-wheelers.

I frankly was annoyed that the electric ferry didn't have a name. Like, say, the *Dolph Camilli,* to honor the Brooklyn Dodgers' first baseman. After all, every ship deserves a handle of some kind, so Howie and I huddled on the matter and in no time at all he had an answer.

"How about we call it the *Sidney Dinnerstein,*" Howie suggested. "He was important in electrical history."

I couldn't figure that one out, so I asked: "What the heck did Sidney Dinnerstein ever do that made him significant in electrical history?"

Howie stared at me as if I had six heads. "Do you mean to tell me that you didn't know that Sidney Dinnerstein invented the first electric pinball machine!"

And with that important note, the newly-named *Sidney Dinnerstein* slowly pushed away from its Brooklyn dock to an exotic island still unknown to us.

"We're on the high seas," I chortled to Howie as we passed the Henry J. Kaiser Shipyards. Kaiser built cargo ships, known as Liberty ships, for the war effort. I happened to have loved the motto he quoted, apparently from the U.S. Army Service Forces: "The impossible we do at once; the miraculous takes a little longer."

One of the electric ferry workers told us that Liberty ships were built there at a record pace. They were badly needed to supply the Allied forces overseas. One ferry guy told us about Kaiser's fast ship-building. A woman, he said, was asked to launch a ship. She stepped forward to the appointed place in the Kaiser shipyard, holding a bottle of Champagne, but couldn't see a ship.

"There's no ship," she said.

"Just start swinging the bottle," Kaiser replied, "and there will be!"

After we had sailed past the Kaiser yards, Howie pointed to a land mass in the distance. "Hey," my pal observed, "that must be Staten Island." And it was.

The good-ship *Sidney Dinnerstein* eased into the ferry slip, after which we walked our bikes into a completely new world. It was not quite a paradise, but it did pass the requirements for civilization. It had a movie theater.

We peered around, possibly expecting to find Martians, but everything looked Sioux Falls-normal. People who closely resembled Brooklynites walked the streets, though not too many.

A billboard even offered a greeting: *Welcome to St. George*. Then we noticed a street sign for Victory Boulevard.

"The war isn't over yet," Howie wondered out loud. "What's with the 'victory' in this boulevard?"

"Never mind," I shot back. "Let's start riding and discover Staten Island."

Once we got going, it appeared that Victory Boulevard could have more aptly been named Tough Hill to Climb Avenue. It meandered up, up and more up until the winding road finally leveled off at a stretch of greenery.

Off to the right we noticed a sign for Silver Lake Park and decided to check it out. We made a right turn and pedaled down a path until we concluded that there was no silver lake at Silver Lake Park. In fact, it had no lake at all.

"Onward and upward," I suggested, and we did another mile or three along Victory Boulevard until another posting caused us to brake. This sign was for Clove Lake Park.

Hurray! There actually was a lake in Clove Lake Park. Not only that, but it was sprinkled with boats being rowed about by natives of this new world called Staten Island.

"What are we waiting for?" Howie exclaimed. "Let's go row."

And so we did, for a good hour and a half, without capsizing or being arrested for spitting our cashew shells into the so-named clovey water. Finally, we realized it was early afternoon – time to return to a more familiar civilization.

Heading downhill on Victory Boulevard was roughly equivalent to three rides on Coney Island's Cyclone. There was the seemingly endless free fall, followed by crazy curves and finally the terminal.

More important, we still were alive.

We boarded the *Sidney Dinnerstein* and took a sentimental, reflective look back at this amazing land of one legitimate lake.

Upon landing back in Brooklyn, we pedaled to the bike shop, got our deposit and sought our pals. We wanted all the gang at Al and Shirley's candy store to know about our astonishing discovery.

Mind you, we were dead serious about this find of ours.

Sure enough, a bunch of the fellows were there sipping egg creams and downing ice cream sodas. Gilbert Birnbaum wanted to know where we had been.

"Guess what?" Howie announced to the faithful: "We discovered Staten Island!"

We detailed how we rode our bikes on Fort Hamilton Parkway, how our expedition continued on something called an electric ferry, how we found a park called Silver Lake without even a pond. And so on, with much intensity.

The boys listened with rapt attention and actually applauded when we finished our travelogue. "It was quite an adventure," Howie proudly concluded.

Our moment of candy store glory should have ended then and there. But, alas, sorry to say, it didn't.

As it happened at Al and Shirley's candy store, there always seemed to be one character who had to one-up everyone else. On this particular afternoon, it was Chubby Wexler, Howie's older cousin and not the brightest bulb in the socket.

"Guess what?" said Chubby, putting down his Coke glass filled with seltzer. "I also had an adventure today. I took the BMT to Coney Island and went swimming, but I almost drowned. Luckily, a lifeguard pulled me out."

Gil Birnbaum shook his head in disgust and said, "Well, wise guy, did you learn your lesson?"

"Yeah," snapped Chubby. "I swear I'll never go into the water again until I learn how to swim!"

The 69th St. Electric Ferry

RIIS PARK, THE POOR
MAN'S OASIS ON
THE ATLANTIC

As New Yorkers go, there was nothing especially special about the Fischlers of 582 Marcy Avenue. We had no cars, paintings, jewelry or fur coats. Nothing! Not even a kid sister for me to badger.

Well, maybe there *was* one thing unique about us. We had a beach that nobody else in our neighborhood had ever known about.

Actually, it was a beach without "beach" in its name, like Jones Beach, Orchard Beach, South Beach or Brighton Beach.

Our very special Fischler beach simply was called Jacob Riis Park in honor of the muckraking author of long ago.

It sits comfortably in the Rockaways on the Atlantic Ocean between a place called Neponsit and another called Breezy Point. Riis Park was opened for business in 1937, when I was five years old.

For the Fischler family, Riis Park became our oasis by the sea. It was -- in those Great Depression times -- exceptionally cheap, although not so splendidly accessible, unless you owned a car.

No matter, a trolley car trip plus a bus ride would do the trick.

What amazed me beyond all reason is that nobody -- and I do mean *nobody* -- I knew on either Marcy or Vernon Avenues had ever heard of Riis Park. For them, it didn't exist, and I'll give you a for-instance.

One Friday in August 1938, I was minding my business in Al and Shirley's candy store, when Chubby Wexler asked me what I was going to do on Sunday. I simply said, "I'm going to Riis Park with my mom and dad."

To which the avid Brooklyn Dodgers fan Wexler exclaimed, "You mean they named a park after [shortstop] Pee Wee Reese?"

Actually, Riis Park was a relatively recent Fischler discovery. Up until 1937, we took two subways, the IND and BMT, to Brighton Beach for our dips in the Atlantic. But neither Mom nor Dad liked boorish Brighton.

Brighton Beach had no bath houses in which to change into a bathing suit nor out of one as the case may be. Ben and Molly didn't go for that. It would've meant they had to do a striptease inside a large towel to get their bathing suits on and off. (Vegas odds were 5-1 they got exposed naked at some point in the strip finale.)

But there was none of that nonsense when Riis Park opened. It instantly became the poor man's oasis in the Rockaways. And since we were poor and liked a new oasis, my parents found it fast.

For me, getting there was half the fun. The excursion began with a 20-minute Nostrand Avenue trolley ride to the Nostrand-Flatbush Avenue junction to connect with the Green Bus Lines coach to Riis. On the way, Flatbush Avenue melded into a two-lane highway, after which was a vast expanse on the left. I instantly noticed it was dotted with airplane hangars and a small terminal sandwiched in between.

This was Floyd Bennett Field, notorious for Douglas "Wrong Way" Corrigan, the mis-informed chap who was supposed to fly his plane from Floyd Bennett's strip to California. Instead, he landed on a runway in Ireland!

Fortunately, our Green Bus Lines driver was a Right Way Kelly who had no trouble finding Riis Park; and it *was* an eye-opener. Riis Park had a spanking-clean, white, brick entrance, flanked by two, huge, round towers that were veritable beach skyscrapers. At the box office, Dad paid the pittance for bathhouse use and came away with a pair of keys.

The keys were for lockers across from banks of shiny-brown brick outdoor showers. "You won't find this at Brighton, Sonny Boy," Dad proudly announced as if he had just discovered Miami Beach.

Ahead of us were shuffleboard courts, handball courts, paddle-tennis courts and even a pitch-and-putt golf course. On the ocean side of the wide concrete boardwalk were the white, sandy beach and ocean.

"When you're ready," Dad suggested, "go in for a dip -- but be careful." It was good advice. Swimming in Riis Park's ocean was not for the faint of heart. No way.

The surf was harsh. Huge, high waves thundered in at a rate of about one every ten seconds. This required a couple of survival techniques:

1. The synchronized jump. As the wave crashed, you jumped as high as possible and took the whack on the side of your rib cage. That would send you down for a 10-count and, hopefully, up in about five seconds.

2. The daring dive *into* the wave. As the onrushing water reached a peak of about a dozen feet, you plunged as low as possible into the briny. With luck, you didn't feel a thing as the wave crashed beyond you.

The pounding, submerging, dancing and otherwise trying to battle the waves was a ton of fun. After a few hours, we repaired to the bath house to see what a brand-new public facility was like.

The outdoor showers looked like they'd been imported from the Waldorf-Astoria. No need for the hideous Brighton Beach towel-ass routine. Riis Park was paradise.

Starting in 1942, the bus ride home offered an added attraction. Floyd Bennett Field had been converted to a naval air base. This was serious World War II stuff right before my very eyes.

U.S. Navy fighters, bombers and seaplanes were right across the way on the other side of Flatbush Avenue, almost too close for comfort.

There were my favorites, the gull-winged carrier-based fighter, the Corsair, as well as the workhorse Grumman Wildcat and the magnificent twin-engined PBY Catalina flying boat that would take off from nearby Jamaica Bay.

Arguably, the best day I ever had at Riis happened when my Aunt Lottie briefly lived with us at 582 while her hubby, my Uncle Joe, was serving in the Navy Seabees. Lottie decided that a day at Riis would be fun. It was.

My *laissez-faire* aunt had no compunctions about letting the Riis surf beat the crap out of me -- back and front -- all day. Finally she shouted, "Stanley, time to go and see a movie."

For some reason, she had targeted the RKO Kenmore on Church Avenue, just off Flatbush. I don't remember the main feature, but I vividly recall the very-B-minus flick comedy that sent me reeling with laughter: *Prairie Chickens*.

I remember it primarily because I was punch-drunk from my all-day wave-beatings. This led to a first in my young life; I wound up falling onto the RKO Kenmore's floor and out into the aisle.

Some crazy scene in *Prairie Chickens* simultaneously attacked my funny bone and my punchy head. I couldn't stop laughing until Aunt Lottie grabbed my T-shirt and hauled an exhausted me back into my seat.

Riis Park remained a part of my life long after Shirley and I married, the only difference being that we drove a 1963 AMC 4-door Rambler sedan there instead of taking the Green Bus Lines coach.

Our last visit to Riis Park – near Riis, at least – was way back in the summer of 1968. It was ironic in the extreme. Shirley and I were hosting former NHL defenseman Carl Brewer and his wife, Marilyn.

The day was swimmingly hot, so we decided to take them for a dip in the Atlantic. After we crossed the Marine Parkway Bridge, I foolishly said, "Why don't we go next door to Neponsit? It won't be so crowded."

And so we did, except that Neponsit didn't have bathhouses or any Riis Park amenities for that matter. Which meant that before and after taking our swims, we had to do the towel striptease.

This was something new -- and I daresay embarrassing -- for the Brewers of staid Toronto. But what could they do? Shirley gave them the big towel and they dutifully did the strip.

Later that evening, after we had dropped our guests off at their hotel, I asked Shirley what she thought of Neponsit. She didn't hesitate.

"I'd rather go to Brighton."

The beach at Riis Park

CAMPING OUT

"You're going to camp," said the mama.

"What's camp?" said the son on a June 1939 morning in Williamsburg, Brooklyn. The kid was only seven. What did he know from camp?

"Camp," replied Molly Fischler, unable to contain her enthusiasm, "means you're not going to Aunt Hattie, Aunt Lucie or Aunt Francis. You're going to where the air is fresh and there are kids. KIDS -- *for three big weeks!*" She then flashed a big Molly smile.

Not that I needed more kids in my life than there were on Vernon Avenue, between Marcy and Nostrand, but that didn't matter. I was going to camp and that was that. It meant a vacation for me and R&R for Mom and Pop.

Camp Sussex, I later learned, was what we Williamsburgers called a "Jewish charity camp." Kids whose folks were precariously living on the fiscal border went to poor kids' camps like Sussex, run by philanthropies like B'nai B'rith.

After a 15-minute ride on the Nostrand Avenue trolley, Mom took me to the Talmud Torah on Crown Street. Next thing I knew, I was on a bus surrounded by strange kids, heading for a remote section of New Jersey I never knew existed.

Camp Sussex was aptly named. It was near a village called Sussex, across the Delaware River from New York and Pennsylvania. At first smell, it was as refreshing as Pulver's Hot-Chu gum, my favorite 1939 mouthwash.

Along with me were all the necessities of camp life: toothbrush, toothpaste, underwear and a cheap baseball cap that didn't even have a *B* for the Brooklyn Dodgers on the crest. Missing were six pair of socks. Nobody told Mom.

For no cost at all, my folks were gifted with three whole Stanley-free weeks during which their only obligation was to write daily letters. The missives assured that I still was alive -- and they were surviving as well.

Unfortunately, in not a single latter did Mom get around to asking if I had enough socks. Pity, because I was determined to get my one pair through the next three weeks, an Olympian challenge if ever there was one.

Sussex was fun. I learned the official camp song ("We welcome you to Sussex camp, we're mighty glad you're here"). Turns out, I later discovered, that it was the official song of 376 other kids' camps. Just replace "Sussex" with "Kiowa."

I also learned my first joke at Sussex, thanks to Miss Jo, the little entertainment impresario with more non-caffeine energy than ten campers put together. Miss Jo's weekly stage specialty was what she liked to call Blackouts. A quick joke was told on stage. Right after the punch line, the stage blacked out until the next joke came along. It was guaranteed to keep restless campers riveted.

The first joke I ever heard in my life involved two guys talking on stage about how dumb their pal, Solly, was in synagogue during the High Holy Days.

"How dumb is he?" Shelly asks Yussie. Yussie shoots back, "Solly is so dumb that in *shul,* he thinks 'Be seated' is part of the prayer." Blackout followed, and I was still laughing.

I ate well at Sussex, played outfield, along with a nation of grasshoppers, and did other neat camp things, except I never asked my counselor for a pair of socks. I was going to see this one indomitable pair through, no matter what.

As a result, when I returned to Brooklyn -- welcomed by Mom and Pop because I still was alive -- Molly Fischler did a double-take when I removed my official Boy Scout shoes.

My unfairly well-well-worn, three-week-old socks looked as if they had faced five firing squads. There were holes next to holes, next to more holes and smelly, worn threads that actually looked like they once had colors. No more.

"Ma," I tried to explain in advance of the inevitable Molly inquisition, "I forgot. I forgot to ask my counselor."

Molly Fischler: "You forgot? YOU FORGOT? What did you expect that your old socks were going to do, drop seeds and grow another pair in your shoes?" I dropped my head in despair, the universal sign of kids' surrender.

Armed with seven pairs of socks a year later, I found Sussex a good camp, but not great. Great would come in 1942 when my folks dispatched me to Camp Pythian in Glen Spey, New York. It was the Waldorf of poor Jewish camps. The bunks were new, the sky was blue and a tall, dark and handsome 20-year-old greeted me at the top of the steps.

"Hi! I'm Uncle Eli," he said, shaking my hand. Male counselors at all Jewish charity camps were called "uncle." Of course, there was no way of my knowing it at the time but this Uncle Eli guy would be like my favorite real Uncle Ben, times ten. Already, good things were happening. To wit:

1. I came to camp with the confidence of a college senior. Two years at Sussex provided good basic training.

2. There were girls on the other side of the brick wall. Lots, especially one named Sheila.

3. Uncle Eli shared my musical tastes.

Ours was Bunk 16. It had a wooden railing where I could sit and play my semi-musical instrument, a plastic "Hum A Zu," which was a variation on the traditional kazoo but was round, kind of like a cigar. I hummed a tune into it and melodies emerged like it was Glenn Miller's Orchestra. Okay, almost.

My first night, I performed a hit parade. It included "Don't Sit Under The Apple Tree," "Jersey Bounce" and "Tangerine."

Uncle Eli endorsed my concert and asked me to do a few more every night before "Taps" was played. But I didn't go to Pythian to play music. I went to play ball, as in softball.

Up until my arrival at the Pythian batting cage, I was what a scout would have pegged as "good field, occasional hit." But something unusual happened when I scanned the bat pile. An oxblood-colored Louisville Slugger caught my eye.

I grabbed it and decided to give it a shot. What a shot! On my first whack, I almost drove the ball into Camp Achvah across the Delaware River. If this happened today, Uncle Eli would've tested me for performance-enhancing drugs.

After that bit of super-hitting -- always armed with that oxblood-colored-Louisville Slugger -- a mere single was a waste of my time. A double was passable, but not up to my new ball-walloping standards.

My idol was Stan "The Man" Musial of the St. Louis Cardinals. That helps to explain why, every time I came to the plate, I expected to hit nothing less than a triple. This was all part of the Pythian paradise.

My bunkmates were swell, the food delicious and even arts and crafts was fun. I brought home a handsome plaster of Paris bulldog that pleased my dad, but two days later the bulldog became neutered when it fell off our mantelpiece.

One thing really set me apart from my bunkmates: mail call. My parents rolled out letters like they had a printing press at 582 Marcy. Mom wrote five days a week and Dad the other two, but my father's mail was extra special.

Every letter he ever sent was in a bulging, white envelope filled with news clippings of important baseball games, mostly the 1942 National League pennant race between the Cards and Dodgers. My bunkmates were jealous.

The three weeks at Pythian went way too fast, and when I hugged Uncle Eli, I whispered, "See ya next year." What did I know?

When July 1943 arrived, Mom announced that I was going to camp, only it wasn't Pythian with Uncle Eli eagerly awaiting my return. Inexplicably, she sent me to NYU's Camp White House on Lake Stahahe at Bear Mountain, New York.

Apart from taking swimming lessons and learning the kid-insult-of-the-year ("You're a homo"), White House was a bummer-to-the-power-of-50. Maybe worse.

The good news was that Mom promised me next year I'd be back at Pythian, and she was true to her word. I had it all figured out: I'd have a reunion with Uncle Eli and enjoy another super Pythian run as I had in summer 1942.

Never, ever, did it dawn on me that my hero counselor, my role model, my pal, Uncle Eli, would not be there. The Erie Railroad took us to Port Jervis, New York, then a bus drove us to Glen Spey and another round of "We welcome you to Pythian Camp."

When we were assigned bunks, it was like Old Home Week, except for one thing: Uncle Eli wasn't waiting for me at Bunk 16. Instead, I was introduced to a nice, upstanding fellow named Uncle Moe.

"Excuse me," I said, "but do you know where Uncle Eli might be?"

Uncle Moe didn't know who I was talking about. When I explained, he politely told me to check at the office, so I did. Sadly -- very, very sadly -- I learned that Uncle Eli was now a camper in the U.S. Army.

It took me about a day and a half to get over the "loss" of Uncle Eli, and I can thank Uncle Moe for that. Not that he was a music lover like his predecessor, but Moe loved jokes.

Turned out that Uncle Moe was to Pythian Camp what Miss Jo had been at Sussex. He was the entertainment guy as well as Bunk 16's counselor. At our post-lunch Relax Hour, Uncle Moe worked at his humor.

One of his favorite things was teaching us what he called "Jewish culture." Uncle Moe would say, "Listen carefully, boys, and you'll know how you grew up Jewish."

Then, I would shoot back, "How, Uncle Moe?" Uncle Moe would take a deep breath and then roll off the following:

You know you grew up Jewish when:

You spent your entire childhood thinking that everyone calls roast beef *brisket*.

You were as tall as your grandmother by the age of seven.

You can look at gefilte fish and not turn green.

Your mother smacked you really hard and continues to make you feel bad for hurting her hand.

Uncle Moe also told real joke-type jokes. One I remember was about an old Jewish lady named Sadie who goes up to a man at a bus stop on Flatbush Avenue near Church Avenue.

She tugs on the man's coat and asks, "Farshtayn Yiddish?" (Do you understand Yiddish?) The man replies, "Yaw isch farshtay." (I understand Yiddish.)

Sadie then says, "Vot time is it?"

Of course, by this time, we kids had heard of dirty jokes, but we really didn't know any. We pleaded with Uncle Moe to tell us one, but he was smart enough not to get himself in trouble. He pulled off a hybrid gag.

"Okay, boys, just don't tell this one to your parents," Uncle Moe warned. "Here goes. One day, I came home early from work and I saw a guy jogging naked. I asked him, 'Hey, buddy, why are you doing that?' He said, 'Because you came home early!'"

When it was time to leave Pythian on the bus back to the city, I hugged Uncle Moe as hard as I had embraced Uncle Eli. I cried a bit, too, hiding the sob as best as I could, which meant almost.

I knew I'd never see either Uncle Eli or Uncle Moe again. On the other hand, to this day I haven't forgotten Uncle Eli's wonderful warmth and Uncle Moe's punch lines.

And that's why I look back at my days at Camp Pythian with a smile.

Oh, yeah, one other thing: In honor of Molly Fischler, I don a fresh pair of socks every morning.

Stan, Molly and Ben Fischler in the Catskills

GOING TO THE 1939-40 WORLD'S FAIR, NEW YORK'S ANSWER TO OZ

D orothy Gale and her pet dog, Toto, from Kansas, found paradise in Oz via a tornado and a Judy Garland super-song, "Over The Rainbow."

Stanley and his pet mom, Molly, from Williamsburg, found their Oz in Flushing Meadows, Queens, via the IND subway -- and without a song.

Both events took place in 1939, when I was seven years old. *The Wizard of Oz* was everybody's favorite movie. The World's Fair of 1939 was to be every New Yorker's favorite show that hot summer before World War II.

Dorothy's Oz was -- um – who knows where? Mine was a half-hour subway ride on the GG (Brooklyn-Queens Crosstown) line from the Myrtle-Willoughby station conveniently located under my house.

Originally proposed in 1935, the Fair was built on what had been a 1,202-acre ash dump and orchestrated by the all-time Big Apple power broker, Robert Moses. (I liked him only because he built a mini-park in our nabe.)

Like most Brooklynites, I got my hands on a World's Fair events brochure weeks before it opened. The promo promised just about everything, from a sky-chasing parachute jump to brand new automobiles from Detroit.

The Fair's world premiere was April 30, 1939. By then, I knew by heart that its slogan was "Dawn of a New Day," and the Fair was celebrating the 150th anniversary of George Washington's inauguration in New York.

What everyone -- and I do mean *everyone* -- also knew by then was that the Fair featured twin symbols: the Trylon and Perisphere. They quickly became as familiar to a New Yorker as the Empire State Building.

Situated next to each other, the all-white contrasting structures were amazing sights to behold. The Trylon was a giant, three-dimensional triangle that came to a point 700 feet up.

The adjacent Perisphere was wrapped with a winding stairway leading to what was called the World of Tomorrow inside. The twin structures were featured on a three-cent stamp, plus a Trylon Theater had just opened on Queens Boulevard in nearby Forest Hills.

In mid-July, Mom and I subwayed to the Fair. The GG local sported brand-new, shiny rolling stock made by the American Car & Foundry Company in Berwick, Pennsylvania. (I memorized the plaque's copper plate wording.)

The GG's front-door window was armed with an iron handle that easily could be moved one inch to the left. A tug on the handle allowed me to pretend that I was starting the GG as a major help to the motorman.

The beauty part was that our GG went directly to the Fair; no train-switching was necessary. Beyond the Continental Avenue station, the tracks swerved north and surfaced out of the tunnel into Forest Hills daylight.

Our local then rolled onto a bridge spanning Grand Central Parkway, finally reaching full speed on a new trackbed installed exclusively for the Fair. (The tracks were ripped up in 1941, long after the Fair closed.)

The GG sped past the IND storage yard and rolled straight ahead to a nifty un-subway-like Art Deco terminal. We exited and gaped at our New York Oz, the truly awesome, handsome Trylon and Perisphere. We were here.

"Where to first?" Mom inquired, and I wasted no time replying, "Let's go see the new cars."

The Chrysler exhibit was first and it was starring the company's brand-new 1939 Plymouth. That instantly knocked me out because it was the newest car design with front lights imbedded inside the fenders. (Great stuff!)

The Chrysler pavilion also featured a film in 3-D that explained how that '39 Plymouth was assembled. It was compelling, but nothing compared to the Ford exhibit next door.

Ford's big deal was an eight car, rooftop track, where race car drivers put on a show that never would have been approved by New York State troopers. I also was crazy about the streamlined Lincoln Zephyr.

"Let's go to General Motors," I urged Mom. "That's supposed to be the best."

GM sure had the longest lines, but it was worth the wait. Finally inside, we found ourselves on a moving carpet transporting us over a huge diorama, The World Of Tomorrow, that kept getting bigger and bigger.

It was GM's vision of highways and more highways. It was both prescient and clever. At the end, we were deposited into the company's dealership pavilion of Chevys, Pontiacs, Buicks -- all the latest that we'd never buy.

"Enough with the cars," Mom insisted. "I want to see what this television thing is all about."

We visited the RCA Pavilion and, yes, this thing called "television" was intriguing. But the exhibit seemed so primitive and so far off in the future that I couldn't even imagine how it would work. Mom agreed.

Since there was so much to see, we hustled over to the Information booth, where a pretty damsel was dressed in the Fair colors of orange and blue. She told us there were seven zones and 60 foreign-government exhibits.

Being Jewish, we were intrigued by a Jewish Palestine Pavilion, which prompted Mom to ask what that was all about.

"It introduces the concept of a modern, Jewish state," the lady explained. "Check it out. The entrance has three copper relief statues: a scholar, laborer and toiler of the soil." We did, and were impressed.

Right across the road, the Japanese Pavilion included a garden and Shinto shrine. (No battle plans for Pearl Harbor yet.) Nippon's motto stated, "To eternal peace and friendship between America and Japan."

(There's got to be a punch line there somewhere.)

Our stomachs informed that it was lunchtime, so we hustled over to the area dubbed Food Zone. It was sprinkled with goodies galore, especially if you liked pickles and white bread.

The Heinz Exhibit not only had free samples, but everyone got a green Heinz pin of a pickle, which I still have. Next door, the Continental Baking Company was giving away freshly baked Wonder Bread.

Best of all was the Borden's – its slogan was "If it's Borden's, it's got to be good!" – exhibit because our home milk happened to be Borden's. The exhibit was a cavalcade of bovines – no less than 150 live pedigreed cows.

The prized cattle collection was mechanically milked, which put the cows in a good *moo-ed*. Even Borden's famed, live Elsie The Cow was there to greet us. She didn't sign autographs.

"It's getting late," Mom said, checking her watch. "Pick out a couple more things, then we gotta get going. You want the rides, I know that."

She did know, of course and, sure enough, there was the obligatory roller coaster. Also, Life Saver's towering parachute jump and many other goodies, but the one that caught my eye was The Flying Turns Bobsled.

It was a cousin to the roller coaster, only it aped a real bobsled run, flipping its car-bobsleds from side to scary side rather than up and down. I loved it for three reasons. It was fast, a thriller and I survived.

"One more and we go," Mom insisted.

I saved the best for last. That happened to be in the Transportation Zone. The exhibit was titled *Railroads On Parade*, which turned out to be, for me, the Oz of all Ozzes.

With real, live locomotives, the exhibit traced the growth of American railroads, starting with a replica of the first American steam engine: Baltimore and Ohio's Tom Thumb. Then there were the new giants.

England's Coronation Scot Express was the epitome of streamlining, but it couldn't match up with a real, live version of my Lionel Pennsy Torpedo electric train. Yet, there it was in all its enormous splendor. The state-of-the-art Pennsy S1 engine was mounted on rollers and running in place at 60 miles per hour, all day. My eyes were riveted on that beautiful hunk of steam loco for a good five minutes.

Finally, Mom yanked me away to our more prosaic GG Local and the gleeful ride home. I thought about the Fair all winter and wanted to see it again, but doubted that I would.

I later learned that my buddy, Jack Goldstein, got in for nothing. His dad, Moe, had a pastry wagon that serviced the fair. "My brother Stan and I hid in the back," Jack recently revealed. "When Dad got past the entrance, he let us out, and we saw the Fair for nothing!"

Since none of my relatives had a pastry truck -- and I didn't know Jack then -- I figured I'd never get a second chance at New York's Oz. But late in June 1940, my Aunt Lucie came up with the invite.

Always a favorite of mine, Aunt Lucie escorted me to the foreign-government pavilions. Since Lucie was from Antwerp, I suggested that we check out the Belgian tower.

"Sorry, Stanley," she reminded me. "There's a war on, and there's no more Belgian Pavilion. In fact, there's no more Belgium as I knew it. The Nazis conquered it."

She paused and said: "And don't ask me to take you to the Netherlands exhibit and, for that matter, Czechoslovakia and France. Hitler took them as well."

Aunt Lucie quickly deleted her downer by hustling me to a double-chocolate ice cream cone and then over to Billy Rose's Aquacade. This was like a Broadway musical in the water with a 10,000-seat amphitheater.

Johnny Weissmuller, an Olympics gold medalist who later played Tarzan in Hollywood, was the featured swimming hunk, outshined only by the sexiest, loveliest great swimmer I ever lived to see, Eleanor Holm.

The Aquacade was a swell *coda* for my second and last Fair visit.

Aunt Lucie and Uncle Ben let me sleep over at their apartment in full view of the Fair. The next afternoon, my sweetheart of an aunt took me to the nearby Trylon Theater to see *The Wizard of Oz*.

I returned home that night and told Mom and Dad what a great time I had at the Fair, plus the second-day bonus -- Judy Garland on the yellow brick road leading to Oz and the wizard.

"How was the movie?" Dad wondered.

"Aww," I said, "it was all right. But I liked the Fair better. You know what, Pop? I'll take Eleanor Holm over Judy Garland any day!"

"But," Ben Fischler shot back, "Eleanor Holm can't sing."

"Yeah," I conceded, "but she sure can *look!*"

Aerial view of the 1939 World's Fair

THE DAY MOM GOT ARRESTED BY THE STATE POLICE

I still can't believe, 70 years later, that kindly, sweet, often-humorous Molly Fischler once got arrested by the New York State police.

It happened on a hot, summer day in August 1951. You can look it up or, better still, I'll tell you all about it.

The actual arresting process took place on the porch of Pollock's Hotel on Swan Lake Road in Ferndale, New York, during the Golden Age of the Catskill's Borscht Belt, as the area filled with Jewish hotels for summer vacationers was known.

But why arrest this sweetheart? Mom had no record. She was so clean that she wouldn't even let me sneak under the subway turnstile down the block at the Myrtle-Willoughby GG local station.

Accidents happen; we all know that. But Molly Fischler's arrest happened because of an incomparable chain reaction of mishaps worthy of Robert L. Ripley's *Believe It Or Not* comic strip in the Sunday funnies.

The root of it all was my love for drums. In 1950, I had played in a quartet at Greenfield Manor Hotel in Greenfield Park, New York. It wasn't much of a hotel, but, then again, we weren't much of a band.

For $12 a week plus room and board, who could complain? Not Irwin Tuchfeld on clarinet and sax, Bernie Rappaport on trombone, me on drums or the infamous Ivan Margolin at the piano.

Margolin's nickname said it all: "Ivan The Terrible Piano Player." (Notice, there's no comma after "Terrible.") But we'll get to him later. (Unfortunately.)

Suffice it to say, we survived that summer. Nothing against Tuch, Rappy and Ivan, but a year later, in the summer of 1951, when this tale took place, I connected with another group, hoping for bigger and better things in the mountains. Maybe even $15 a week.

My new colleagues included Ruby Grossman on trumpet, Bob Emen on sax and a fellow named Howie tickling the keys. As you soon will see, I have an eternal block on the piano guy's last name.

Throughout the fall, winter and spring, we practiced hard until we were ready to audition. The management of two hotels liked us, and we accepted the invitation from Pollock's, the pride of Swan Lake Road.

For me, this was big stuff. Unlike Greenfield Manor, Pollock's had a swimming pool, a tennis court and a handball court, plus Rita Biegelman. But we'll get to her later, as I tried innumerable times to do.

The deal with Pollock's was that in addition to playing dance music, we had to "cut" shows. Live entertainers would arrive on weekends, and we had to accompany each of the acts: a singer, dancer and comedian, say.

No question, the key to any band's show-cutting was the man at the keyboard. The piano man had to "sight-read" the act's music and our man, Howie, was good at that. The rest of us went along for the ride.

We were due at Pollock's a few days before the July 4th weekend and then *it* happened. I have taken torpedoes amidships in my lifetime, but this was the blitz beyond all blitzes. First-class musical sabotage, if you will.

Exactly five days before we were to leave the city for our Pollack's rendezvous, Piano Man Howie quit on us. Disappeared, just like that.

This was doom-to-the-power-of-50-times-100. If we don't have a piano man, we don't have a gig; if we don't have a gig, I have to get a real job, which was out of the question.

What to do? Good piano men don't grow on trees. As a matter of fact, paid summers in the mountains don't grow on trees for 19-year-old Brooklyn College sophomores. I had to find a replacement for Benedict Howie.

Since I only knew one piano man, I phoned Ivan Margolin and suggested that we meet for an egg cream at the Sugar Bowl, on Tompkins Avenue. Ivan never would reject a gift egg cream, and he showed up in ten minutes.

"I need you for a summer gig," I implored. At first, Ivan alibied that he was going to work in his father's container factory. I had to top that with a promise -- my ace -- lots of *nofkies* – single, Jewish girls.

"Ivan," I assured him, "you'll meet girls, and more girls and more girls after that." Then, I leaned forward and put my right index finger to my lips. "Shhhh. You might even get laid."

BINGO!

We now had a piano man. But did we have one who could cut shows? Frankly, I was so thrilled having pulled Ivan out of a hat, that show-cutting was not even in the back of my head, although it should have been.

After arriving at Pollock's, we checked out the facilities and were pleased. In addition to all the amenities mentioned above, there also was the majestic casino, where we would play dance tunes like "My Foolish Heart" and "Miami Beach Rumba" as well as cut shows, starting on Saturday night. It, therefore, inspired a harsh question: Could Ivan the Terrible Piano Player sight-read? Could he cut a show?

Then a Catskill miracle happened. Actually two, as I also met the lovely Rita Biegleman that night. (That meant not one but two novelty acts in one evening.)

The musical miracle was the show. We only had to cut one act and it was a dancer who, incredibly, only had one tune. It was "Rose Room," played in stop tempo, which made it even easier. And Ivan actually knew "Rose Room" from past gigs.

We did it! Not only did we do it, but the gorgeous Rita and Pollock's drummer – yours truly – became an item. One night, she even invited me to her hayloft. But I digress. (Fortunately, Rita didn't.)

A week went by. We played danceable music, we swam, we whacked the handball and beat the Gottlieb pinball machine many times. Man, this was paradise in our mountain greenery -- right up until lunchtime on Friday.

Pollock's son-in-law, Irwin Riven -- the not-very-nice fellow who really ran the joint -- came to our table with startling news: the Friday act had arrived. This was no time for comedy; we hustled our *tushies* to the casino.

Bad news. The Friday act was the "international" singer we had been told -- er, warned -- about. He handed Ivan the sheet music. None of us breathed for the next ten minutes.

Crisis No. 1 was upon us. Ivan did his best but the "international" singer thought it was the worst, and told Riven so. Not that Riven had to be told. He also had ears that could detect good from Margolin.

Which is where the ever-fetching Rita entered the melodrama, stage left, to get us a reprieve. She liked me, and her grandpa Pollock liked the idea that his *bubbele* liked me.

The short but very sweet Biegelman-Fischler romance saved our jobs. Since Cupid was on our side and Pollock didn't want the Rita-Stan act uncoupled, we had to work out a deal – and did.

The "international" singer would henceforth import his own pianist every Friday night and we would pay for him out of our already meager salaries.

No sweat. I still had the sensuous Rita, while Bob, Ruby and Ivan had the swimming pool, the handball court, a beatable Gottlieb's pinball machine, three good meals a day and chump change left over.

Meaning: Why leave Paradise on Swan Lake Road? No way!

Unfortunately, we didn't do such a hotsy-totsy job of cutting the Saturday night show, hence we were summoned on Sunday morning to Lord Riven's office for a high-level conference.

And another deal was cut. This was not quite the Treaty of Versailles but more like The Treaty of our Sighs. Another pianist would visit from the city to cut the Saturday night shows, and we -- sigh! -- took another pay cut.

Now we were getting a few pennies more than ten bucks each a week. But, so what? I still had the buxom Biegelman, and Ivan's parents checked in to Stier's Hotel down the road and brought us many goodies.

Unfortunately (again), by the third weekend – this was mid-July 1951 -- the treaties began unraveling. On Friday night, the "international" singer's piano man was a no-show, and the Saturday visiting pianist didn't show either.

Lord Riven asked us to rehearse all of the acts and promised to pay us the deducted dough. We did our best and it wasn't a disaster, except that we didn't see the promised booty. We were more than mildly pissed.

A couple of weeks later, another double-no-show-pianist episode unfolded. Pollock promised, we acceded and, somehow, managed to salvage both shows. But the promised dough-re-me again was a no-show.

Otherwise, we were loving the place. The food was good, our softball team was winning, the ravishing Rita was becoming more progressive in her romantic attitudes -- but not progressive enough -- and guess what? My letters home were so brimming with fun and frolic that my Mom decided that she needed R&R at this marvelous mountain manor. Also, she'd see her favorite – also, only -- son in his sym-phony orchestra.

Too bad that none of us saw the storm clouds gathering over Swan Lake Road. What would become The Weekend In Hell already was loaded with warning asterisks:

* ONE: Bernie (Rappy) Rappaport, my trombone player from the Greenfield Manor band, unexpectedly showed up. He figured we could sneak him a weekend freebie, and he was right. (But we were wrong.)

* TWO: Eddie Margolin, kid brother of Ivan the Terrible Piano Player, also showed, and also was promised a sneak-freebie. Unlike the subdued Rappy, Eddie was a certifiable nut case; he was trouble spelled with a capital *T*.

* THREE: Mom's friends were driving to their mountain lodge in nearby White Lake. They'd drop her off at Pollock's and pick her up on Sunday afternoon for the trip back to the city. It seemed smart. It did not turn out so!

At 3 p.m. on Friday afternoon, the 1950 black Dodge sedan pulled up as advertised. Naturally, the drummer son was there in Pollock's driveway, hailing the mama from Marcy. So far, so good.

My very sociable mom immediately found friends, enjoyed dinner and headed to the casino for more entertainment.

As luck would have it on this night, Irwin Riven replaced his "international" singer with a movie -- *David and Bathsheba*, starring Gregory Peck and Susan Hayward.

Mom loved the flick and also enjoyed a midnight supper with friends. By this time, she had almost as many pals as Pollock had guests. Life was dreamy. Even sneaky Rappy and Crazy Eddie had remained undetected.

The nightmare was yet to come.

On Saturday morning, the cocks crowed, the stowaways got their purloined breakfasts and our quartet got word that Irwin Riven wanted to see us in his office for yet another high-level, but off-key, music conference.

"Boys," he intoned very seriously, "our pianist is stuck in the city. You guys'll have to cut the show; the acts will be here at eleven."

Almost instinctively, not to mention simultaneously, the four of us remembered that on too many weekends the paid -- out of our pockets -- pianists never made it, and we were compelled to cut the shows.

Out of character, Ruby, the mild-mannered trumpet man, rose and summarily snapped. "Where's our money?" he shouted. To that startling statement, Riven swallowed, winced and offered solace but without simoleons.

"Just do the rehearsal," he demanded, "and don't worry about the money."

Riven didn't get it; he just didn't get it. Sax man Bob did.

"No dough," he shot back, "no show."

Bob rose, adding to the growing defiance and, one by one, trumpet, piano and drum followed him out the door.

Bear in mind that Mama Fischler had no idea that any of this nastiness was going on; she was having too much fun devouring Nova lox, cream cheese and *smetena* (sour cream) in the dining room. Mom was all enthused, musing about her impending wonderful evening at the casino, the poor man's – very poor! – Radio City Music Hall.

Meanwhile, the three new acts invaded the casino, prepared to rehearse. But where's the band? We had retreated to our miserable hovel – we shared it with the lifeguard -- awaiting Riven's next move.

"We gotta hang tough," Ivan insisted, and nobody disagreed.

We skipped lunch. Finally, at around 3:00 p.m. Riven summoned us to his office. He capitulated -- sort of -- and peeled off a few bills -- but not nearly what we were owed -- and promised the rest later.

"Start rehearsing!" he ordered.

Taking the compromise cash, we marched to the casino for the prelude to a show business disaster of disasters. This time, the music for each of the three acts was beyond challenging.

Even the comedian had tough rim shots for me on drums. I rimmed either too soon before or too late after the comic's lousy punch lines.

No need to go into the gory details. Everything about the show went wrong. I mean, WRONG, right down to my rim shots. Mercifully, when the last act had ended to tepid applause, I sneaked a look over at Mom.

There was nothing but candor about her response. She grasped her nose with her right thumb and index finger. Not that I needed a translation; it told me that our show-cutting stunk, and that was an understatement.

In fact, the only thing that worked for us that night was the successful hiding away of the hotel stowaways, Bernie Rappaport and Crazy Eddie Margolin.

By morning, we all had shaken off the disaster. That included Molly Fischler, who was doing what she did best: *schmooze,* make still more friends and work out details for leaving with her ride home

The pick-up Dodge sedan was supposed to arrive right after the noon meal and drive back to 582 Marcy. It was all set.

Meanwhile, Rappy and I hitchhiked into Liberty, killed some time just walking around town and then got a quick hitch back to Pollock's.

As soon as we reached the entrance, my Brooklyn street smarts sniffed trouble. Ruby, Bob and Ivan soon found me and delivered the fateful news.

"We got fired," Bob said. "Riven just gave us the news."

We immediately confronted him in the office to collect the unpaid dough owed for all the shows we cut when the hired piano guys never showed.

Our confrontation was short and bitter, not to be confused with bittersweet.

Riven broke all previous Borscht Belt records since the invention of the *kuchalein,* telling us we'd be lucky if we got one penny out of him. He did have one kind word in parting.

"OUT!"

We would learn that Pollock already had planned for our musical Dunkirk and had hired a band from down the road. The new outfit was due later that day.

First thing I did was tell Mom that we were finished for the season, a fact she took well, figuring the music she had heard us play deserved another band, if not Guy Lombardo and his Royal Canadians.

No sweat; right after lunch, she'd get her ride and be off. And as a special favor to her favorite son, she would take my bass drum and put it in the car trunk. That part of The Great Escape went easier than I thought.

I quickly rejoined my band mates who already had declared war on Riven. The not-so-secret-word was *revenge*. Two attack targets were planned: our hovel and the casino.

Ivan -- with something akin to a Bowie knife in hand - began slicing up pillows, sheets and mattresses. In five minutes, there was a million-feather convention on the cabin floor.

For an encore, I opened two gigantic jars of uneaten dill pickles and gently poured the contents on the mattresses. The remaining pickle juice went into a few empty drawers.

Although nobody knew it, Crazy Eddie Margolin had sneaked into the kitchen, grabbed a knife and a few chicken breasts and marched to the empty casino.

With knife in hand, he surgically severed the piano strings, and with chicken breast he rubbed a few slices over the strings for good measure. If he had added some gravy, he would've seasoned the Steinway as well. End of piano.

Now that our equal-opportunity sabotage had been completed, it was time for an orderly retreat. Once again, the exit plan seemed flawless. This was the plan:

1. Ivan and Crazy Eddie would hitch down Swan Lake Road to Stier's Hotel, where their parents eagerly were awaiting them.

2. Ruby and Bob -- with trumpet, sax and valises in hand -- walked to a motel near Liberty, where they planned to stay overnight.

3. Vagabond Bernie Rappaport and I decided to camp at Liberty's New York, Ontario and Western Railroad station and take the next train to Manhattan.

Without informing my beloved mother about our anti-Pollock guerrilla assaults, I kissed her goodbye and wished her a happy drive home. Her car was due in a half-hour. My big, bass drum was at her elbow.

Amazingly, the New York, Ontario and Western Local, which usually ran as erratically as a Toonerville Trolley, chugged into Liberty station only ten minutes after Rappy and I had purchased our tickets.

Triumphantly, like French *maquis* guerrillas who had just blown up a Nazi bridge, we contentedly found seats and relaxed for the railroad ride home. We felt secure in the knowledge that we'd defeated the Riven-Pollock Axis.

At this point, it's important to understand some of the developments that would lead to the melodrama ahead.

1. Nobody in the incoming band had realized the extent to which Crazy Eddie Margolin had destroyed the casino's piano. That bit of sabotage was a one-man operation and would have been rejected by our Politburo.

2. My mother's ride back to the city was conspicuously late. She killed time with her new-made friends schmoozing on the terrace, totally oblivious to the pickled hovel and the former piano.

3. The new band arrived early. Typically, the piano man tried out the upright. Every time his fingers hit a key, it popped up at him just like in a Bugs Bunny cartoon.

4. The lifeguard who shared our hovel -- or what was left of it -- was allergic to ripped mattresses, torn sheets and pickled drawers. Furthermore, he hastened to Riven's office to tell him so.

5. Supplied with harsh communiques from the new pianist and old lifeguard, Riven phoned the state police.

When the cops showed up, they found my mother on the porch sitting next to a bass drum. They put Mom and drum together and arrested her on the spot. The fuzz had mistaken her for part of the band.

Eventually, she got a break. Somebody tipped off the cops that Trumpet Ruby and Sax Bob were hiding out at a motel down the road. *They* were the genuine culprits, not Molly Fischler.

Sure enough, one cop car took off and returned with half our band. Ruby and Bob co-signed a document that they -- actually the four of us -- would pay Pollock once the damages were totaled.

Mom was released from custody and soon would pack the bass drum in the trunk of her friend's car and head for New York City.

Meanwhile, Rappy and I finally made it home to 582 Marcy and sat on the front stoop, recapitulating how we got even with the evil Irwin Rivin.

Not knowing that Mom's ride was late or anything about the arresting process, Rappy and I expected her car to arrive about 6 p.m. But that estimated time came and went. So did 7 p.m. and 8 p.m.

Needless to say, I was worried, big-time. Finally, at a little after 9:00, the black Dodge sedan rolled up to 582. Mom thanked her friends, fetched the bass drum from the trunk and said nothing to me or Rappy.

Then, with a firm swing of her right arm -- not unlike a tennis backhand -- she waved Rappy away, ostensibly to his DeKalb Avenue apartment.

There was an assumption in Molly Fischler's dismissal of the trombone player that Rappy was at least partially responsible for her current misfortune. Public Enemy No. 1 would be dealt with next.

Still without uttering a sound, Mom waved me upstairs for what would amount to a family court martial. And it *was* bad – no getting away from that. Bad, bad, bad!

When we reached the living room, she unleashed her tale of woe. Ignominy piled on ignominy like Sunday pancakes at the breakfast table. Embarrassment in front of her new friends, the state police, being arrested-- even if it was only momentarily -- and the miserable trip home.

Then Mom pulled out the final stop, like Gladys Goodding on the Madison Square Garden organ. She wept. Fortunately, Dad was away, visiting his kid brother, Julius, a lawyer who would come in mighty handy in days ahead.

I apologized about 325 times and vowed I-don't-know-what, but I did know that I had to repent in record time. Hustling into bed, I began figuring redemption plots and then *plotzed* to sleep.

Awake at 5:30 a.m., I bolted out of the house before anyone was up and bought a copy of *The Times* and -- breakfasting on Myrtle Avenue at the local luncheonette – pored over the classified want ads.

Ah, there it was: The Minneapolis-Honeywell outfit on Park Avenue South and 27th Street was looking for an office boy. I subwayed uptown for an interview and got the gig.

My main role was operating a "blueprint machine," which was about as easy as yawning. The dough was better than expected and the office chickadees were good for the optics.

All of which was small potatoes compared to the big issue: at least semi-pleasing-consoling Da Mama on my return from real work.

For starters, she seemed happy to see me and betrayed none of the Pollock-induced scars. With that, I jumped into the hot news that I had joined the workforce.

I explained my job -- that got a much-needed nod of approval -- and added that I'd be making far better dough than what that *gonif* Pollock was paying us. That upgraded her approval-nod to a big Molly smile.

Now that the big war was over, the Pollock adventure turned to a final, yet scary, skirmish.

Back at the hotel, Pollock had totaled damage to the well-pickled hovel and his castrated piano. He then dispatched the same bill to each member of our quartet and demanded immediate payment.

Forget about the exact amount. Suffice it to say that it would have bankrupted Ruby, Bob, Ivan -- well, maybe not Ivan -- and me, for sure. That inspired an immediate convening of the troops and final counterattack.

The first thing we did was total the unpaid money Pollock owed us for the many nights of pinch-playing when the hired pianist didn't show. We then matched our figures with those on the Pollock bill.

Eureka! It was almost even.

I remembered that my Dad had visited Uncle Julius, the lawyer.

"Boys," I said, "I got a guy who'll handle this for us: my uncle. He's an attorney and it won't cost us a cent."

In record time, the ayes had it.

They didn't call Julie Fischer of 469 Miller Avenue in East New York "a helluva good lawyer" for nothing. Exhibit A was the letter he wrote to Pollock.

In plain English, it explained that since he owed us as much as we owed him, the case was closed.

We never heard from Pollock again.

Before completing this tale of abject musicianship and guerrilla warfare in the Catskills, a couple of postscripts are in order.

* Rita Biegelman, the Sweetheart of Steinway Street in her native Astoria, Queens, had returned home the week of the chaos. When she did return, there was a new band – and no Stan. End of romance.

* The musical fallout: The replacement band did not consider their pickled cabin an acquired smell and wasn't crazy about the repaired piano either. They told other bands about our assaults and we earned a bad rep.

* Pollock's a year later: In a total coincidence, the band at Pollock's in 1952 was gifted with my original drum teacher, Larry Subin. When he returned from the summer gig, he filled me in on the aftershocks of 1951.

This was Larry's direct quote: "If I were you, I wouldn't be seen within fifty miles of Pollock's. Irwin Riven would like to place a 50-calibre machine gun on the roof fitted with radar that could identify you, Ruby, Bob and Ivan!"

He was kind enough to leave my mom off the wanted list.

Mom was kind enough to let the Pollock bygones be bygones, but with one condition.

She would not allow me to ever again play in a group with Ivan The Terrible Piano Player working the ivories.

In case I thought she was kidding, she added, "And I don't mean 'maybe,' either!"

P.S. Molly Fischler's incident on the porch at Pollock's proved to be the first and last time she ever was arrested!

You can look it up!

Pollock's lifeguard with Stan, 1951

PART THREE
Riding The Rails

THEY BUILT A SUBWAY UNDER MY HOUSE

Over the years, many friends have asked about my obsession with sub-ways, trolleys and railroads in general. How did it all come about?

Simple. When I was three years old, they built a subway in front of my house. ("They" being the New York City Department of Transportation.)

I kid you not. One day in the year nineteen-hundred-and-thirty-five, my mother took me on a neighborhood shopping expedition. The moment we walked out of 582 Marcy Avenue, I noticed a dozen men digging up the street.

"What are those men doing?" was my question.

"They're building a new subway for us," was her answer.

Then, a pause; finally, I came back with the dumb-and-dumber ques-tion: "You mean for you, me and Daddy?"

Mom: "No, silly. This subway will be for everybody who wants to go somewhere for a nickel. It will even go to Coney Island."

Sounded good to me. Then, I asked more questions and found out why the Marcy Avenue trolley cars had suddenly disappeared from our street.

That's right; my beloved Marcy Avenue trolley had become extinct. Its tracks were being extracted from the ground like broken teeth. "Dig, we must!" was the transit system's theme, and for three years I never was bored of the boring.

They called it "cut and cover." First, you cut the guts out of dear, old Marcy Avenue. Then you build the tunnel's insides, lay the track and, finally, cover it all up with a roof that becomes Marcy Avenue once again.

I was three years old when the business began and six years old when it was done. By the time the GG Line started rolling, I was an out-of-my-mind subway nut.

You would have been, too, had you lived at 582. Not only did the Brooklyn-Queens Crosstown Line -- its official name -- roll between Red Hook and Forest Hills, but the transit bigwigs conveniently placed a station directly under our house.

Can you believe it? Right underneath Grandpa's basement!

The station was called Myrtle-Willoughby, which meant that it extended two blocks under Marcy Avenue. One entrance was placed at Myrtle and Marcy and the other entrance at Willoughby and Marcy.

Our house, at 582, conveniently was a mere half-block from the Myrtle Avenue entrance. Couldn't beat that, and since my parents never owned a car, we became instant GG fans.

At night, in my third-floor bedroom, I'd listen. My head was on the pillow at about 9 p.m., I could hear the local roll in and I even could hear its doors open and close. Those subway sounds became a part of my psyche.

In its own quirky way, the GG was a curious line. For one thing, it was the only subway line that did *not* enter Manhattan. For another, its very-elevated Smith-9th Street terminus in Brooklyn was the highest station in the city.

It was so high that you could see the Statue of Liberty and New York Bay's flotilla of freighters and ferryboats from the el's outdoor platform.

The GG's subway cars were designated as R-1 to R-9 and built by the American Car and Foundry Company in Berwick, Pennsylvania. Each car was spacious and adorned with four huge fans in the ceiling.

There was, however, a major downer about the new cars. Unlike the BMT Standards, which featured a kid-friendly front window that opened, the GG's panoramic pane was sealed, never to be lifted.

But the window was very big, and at the bottom right of the locked front door was a brass handle. A kid like me could pretend to be the motor-man by pulling a half-inch on the brass handle just as the train was about to move.

Since the GG was a local, it operated north-south on two tracks. But here's the kicker: The next station after Myrtle-Willoughby heading south was Bedford-Nostrand.

For decades, the Bedford-Nostrand station baffled me because -- unlike any other station on the GG -- it had a center (third) track dividing the platforms.

This, I couldn't figure. After the GG left the double-track at Myrtle-Willoughby and approached Bedford-Nostrand, the double track went to the left and to the right and, suddenly, a center track appeared in the Bedford-Nostrand station.

For a good 70 years, I never could understand why there was a center track. Then, one day, I read a book about subway projects that never were realized. In one section, the author explained that when the original Second Avenue subway was blueprinted in 1928, it had a proposed Brooklyn link. Part of that link included a new tunnel under the East River leading into Brooklyn and eventually to Coney Island.

There was going to be a Super Second Avenue Express, with stops at Hoyt-Schermerhorn -- that explains the extra fifth and sixth tracks -- and Court Street, which now houses the Transit Museum.

As it happened, the center track at Bedford-Nostrand was going to be part of the Second Avenue subway's grandiose Brooklyn extension to the Atlantic Ocean beaches. Glad I found out about it 70 years later!

One of the beauty parts of my downstairs GG was that in 1939 it had a connection to the grandiose World's Fair at Flushing Meadow. The trip took me no more than a half-hour from my station to the Art Deco train terminal at the Fair.

Better still, the New York City Pavilion at the Fair included a model electric train just like the GG. It sped around the pavilion's perimeter similar to my Lionel 027 set that rolled around our living room rug at 582.

On every one of my World's Fair visits in 1939 and 1940, I made a beeline to the New York City building to watch the model GG circle City Building's main exhibition room.

The genuine GG had a major connection at Queens Plaza with the E and F express trains that sped all the way to Jamaica-169 St. This express route turned out to be one of my regular favorites because it was the speediest.

My Uncle Ben, Aunt Lucie and Cousin Joan lived in Kew Gardens, and I savored every visit because I could stand at the front window on either the E or the F as it tear-assed underneath the borough of Queens at 45 miles per hour.

The GG also got an assist for my Sunday afternoon hockey games at Madison Square Garden. In order to get to The Garden, I'd ride to Hoyt-Schermerhorn, grab the A train to 42nd and Eighth, and walk to 50th and Eighth.

By the end of World War II, some genius planner at the transportation department decided that a change booth was unnecessary for the Queens-bound entrance at Myrtle-Willoughby.

So, they boarded up the change booth and installed a full-length turnstile. That provided me and Larry Shildkret with a genius idea: The two of us could squeeze into the opening and thereby save a nickel. That was a big deal then!

That worked -- but just barely -- and then we made another monumental discovery. Between the bottom of the moveable gate and the floor, there actually was enough room to creep under the gate.

This was a chore for Larry, since he was a bit plump. But to save a nickel, he made himself skinny enough to get under. Hence we saved a big dime and enjoyed our ride to The Garden twice as much!

Before I moved from Brooklyn to Manhattan in 1956 -- I had begun newspapering -- I took my last ride on the GG and didn't return for another four decades.

By that time, my personal GG Local dramatically had changed. Myrtle-Willoughby still was there but the station's glisten had given way to grime. There even was talk of abandoning the Brooklyn-Queens Crosstown Local altogether.

Worst of all, it was not the GG anymore. The Transit Authority brain-stormers got an idea one day and, for no good reason, removed a G from GG. Now, in its 70th year, it was just the G Line. Ugh! (Where did they hide the surplus Gs?)

Instead of terminating the now-G in Queens at Continental Avenue in Forest Hills, the Metropolitan Transit Authority decided that it should run only in Brooklyn and that the G's new last stop was placed in Greenpoint.

Also gone but never forgotten were those neat R-1-R-9 cars that rolled along the original line. I'm talking about the trains that featured those big front windows that allowed a kid to play motorman on every ride.

On the G's new cars, the front window is completely blocked off so nowadays a kid can't even see out the front pane and pretend to be a motor-man anymore.

That's not my idea of progress!

Or, as my father-in-law would have disparagingly said, "GG-Whiz!"

Or, as I say: What a pain; no pane!

Ben, Molly and Stan at 582 Marcy

ABOUT LOVING THE MYRTLE AVENUE EL

The Myrtle Avenue el (that's *el* for *elevated train*, as opposed to a below-ground subway) had to be seen to be believed.

I'm talking about 1939, when I was seven years old and a regular el passenger as well as keen observer of its architecture and listener to the el's own brand of cha-cha-cha.

I rode the el because it took me to neat places: downtown Brooklyn for Fulton Street shopping, over the Brooklyn Bridge to City Hall in Manhattan or all the way to Dexter Park to see the Bushwicks play baseball.

Actually, when I was three years old and before I ever rode the el, I began listening to it. Yeah, listening. Myrtle Avenue was only a half-block from our house on Marcy Avenue, which meant that I got to know all the el sounds.

A block away -- at Nostrand and Myrtle -- the el stopped at the Nostrand Avenue station. Just two blocks away was the Tompkins Avenue station.

This meant that once the el departed Nostrand and got up to speed, the sounds of its wheels over the rail gaps were distinct, with a drum cadence: *ta-dum, ta-dum,* faster and faster and then slower and slower until it came to a stop.

A ride on the Myrtle was like being cast into the 19th Century. The rolling stock dated back to the early 1900s -- and looked the part. These were mostly wooden cars with an open steel platform at each end. A conductor manned each platform, and when the train braked to a stop, one conductor would pull two iron handles to swing the two gates open. After all passengers had boarded or alighted, the conductor swung the gates closed.

The last car conductor then would pull an overhead cord that rang a bell in the car ahead, whereupon that conductor would do likewise until the bell on the front car signaled the motorman to start his train.

For any kid who liked trains, riding the Myrtle El was the next best thing to being on a Coney Island roller coaster. Sure, the open el platforms were safe, but being outdoors on a moving el provided a special brand of excitement.

Back in those late 1930s, nobody thought twice about falling over the gates, but that didn't mean I ever would loosen my grip on the metal bar affixed to the gate. No way!

None of the el cars featured a fan or any artificial device to cool passengers on a broiling August day. But the el had a way of beating the heat.

During the summer, side panels were removed from the rolling stock, allowing zephyrs to circulate throughout the train. Believe me, it was better than air conditioning.

When I began riding the Myrtle el in the late 1930s, it began its run at Manhattan's City Hall and then traversed the Brooklyn Bridge alongside trolley tracks of the Vanderbilt Avenue line.

Once in Brooklyn, the el clickety-clacked through downtown, then Clinton-Hill and Williamsburg (where I lived) all the way to the Metropolitan Avenue terminus in Glendale, Queens.

The final run in Queens was especially fun because the el descended to street level and sprinted past the old-car-barn and storage area along a right-of-way just like that of a regular railroad.

Life below the el was consummately unpleasant in a few neighborhoods, ours included. Just around the corner -- along Myrtle, from Marcy to Nostrand Avenue -- stood some of the most wretched tenements in the city.

Many of the tenants were poor African Americans at or barely above the poverty level. And it turned out that our cleaning lady lived in one of those tenements.

Every Saturday, I was assigned the dubious task of walking halfway down Myrtle to our cleaning lady's tenement. Then I had to climb the stairs to her apartment and hope that she would acknowledge my knock.

By contrast, just another block in a different direction we'd gladly make a beeline to Muller's ice cream parlor underneath the Tompkins Avenue el station.

Of course, there was no way of proving it, but I'd swear that nowhere in the wide world could anyone find a better chocolate ice cream soda -- with or without whipped cream and cherry on top -- than at Muller's.

But all that changed after Pearl Harbor Day (December 7, 1941) when the Japanese pulled their sneak attack on Uncle Sam's armed forces and then Hitler declared war on the United States a few days later.

That's when word spread that Mr. Muller of the ice-cream parlor had cast aspersions on our president, Franklin Delano Roosevelt. Overnight, Muller's name was Mud; within weeks, his ice cream parlor had become a former ice cream parlor.

But enough of these digressions. Since only Brooklyn's Lexington Avenue el was older than its Myrtle Avenue cousin, many trappings of both lines were right out of the late 1800s, when both were built.

For example, the tiny waiting room had not changed a bit from the day it opened. Among its more endearing pieces of equipment was a pot-bellied stove that could produce equator-type warmth. A winter joy while awaiting the local was just standing in front of the pot-bellied stove while watching the red coals transmit an incredible amount of heat.

Speaking of heat, one way to beat it on a sultry summer day was to camp right outside the front door of the first car. Conveniently, the motormen would leave that sliding door wide open, which enabled the breeze to cool the lead car once the train got going.

By the way, I don't want to leave you with the idea that the el ruined neighborhoods; far from it. For example, just a block away from the decrepit tenements around the corner on Myrtle, the nabe was just fine.

On my way to school, I'd walk under the el from Nostrand to Sanford Street past a pizzeria -- rare in those days -- and other well-kept businesses. It was that way on Myrtle all the way west to the downtown section.

Some of my favorite el rides took place during the baseball season. On Sundays, my dad would take me to see the Bushwicks, a semi-pro team that played at Dexter Park on the Cypress Hills, Brooklyn-Woodhaven, Queens border.

Reaching Dexter Park was as much fun as the ball games themselves. Fun because we had to take not one but two els to get there. We'd leave 582 Marcy, turn left to Myrtle and walk the long block to Nostrand. Then it would be up the creaky old stairway to the waiting room. The fare was a nickel, but the shiny, gold turnstile was not automatic. You had to give the five-cent piece -- or get change -- from the attendant and then push the turnstile.

That led us out on to the rickety wooden platform that always seemed two hours away from complete collapse. Looking west, we could see as far as the Franklin Avenue station, and peering east was Tompkins just two blocks away.

Once the el rolled toward us from Franklin Avenue we could distinctly hear the da-da, da-dum drumbeat as our train hove into view. It was doubly exciting. The closer the train, the more the wooden platform vibrated to a point where you never knew whether this was IT. Complete collapse or not? One never knew.

Dad and I never would go inside the car; we wanted the roller coaster feel being on the open platform. So, it was on to Tompkins station and then Brooklyn's Broadway junction.

This is where we had to switch to the Broadway el, which was situated right one level under our elevated tracks. Unlike the Myrtle Line, the Broadway el featured the newer BMT (Brooklyn-Manhattan Transit)

67-foot Standard cars. Standards were state of theart in 1914 and enjoyed improvements for the next decade, when newer models appeared. Still, the Standards had an appeal of their own and lasted until the 1970s.

To me, the big deal was a front window that opened. Alongside it, on the left, there was a jump seat that a lad could stand on and thereby stick his head out of the window for a very special breezy treat.

From the Myrtle-Broadway junction, the Standard thundered above Bushwick and its assorted breweries (Trommers, Rhinegold, Piels, among others) to the Canarsie Line connection and then the Cypress Hills swimming pool.

Next stop was Elderts Lane -- one of my favorite station names -- and Dexter Park. For about a buck, we'd see the Bushwicks play one of the black teams from the Negro National League and then double-back to the double-els.

The return from Dexter always had a neat twist to it. Instead of getting off the el at our Nostrand Avenue station, we remained on until it reached Downtown Brooklyn.

This was exciting stuff for two reasons: Dad would treat me to dinner at the Automat and we'd get the latest Sunday afternoon baseball scores. The first was as important as the second.

We got off at Sands Street, walked a few blocks to Fulton, where the spacious Automat sat across the street from Loew's Metropolitan Theater, MGM's flagship movie house.

Upon entering the Automat -- fast food long before McDonald's -- you immediately were greeted by a change booth, usually with two change-makers.

These were important people because everything at the Automat was paid for with five-cent pieces, alias nickels. To get nickels, you had to toss your quarters or bill on the counter and, with enormous speed, the nickels were returned.

Many favorites such as baked beans (with a slice of bacon) were featured behind glass containers. You put in a couple of nickels, turned the crank, the window flew open and out came your order.

In addition to baked beans, my favorites were creamed spinach, mashed potatoes and -- hard to believe -- mashed turnips.

After the Automat, we crossed the street to where the then daily newspaper, *The Brooklyn Citizen,* had its offices. On Sundays, during the baseball season, the *Citizen* placed a giant blackboard-scoreboard on the sidewalk.

Every game in the National and American Leagues was chalked. After perusing the scores -- hoping, of course, that the Yankees lost -- we headed to Myrtle and the sweet el ride home.

Between riding the el, watching the Bushwicks and eating baked beans with bacon at the Automat, my Sunday was made.

The only regret was that the el stopped running in 1968, soon was demolished and went the way of its cousins on Manhattan's Sixth, Third and Second Avenues, to name but a few lost elevated lines in The Big Apple.

Yeah, the music stopped but the melody lingers, albeit in a curious Myrtle-Avenue-el sort of way. To this day, I still get a kick out of tapping my right index finger on a table with the rhythm of the rails -- *da-dum, da-dum* -- clear as it was 80 years ago.

And when I do, I can "see" the Cascade Laundry building, William Davis' newsstand, the decrepit, sad tenements and, yes, even Muller's ice cream parlor -- before Herr Muller got nasty with FDR and got caught doing so.

At least in my head -- and on my fingertips -- the beloved Myrtle Avenue el remains alive and running -- still on its way to Tompkins Avenue Station!

The Myrtle Avenue El

HEBREW SCHOOL, A TROLLEY RIDE, A BLIZZARD, A BAR MITZVAH LESSON AND NICK PIDSODNY

During the winter of 1943, a running battle took place in my 11-year-old head. It was a tug of war between two demanding forces, Hebrew and hockey.

On the Jewish side, it was all about attendance at the New Hebrew School three blocks away, on Stockton Street near Tompkins Avenue. My dilemma blended into a migraine: Should I continue with my religious lessons or should I forsake them so I could get to the Sunday afternoon hockey games at Madison Square Garden on time?

Sunday Hebrew classes ran late. Hockey games started in the early afternoon. My icy mind kept telling me it would be sinful to miss the opening face-off, especially for the Sunday afternoon doubleheaders at The Garden.

This was a tough equation because -- ironically -- my mother never wanted me to start Hebrew school in the first place. And I can remember the phone conversation like it happened ten minutes ago.

It was three in the afternoon. I was home from P.S. 54 and, according to house rules, I did what I was supposed to do: phone Mom at work to assure her that I still was alive and didn't flunk penmanship again. The dialogue follows:

"Hi, Mom."

"How are you, Stanley?"

"Good, Mom. Listen, I want to start Hebrew School."

"No, you don't!"

"Yes, I do."

"Give me one good reason why."

"Because Jay Koslo is going!"

Just the mention of Jay Koslo stopped Mom in her tracks. What does that spoiled brat have to do with Hebrew school? But before she could lay out her case, I pointed out that Jay lived down the block on Marcy Avenue and that he and I could walk together to the New Hebrew School.

Before Mom could rally and speak for the prosecution, I tossed my knuckleball for strike three. "And The New Hebrew School," I argued, "will make me a better Jew." Mom thought for a moment and relented.

Two days later, I enrolled at the New Hebrew School and already had my doubts. The big sign in front proclaimed NEW HEBREW SCHOOL, but it looked like "new" had been well before General Sherman burned Atlanta.

The second doubt was my teacher, Mar (Hebrew for *Mister*) Rosenberg, who had an attitude that must have inspired the invention of spitballs. But there was no quitting now, and when my buddy, Howie Sparer, enrolled a week later, I decided I just might become a good Jew after all.

Nobody bothered to tell me this when I enrolled, but part of the deal was that I was required to attend Shabbat services on Saturday mornings, and, in the end, that was the deal-breaker.

Yeah, I showed up as required, took a look around at everyone praying, then realized that I was lost. Mar Rosenberg never taught us how to pray. I might as well have been holed up in a Tibetan monastery.

When I told Mom, she understood -- gleefully -- and that was that -- no more Hebrew school, a TKO for hockey.

But that didn't mean I was done with Hebrew, because somewhere down the calendar -- when I turned 13 -- I had to have my bar mitzvah. Mom quickly discovered a Conservative *shul*, Shaari Zedek Synagogue, and a cantor who'd give me early Sunday morning lessons. Hallelujah!

The lessons cleared me for hockey, and my instructor, Cantor Kwartin, was a sweetheart who made the lessons as easy as reading Dick and Jane. But even that wasn't the beauty part. The icing on my cake -- or matzo, if you will -- was The Ride. I had to take a trolley car to get to Shaari Zedek -- the Tompkins Avenue trolley, to be exact, so as to be there by 7:30 a.m. Everything was falling into place so neatly that I couldn't wait for Saturday night to be in my rearview mirror.

Sunday arrived and I was out of there, already musing about after-noon hockey. The Rovers were playing my favorite team, the Baltimore Blades. I loved the Blades because their goalie, Nick Pidsodny, was a neat, tough guy who liked to hit his opponents with his big, fat goalie stick.

But first, the trolley ride. How would I know it would be a once-in-a-lifetime classic?

I was on time at the streetcar stop but freezing my *tush* off. *Oy,* it was the coldest day of winter, and the predicted blizzard already was blizzard-ing. Good, 'cause I prayed for snow. I loved it the way I did chocolate ice cream sodas at the Sugar Bowl.

I saw my trolley in the distance. It's what they called a Peter Witt car, named after a Cleveland fellow who designed it as state of the art in 1922. It still looked good to me. I listened to the *ch-ch-ch-ing* of the brakes as it rolled to a stop at Tompkins and Vernon.

The twin wooden front doors banged open. Down plunged my nickel in the Johnson fare machine -- ka-ching! -- and I did a two-step to my jump seat to the left of the motorman so I could check his every move. But then I realized there was something unusual inside the trolley: I was the only passenger. This was a lifetime first; I got a limousine streetcar all to myself.

The motorman pulled on the big metal controller with his left hand, and off we went, as fast as a Peter Witt could go, which is not very fast … but fast enough for me. The occupants were just the two of us, Stanley and the motorman. I looked outside: No pedestrians on the sidewalks, no autos in the streets, just a surreal, snowy city scene.

As we blew past DeKalb Avenue, then Lafayette, then Gates, it suddenly dawned on me that we'd made every green light and not a single man nor woman flagged my trolley limo for a stop. Could it happen? Could this Peter Witt make it into Ripley's *Believe It or Not* and go all the way to my shul without a stop?

Now, the Make the Green Light Game was getting serious and I was really into it, leaning forward, holding my wooden jump seat hard with my left hand as we approached Fulton Street. Wow! Another green light, and still another greener as we veered right onto Kingston Avenue.

I wanted to talk to Mister Motorman to urge him on as if he were a jockey in the homestretch, but I knew that a non-stop trolley also was the operator's dream come true. Now I was counting streets and figured that Sharri Zedek was just a dozen blocks away. I saw through the snow that Bergen Street was visible out the front window. Yikes! It looked like another green light at Bergen; we're hitting the jackpot. But wait – I saw a figure through the snowflakes. Oh, no! No, please, no! But, alas, it's a yes.

A lady stood on the sidewalk, hunched over, head away from the wind-blown snow. She stepped off the curb and did what I was praying she wouldn't do: waved to the motorman so she could board. My no-hitter, as it were, ended in the eighth inning as the trolley skidded to a halt. She got on and, in a minute, I got off, still pleased that we got so far without a red light or another passenger.

I crossed Kingston, entered the shul's back door, and took the staircase up to the cozy, organ loft where Cantor Kwartin awaited me. He thanked me for braving the snow and we breezed through the lesson so swiftly that I was hoping the bar mitzvah would be held the next week, not in April.

Cantor Kwartin's farewell had a slightly European twang to it -- "See you next Sunday at seven-SURTY" -- and I was out of there, savoring the fast-piling snow. My Tompkins Avenue Trolley took me home and, even though we hit four red lights and picked up ten passengers, I couldn't have been happier.

I made the obligatory stop at Shlukers' bakery, diagonally across from my house, bought a usual small rye bread, sliced, without seeds, came home, ate breakfast, read the papers and waited for my buddy, Larry Shildkret, to ring the bell at noon.

That he did, and off we went to The Garden where my Baltimore Blades would beat the Rovers. Nick Pidsodny was belligerently beautiful in goal, thereby completing one of the best days of my life.

P.S. My April bar mitzvah went off well and, 76 years later, I still remember the speech opener, prepared by Cantor Kwartin: "My dear parents, grandparents, relatives and friends, this is the most important day in my life ..."

Who was I kidding? The trolley ride in the blizzard and Nick Pidsodny beating the Rovers was ten times more important!

Howie Sparer at his Bar Mitzvah, 1945

THE GREAT TROLLEY
STEAL -- ALMOST

I always wanted a trolley car of my own. Not a toy; a real one, built by the Brill company in Philadelphia, if you please.

Who wouldn't?

Once you have the streetcar, all you need is a few miles of track, an overhead wire generating electricity and a year's worth of chutzpah.

I had neither track nor wire, but I did have a ton of nerve and a best friend named Howie Sparer, whose running theme was: What's life without a little adventure?

Howie and I enjoyed that adventure and almost got that genuine Brill car. Not too legally, either, as you'll discover in a moment. In the meantime, consider this pressing question: What could be a greater adventure than stealing a Brooklyn trolley right out of its own home? In this case, the Sea Gate yards in the shadow of Coney Island.

But first let me explain that my obsession with streetcars began when I was a kid and discovered that I was surrounded by them.

The Tompkins, Nostrand, Myrtle, DeKalb and Lorimer Street trolley lines either were just around the corner or a few short blocks away. Who needed a car or a taxi? Surely not the Fischler Family.

We never owned a car and would be more likely to charter a rocket to Venus before we'd ever hail a cab.

If you were a school kid in 1944, during the school year three pennies got you a trolley ride; it was a nickel for everyone else. Plus a free transfer if you wanted to switch to the Flatbush Avenue line and go to Ebbets Field and watch the Dodgers play baseball.

One day, while my father and I were shoveling snow after a freak Thanksgiving Day blizzard, Mr. Meyers, a next-door neighbor, stopped by for a schmooze.

After gabbing with my dad, Mr. Meyers asked me what I want to be when I grow up. "A trolley car motorman," I shot back. Meyers laughed.

"Nah," Meyers answered, "you don't want that job. They only make $35 a week."

I respectfully told Meyers that I liked trolleys so much I'd do that job for nothing,

Meyers walked away shaking his head and I kept nodding my noggin, still wishing I could be a motorman. As luck would have it, my fantasy almost was miraculously fulfilled a few years later.

It happened this way.

In the summer of 1944, I spent a few days at Brooklyn's private seaside enclave called Sea Gate, just a skee-ball's throw away from Coney Island.

My best friend Howie and his parents rented a house inside the gated community that sits right on the Atlantic. It was a nifty place for a couple of 12-year-olds to be when the sun got hotter than hot.

There was the ocean for swimming. There was the beach for girl-watching, and there was the rest of Sea Gate -- once the Prohibition-era hideaway for bootleggers -- to explore.

There happened to be a grand total of two gates at Sea Gate. The main portal -- closely guarded like a toll booth -- was for cars, pedestrians and people who lived there.

The other gate, which was about 30 yards north of the main portal, was unobtrusive because the only things that were allowed to go through that gate were the Norton's Point trolley cars and their operators, alias motormen.

Just inside that gate, the Norton's Point streetcars "slept" at night, later to be awakened for the morning rush hour. About four were taken out of the yard for the a.m. run -- mostly past Coney backyards -- to the BMT's Stillwell Avenue el terminal.

The Norton's Point line was more like a shuttle -- or Toonerville Trolley -- than anything else. It was the kind of streetcar that I dreamed of piloting, although I knew that miracle never would happen.

Until.

It was another broiler of an August day, with the temperature climbing to the 90s. Howie and I hit the ocean for some waves and then checked out the chickadees, but there was just so much chick-checking we could do. So we decided to go biking.

Ah, but there was only one bicycle in the Sparer stable.

No problem. Howie would take a ride, then I would take a ride and then we would do a duet. I pedaled and young Sparer sat on the package rack behind me. For three minutes, we had a ball until that nasty bike-riding sound was heard.

Pssssst! Then, *PSSSSSST!*

It could mean only one thing: a blow-out. We dismounted and realized that there was no bike store within miles of Sea Gate, so another creative move was in order.

Holey Moly! Our bike disaster took place only a few yards from the trolley-car camp. We saw four elephantine streetcars parked back-to-back under a large oak tree. A fifth sat on the rails adjoining a weeping willow.

"Let's check it out," I suggested to my pal.

Howie knew that there was nothing else to do and nowhere else to go, so he followed me as I eagerly hustled over to the lone Norton's Point car.

"Now what?" he wondered out loud.

"I'll tell you what," I shot back. "Let's see if we can get into this thing."

"Are you nuts?" he wondered, knowing it was too late for him to change my mind.

"You grab one end of the door and I'll grab the other," I implored, "and when I say, 'Go,' pull."

Mandrake the Magician couldn't have opened the sesame faster than we did. And without further ado, we climbed the three steps and found ourselves precisely where the motorman would sit -- or stand, as the case may be.

I could tell that Howie had shaken off his I-don't-give-a-damn-about-trolleys pose. He noticed my eyes, knew the look that told him that I was up to no good -- but if we followed through, it just might be good after all.

First, I explained that the Norton's Point line once actually ran to a terminal at the very western tip of Sea Gate.

"You can see the tracks are still there," I pointed out, "and they go all the way to the end and then curve back here."

Then, I explained that the trick was to discover whether there still was "juice" in the overhead wire that was strung above the tracks all the way around Sea Gate.

"I'll show you," I said as we clambered out of the motorman's cave, down the steps and walked to the trolley's backside, where the electric pole was held in place.

"Watch this," I said, pulling the pole free of its clamp.

Never having done this before, I was more than a bit shaky holding the rope while the trolley pole spring moved it higher and higher in the direction of the overhead wire.

The little round wheel at the tip of the pole fit neatly in place on the wire and then came the sound of trolley music-- *UNGA-UNGA-UNGA-UNGA.*

That meant that power was on, and the wire was live. The lovely Brill product was ready to run.

As we strode back to the front door, I visualized our dramatic run. We'd take it nice and slow, crossing the front lawns of summer hotels and other residences. Then we'd complete this historic journey by circling right back to the trolley camp from whence we had come. This would be as exciting as the Union and Central Pacific meeting in 1869 at Promontory, Utah.

Climbing back to the motorman's seat, Howie blandly -- and yet so sensibly -- wondered, "But how do you make it go?"

I pointed to the raised metal handle with a round wooden knob on top situated to the left of the motorman's chair. "You pull on that thing -- it's called the 'controller' -- and it makes the trolley move: slow, medium and faster."

"Yeah," Howie wondered, now getting serious about the melodrama before him, "but what if somebody is standing on the tracks and the trolley is coming right at him or her?"

With my right shoe, I hammered a round steel knob on the floor and the *clang-clang-clang* answered that question.

"So, what if the pedestrian doesn't get out of the way, how do you stop it?"

"Elementary my dear Sparer; elementary. It's like a car or a truck or a subway train," I said dismissively. "You use the brake. Here!"

I pointed to the big, round silver device on the right side of the controller. "That's the brake," I pointed out.

Howie did a double-take. "Brake? What brake? I don't see a brake."

He was right; something *was* missing; namely the brake handle that normally fit snugly over the protruding metal device that I called the brake.

(The scene reminded me of Chin, the neighborhood Chinese laundry man, who liked to say, "No tickee; no laundlee!")

Ergo: No brake handle; no brake. It suddenly dawned on me that brake handles are removed by every motorman after the day's run. Perhaps he stored it behind the controller.

I looked to the left, looked to the right, looked down to the floor. No brake handle.

"What kind of crap is this?" Howie demanded, obviously as crushed as his almost-motorman.

I had to get out of this jam somehow. The ploy machine was working overtime in my head.

"How about this?" I said, pulling my last rabbit out of the hat. "I make the trolley go and you run ahead, waving people out of the way. Good idea?"

"Not good," came the Sparer squelch. "What if I trip over the tracks in front of the trolley and you don't have the brake handle? BAD IDEA!"

Stunned to the core, I could only blurt, "Let's get outta here and walk over to Coney. There are tons of girls at Bay 16."

"You got a deal," snapped Howie, suddenly and sensibly placing his priorities in order. Frustrated, we strode along the boardwalk to Bay 16.

I was right; there were bathing beauties all over the beach. But only one of us enjoyed the sensuous scene. Howie did the chick-watching while I stretched out on the comforting sand, humming a chorus of "The Trolley Song," that Judy Garland warbled in MGM;s technicolor production, *Meet Me In St. Louis*.

As Howie later confessed, my last words to him as I nodded out went something like this:

"I'm gonna dream of one wooden brake handle -- that's all!"

The exact trolley car Stan and Howie almost stole from this Sea Gate locale…

And the cab of that very trolley

ODE TO A BMT "STANDARD" SUBWAY CAR

How can anyone possibly fall in love with a subway car?

For me, it was easy.

The BMT Standard was built for a four-year-old kid. Okay, for me. The year was 1936, and that's when my Stan-Standard romance began. By 1942, at age ten, I appreciated the handsome subway cars even more. Call it a love affair with an express.

By far, the Standard's best youth-friendly item was its front window. It actually opened so wide that even a four-year-old could stick his head through the aperture. It was a terrific way to play a lad's game called I'm The Motorman.

Of course, sticking one's head out of the BMT Standard's front window wouldn't have been possible for a four-year-old without an essential extra -- the all-important jump seat.

Positioned just to the left and below the front window, the jump seat enabled the littlest guy to stand on it and have a window-header, as we liked to call it. In those carefree days, the BMT never worried about insurance problems.

But the strategic jump seat wasn't all the BMT Standard offered a young train cashew like me. Every kid who wanted to operate a train craved the opportunity to actually *see* how the motorman drove his eight-car express.

The added attraction was a rectangular glass panel across the motorman's cab door. It enabled kids to peer through the pane and watch The Man apply his brakes and pull on the controller for more speed.

The BMT Standard originally was designed in 1914, when the company then was called BRT (Brooklyn Rapid Transit.) Following improvements, The Standard became BMT's workhorse, plying all major Brooklyn routes. The West End, Culver, Sea Beach, Broadway, Canarsie and Brighton Lines all featured the Standard. But my favorite, by far, was the Brighton Express. (More on that later.).

I should add that the BMT Standard also was a treat for adults. It measured 67 feet long, by far the largest subway car then built and boasted more seats than any other; not to mention a trio of overhead fans the size of Dutch windmills.

Every kid who ever rode a BMT Standard had his favorite route, but -- from May through September -- mine was the Brighton Express, which ran to Coney Island from Franklin Avenue in Bedford-Stuyvesant.

What differentiated the Franklin-Coney line was that it featured a huge, white disk, attached to the front bumper. No other line in the city had that, and -- since World War II was on -- it reminded me of a logo on the side of a Spitfire.

The beauty part of my ride unfolded after The Express emerged from a tunnel at the Prospect Park station. From there, the train rolled along a four-track open cut interspersed by short tunnels. Above were the lovely homes of Flatbush.

The Standards gathered speed as we reached the first curve -- passing the Parkside Avenue local stop -- at top speed. The clickety-clacks reminded me of a drummer's paradiddle. And that reminded me of the King of Swing.

Benny Goodman's "China Boy" and "I Got Rhythm" – with Gene Krupa on drums -- seemed to move at the same pace as our Express. With my tongue tickling my palate, I duplicated the *clickety-clacks* and Krupa's drums.

Soon, the open-cut ambience changed as we departed Newkirk station. Just ahead, the Standard would be challenged by a climb to an embankment that once was plied by 19th Century Brighton-bound steam engines.

The express tracks went up, up, up until they leveled off at the Avenue H local stop. By now, the clear right-of-way enabled the Express to gallop past landmarks like Wingate Field and the old Flatbush movie studios, still intact.

As the Express relentlessly lurched toward Kings Highway, I indulged in more than my Be A Motorman game. I made sure that every Express ride had a built-in contest called How Long Would It Take Before We Caught A Local?

For me, this was serious stuff. The trick was simple -- catch a local before it reached the Sheepshead Bay express stop. My role as deputy motorman was to spot any Brighton Locals that might be ahead on our right.

Sure enough, as we braked toward the Kings Highway express stop, a Coney-bound local rolled out. I instantly figured that we'd catch it at either the Avenue U or Neck Road local stops, just before Sheepshead Bay. After that, we'd lose.

Our Standard's doors closed at Kings Highway, and off we went in hot pursuit. There was the Local, very catchable, as it lumbered out of the Avenue U stop.

"We can catch it at Neck Road," I confidently said to myself. "We have to --since it's our last chance before Sheepshead."

This subway version of a fox-and-hound chase approached its melodramatic conclusion. My Brighton Express, now at full throttle, began bearing down on its quarry. With my head thrust as far out of the window as possible, I gasped.

"This is it," I yelled to no one in particular as the halted local's doors opened while we flashed by at Neck Road. "Six, seven eight cars ... " and that's it – yet another victory for the Brighton Express!

Ah, but there remained more good train stuff ahead. After Sheepshead Bay, the earthen embankment transferred the tracks to an all-steel el. That meant the muffled clickety-clack became a much louder CLICKETY-CLACK on the old-time el.

Ch-Ch-Ch. The motorman hit the brakes. Straight ahead was the ominous, 90-degree right turn onto (above) Brighton Beach Avenue. As we decelerated, the briny aroma of the Atlantic soothed my nasal passages.

Now we were overlooking Brighton Beach Baths, a Jewish, city-country club replete with handball courts, paddle tennis, a swimming pool and Enoch Light's dance orchestra for waltzing under the stars.

Meanwhile, the Brighton Express stopped at the Art Deco-style Ocean Parkway station, followed by West 8th Street, where the Culver Line joined our tracks. Behind the station's canopy loomed Coney's Wonder Wheel and Cyclone.

The BMT Standard approached the Stillwell Avenue Terminal at a crawl easing around the final, 90-degree curve accompanied by operatic screeches -- wheels rubbing angrily against rails -- and into the last stop.

Only after all the other passengers left did I relinquish my hold on the front window. The motorman opened his cab door and I thanked him for the wonderful ride.

I wanted to tell him it was worth five dollars, not a nickel, but before I could deliver my postscript, he pulled out a pack of Lucky Strikes and headed for the transit workers rec room perched above the platform.

I walked down to Surf Avenue -- Coney's main drag -- met my best friend, Howie Sparer, and we started our tour of The Rides.

We started with bumper cars, then The Bobsled -- imported from the 1939-40 World's Fair and a big winner -- plus The (Gold Ring) Carousel.

A break for Nathan's hot dogs interrupted our expedition, after which we hustled back to the remaining attractions -- Skee-Ball and, finally, The L.M. Thompson Roller Coaster. All things considered, it was a good day as Coney days go.

An hour later, I arrive home in time for dinner at 582 Marcy. Mom is there in the kitchen. A Coney Island veteran, Molly Fischler asks the key question:

"So, Stanley, tell me, which ride did you like best, the Bobsled or the roller coaster?"

I paused for a brief, thoughtful moment and then shot back the one and only reasonable reply: "The Brighton Express!"

The BMT Standard

MY BEST
HANUKAH-CHRISTMAS GIFT

Like Ralphie in Jean Shepherd's classic *A Christmas Story*, I had a holiday gift in mind when I was Ralphie's age.

For religious reasons, gift-giving in December was complicated in our house during the Great Depression. Complicated, yes, but not depressing. Any little gift in those late 1930s was a *mitzvah*.

Being Jewish, we celebrated Hanukah and wouldn't even think about having a Christmas tree. But, like any denomination, we had a right to dream about a present, if not a white Christmas.

However, my eminent mom, Molly Fischler, compromised; I got my Hanukah gift on Christmas morning. That seemed fair enough. But what manner of gift could they afford -- besides a Hanukah *dreidel?*

By the time I was three, my parents realized that I was nuts about trains. There's no need to go into the whys or wherefores except for the BMT Myrtle Avenue el a half block away and the IND subway under 582 Marcy.

To satisfy my train-mania, I was given a set of wooden railroad cars when I was four years old. I pulled them around the living-room floor for a few weeks and then stashed them in the hall closet next to a broken mandolin.

By age seven, in 1939, I had become like Ralphie in *A Christmas Story*. He wanted a Red Ryder BB gun rifle in the worst way and I wanted a set of Lionel electric trains.

Ralphie's mother warned him, "You'll shoot your eye out," and my Dad shot down my wish with his standard, deathless line: "Sonny, don't you know that money doesn't grow on trees?"

And so another Lionel-less year went by and now it was December of '39. Stanley was all of seven-and-a-half years old, with no Lionel locomotive lights at the end of his tunnel. Not that I completely was shut out of gifts.

I did get a high-tech "Ink-O-Graf" pen -- I needed that like a moose needs a hat rack-- a couple of pairs of socks and a dollar bill to buy a few phonograph records, preferably anything by Benny Goodman

No sweat; I had become accustomed to our monetary misfortunes and went to bed secure in the knowledge that there were many Hanukah-Christmases ahead in my lifetime. Who knows, one year I might get lucky.

As I donned my pajamas, about to plunge into bed and turn to *I Love A Mystery* on my tiny Philco Transitone radio, Mom unexpectedly walked into my bedroom. I figured she was back for an encore of wishing me a good night.

"Guess what?" she excitedly exclaimed. "Your Uncle Ben drove up and he wants to wish you a happy holiday."

Great; really great! Uncle Ben was one of my all-time favorites. It wouldn't kill me to miss *I Love a Mystery* for a few laughs with Funny Face Ben.

I put on my bathrobe and walked into the living room. There was a very grinning Uncle Ben, sitting on our green sofa, still in his winter coat and snazzy grey fedora. His 1938 Pontiac was out front.

"Stanley," he said, "I have a present for you."

I said nothing. *Nada.* Except my brain did a few Major Hoople lines: "*Hak-Kaff.*" Then, "*Sput-t-t,*" and, finally, "*Umm-hak!*"

He handed me a big box, gift-wrapped by Loeser's Department store on Fulton Street in downtown Brooklyn. (Among my pals, Loeser's was rated second best, after A&S, for top toy department.)

"What are you waiting for?" my dad insisted, interrupting my reverie. "Let's see what's inside the box."

Nervously, I struggled past the outer wrappings, still uncertain about the contents. At last, I pulled that last stretch of paper off and tossed it on the carpet.

I did a double-take. (Possibly even a triple-take.) It was a Lionel O27 electric train set. The big box was filled with smaller orange and blue containers marked 027 PENNSY TORPEDO.

One by one, I pulled out the cars – first, the grey, streamlined Pennsylvania Railroad's newest locomotive, the Torpedo, followed by its gray tender.

But that was just for starters. Out of other boxes, I impatiently extracted three freight cars. The yellow boxcar had a sliding door in the middle and a Baby Ruth chocolate ad on its side that read, "Candy is delicious food."

Next was a Sunoco Oil Car and, finally, a sweet, red caboose. Oh, yeah, and plenty of track and a transformer to make the set go. I was overwhelmed.

I gave Uncle Ben a big, big hug. "Enjoy it," he said. "I must be going."

The Lionel O27 Pennsy Torpedo was the best Hanukah-Christmas gift I ever got. And it got even better the next December when Uncle Ben added three bright-red passenger cars to the train's stock.

Unlike most kids, I didn't limit my train use to the holidays. I played with my Lionels even into the summer. Not that there weren't issues.

Building a route around our compact, crowded living room was roughly equivalent to completing the first trans-continental Union Pacific-Central Pacific railroad in Utah during the 19th Century.

Instead of mountains to be crossed and tunnels to be built, my track route

bisected my father's large smoking chair as well as the dining room table's legs and my little homework desk.

A great, Lionel train wreck narrowly was averted one night when my Dad carelessly rose from his chair to fetch a cigar and nearly derailed the Pennsy Torpedo with his right Florsheim shoe.

For my 1941 Hanukah-Christmas gift Dad splurged and bought me a pair of manual switches and a miniature railroad hut with a hidden bell inside. As the train approached the hut, the bell rang and stopped in six seconds.

That same winter Jay Koslo, who lived two blocks away on Marcy Avenue, burst into my house one Saturday morning with extraordinarily pulsating news.

"Guess what?" he blurted while interrupting my honey-and-oatmeal breakfast. "My cousin Julius told me that Lionel has a showroom in the city on 26th Street. "Get dressed and let's check it out."

I knew from Pontiac, Dodge, Packard and Ford showrooms, but who knew that Lionel actually had one of its own? Well, Julius Koslo did -- or at least that's what he told Jay.

At 11 a.m. that fateful Saturday, Jay and I found the Lionel showroom in a modest building overlooking Madison Square Park. But there was nothing modest about this eclectic electric train bonanza. Inside, we were stunned.

A table that looked a mile long was festooned with all manner of trains. An orange Union Pacific diesel streamliner was hustling down an express track, while a New York Central freight sat in a siding.

The trains snaked through mountain tunnels, past make-believe cities and across myriad bridges. What more could I say to Jay than, "Do me a favor and tell Cousin Julius, 'Thanks for the tip.' This is fantastic."

Then, there was a pause, and a look at a very special passenger train. "The one I'd love to have," I said, "is that Rock Island route's Wabash Cannonball. It's the only one I know that has a song to go with it." Jay also was impressed.

After about an hour of gaping, I had made a mental note of the best of the best exhibits, and one of them was ... the Wabash Cannonball.

"What do you like?" I asked Jay on the subway ride home.

He thought for a moment. "Definitely the crossing gates, the coal machine that empties into hopper cars and that fast passenger train you just mentioned -- 'The Wabash Cannonball,'" he said.

My nods and grins told Jay that he had good taste in Lionels, and I hoped that our wishes someday would be fulfilled, grandiose as they were.

Alas, they would not.

Not ever, ever, ever!

There was a world war on. Not long after our visit, Lionel's New Jersey factory stopped making electric trains and converted to wartime production for the U.S. Navy. Electric trains turned to cardboard models.

"Do you see what Lionel is selling?" Jay Koslo asked me one day. He didn't wait for an answer. "Cardboard train sets from cut-outs!"

That did it. We had come to track's end. Cardboard Lionels! Were they kidding, or what?

But I simply couldn't leave this disaster at that and finally produced a coda of sorts.

When P.S. 54 shut down for the holidays in December 1943, I took New York Central's Empire Builder to Albany. I decided it was as good a time as any to visit my kid-cousin Ira Sheier, eight years my junior.

I brought along a big box for Aunt Hattie and Uncle Paul to give Ira for Hanukah-Christmas. The box was not as pretty as the one from Loeser's Department store, but the contents were the same.

It contained my Lionel Pennsy Torpedo electric train set, including manual switches and a bell-enclosed hut. "I hope Ira enjoys them as much as I did," I told Aunt Hattie and Uncle Paul.

Leaving my Lionels with Cousin Ira was a bittersweet experience. But I got pleasure out of the giving and obtained sweet memories of that wonderful trip to the Lionel showroom overlooking Madison Square Park.

The best recollection, by far, was watching Lionel's Wabash Cannonball tear-ass along the company's O gauge tracks on a table that seemed never to end.

And on the rare occasion when I get the electric train-missing blues, I turn on Bing Crosby singing -- What else? -- "The Wabash Cannonball."

Listen to the jingle, the rumble and the roar

As she glides along the woodland o'er the hills and by the shore.

Hear the mighty rush of the engine, hear those lonesome hoboes call,

Traveling through the jungle of The Wabash Cannonball!

And if The Cannonball could talk, its message would be as simple as this:

HAPPY HOLIDAYS!

PART FOUR
Sports!

SOFTBALL, HARD FEELINGS AND A BLOWN PICK-OFF PLAY

Bernard Malamud's novel, *The Natural*, was published in 1952. A good three decades later came a movie based on Malamud's work, starring Robert Redford.

In both book and flick, the hero, Roy Hobbs, produces prodigious wallops. Hobbs accomplishes these feats with a bat that he hand-carved and then named "Wonderboy."

Of course, Malamud couldn't have known this, but in 1943, nine years before his best-seller hit the bookstores, I happened to be "The Natural," right out of Williamsburg, Brooklyn. And nobody wrote about me until now.

Unfortunately, I have no witnesses. My best friend, Howie Sparer, would swear by me because he saw my Ruthian hits. Alas, Howie isn't around anymore, so you'll just have to take my word for it.

My saga began the day after I arrived as an eleven-year-old at the Pythian Camp in Glen Spey, New York, a sweet, rural hideaway on a tributary of the Delaware River.

I was assigned to a bunk with three other campers and a counselor named "Uncle" Eli. As I mentioned in an earlier chapter, in those antediluvian days, Pythian's counselors all were called "Uncle." For all I know, he could have been a Goldstein.

Uncle Eli played a part in my becoming The Natural on the second day of camp. That's when he hustled a bunch of us campers over to the softball field for a very simple pick-up game that suddenly became quite important to me.

Up until that point in my softball life, I could be categorized as good-hit/bad-field. Ground balls all looked like sweet peas to me, but, at bat, the Clincher softball reappeared like a white grapefruit.

Not that I was a budding Babe Ruth. I hit okay and if I had been playing in the majors my batting average would be around .250, give or take five points.

Uncle Eli had me hitting third, which gave me time to check out the bats laid out on the turf. One particularly caught my eye because of its color, ox-blood, which also is defined as burgundy.

I had no idea what this ox-blood-colored bat would do for me until I swung it, which I did several times that afternoon. And every time I took a cut, it felt as if someone other than yours truly was responsible for the smash.

One drive after the other went sailing somewhere in the outfield where the outfielder wasn't. And the crazy thing was that I was slugging with remarkable ease. Or, if you don't mind the bromide, hitting was like a walk in the (ball) park.

I was smart enough to realize that it may have been one of those lucky days that never would appear, not even in my wildest softball dreams. But I was happily mistaken.

When we played another game a few days later, I found another ox-blood-colored bat and, lo and behold, I was slugging big again. It finally dawned on me that there was something magical about these hunks of burgundy lumber.

To me, every ox-blood-colored bat was roughly equivalent to what Wonderboy had meant to Roy Hobbs, except that my selection of Camp Pythian bats weren't hand-carved or infused with lightning bolts. They merely were plain dusty.

For the rest of my two weeks at Pythian, I made a point of going up to the plate armed only with an ox-blood-colored bat. It never let me down. I felt the way Hobbs must have felt in both book and flick.

But that was camp, and camp wasn't the city – and most certainly not the P.S. 54 Softball League. I returned home to discover that our Vernon Avenue team was well-ensconced in the cellar. Could the Poor Man's Roy Hobbs help them?

Coincidentally, Howie Sparer arrived home from Camp Achvah simultaneous to my return. We checked in with our Vernon Avenue buddies and learned they desperately wanted us back in the lineup, like right now! We understood the S.O.S. and promised that we would do our best. And we did.

Using any ox-blood-colored bat I could find, I continued to wallop the ball like crazy, mostly line drives. I remember coming to bat one day and disgustedly blasting a grounder between second and short for an easy single.

Yeah, it was a hit, but I was furious with myself for whacking the ball on the ground instead of over an outfielder's head. At that brief time of my greatness, I regarded a hot ground single below my stature as the slugger king.

As it happened, the Vernon Avenue Gold Dust Twins -- me and Howie -- did wonders for the Junior Dodgers. When the P.S. 54 season ended, our club had climbed from the cellar to second place. Not too bad!

But, good as we had been, none of our wins had come at the expense of the Hart Street gang, alias The Junior Yankees. They were hailed as champions of the P. S. 54 Schoolyard League, although we never had a shot at them.

This pissed me off -- and Howie as well. We believed that with Sparer and Fischler in the lineup the Junior Dodgers could beat those cocky, undefeated bums from Hart Street. So we did the natural thing and challenged them.

The Harts' captain -- my classroom pal, Neil Brown -- thought it was a swell idea. But since this was such a monumental game, Brownie insisted it be played on a more professional ball field than the deformed P.S. 54 diamond.

We agreed that Taaffe Park was the perfect place for our tourney. It bordered the Brooklyn Navy Yard and was within walking distance -- underneath the Myrtle Avenue el -- of both Hart Street and Vernon Avenue.

Taaffe Park's softball diamond was laid out just perfectly. It was enveloped by a five-foot chain-link fence running from left field to center and ending at the right field foul line.

Centerfield was deep, but not too deep. It would take a really good swat to clear the left and right field fences for a four-bagger. After checking the fences, our pitcher (also a Howie) seemed quite at ease.

To distinguish him from Howie Sparer, we logically labeled him "Howie Rabbit" because he wore the biggest ears in the neighborhood and featured buck teeth that would have driven Bugs Bunny nuts with jealousy. (Eh, what's up, Howie?)

I played shortstop and Howie Sparer was in center. The rest of our lineup proved irrelevant, but the game was very relevant. Beating the Harts would give us bragging rights for weeks at Al and Shirley's candy store.

Granted, winning was a long shot because the Harts were loaded. They had the hitters, the fielders and the fastest guy in the nabe, Joe DiNapoli, who was even more dangerous because base stealing was allowed in our games.

It was game time, so we flipped a coin to decide which team was first at bat. We won and chose to be the "home" team, batting in the bottom of the inning. The Harts (Junior Yankees) were up first and, brother, were they ever "up!"

What they did to us in the top of the first you wouldn't want done to, well, any self-respecting ball club; not that the Junior Dodgers were remotely close to being good. Staggeringly inept is what we were.

With only one out, the Harts were ahead 9-0.

Not having a white flag of surrender, we requested an armistice parlay with our murderous foes. They agreed and we surrendered, just like that.

Then came a sportsmanlike move on the victors' part. They agreed to a do-over game here and now. Why waste that long walk to Taaffe Park?

The winners graciously allowed our Junior Dodgers to bat first and you know what that meant. Slugger Stan, batting third, finally would get a chance to make like Roy Hobbs and redeem our pride, or what was left of it.

Feverishly, I looked through the bat collection to find an ox-blood-colored wand. Hooray-hooray, there it was, complete with three inches of tape for better gripping at the bottom. I couldn't be happier or more confident. This was *it!*

Batting first, my pal, Howie, grounded out to short. Our left fielder, Howard Gelch, popped out to the first baseman. At last! I now had my chance to make amends.

For a brief moment, my thoughts drifted back to my halcyon clouting days at Pythian Camp. Then, I fortified my confidence with a brief flashback to those drives off P.S. 54's brick wall, an automatic two-bagger. I considered how easy it all was.

I picked up the bat and did two circular practice swings in the manner of my hero and role model, Stan "The Man" Musial of the St. Louis Cardinals. I was ready.

My eye was on centerfield. My mind measured the distance from home plate to the centerfield fence. "It's doable," I murmured to myself.

No point in waiting. The pitch arrived, juicy-slow. I swung -- maybe too hard, perhaps too over-anxious. Still, the ball sailed just where I had hoped, toward deep center.

But about five yards from the fence, the official Clincher softball suddenly looked like a model plane that had run out of gas. The ball parachuted right into their centerfielder's mitt. *Oy vey!*

As I stopped short between first and second, I momentarily wondered what had gone wrong. Maybe I was overanxious. That was it. Certainly, the burgundy bat couldn't have been the problem; it never was.

The good news was that we retired the side in their half of the first, and the even better news was that now we had a real ballgame. Remarkably, the score remained 0-0 through five innings.

Even more remarkably -- nay, tragically -- was my inability to produce even a measly single. I kept going for the centerfield fence and the ball kept surrendering to the centerfielder's mitt.

Still, there was time. It was zip-zip, bottom of the sixth, two outs, nobody on base and Howie Rabbit was making like Cy Young on the mound. What a game!

Joey DiNapoli stood at the plate for the Harts. He viciously lined the ball to right center. By the time pal Howie pegged the Clincher to second, DiNapoli was standing confidently on the base.

The plot thickened. We knew that Joey was gonna try to steal third; that was a given. And we knew, with his speed, that he'd pull it off, unless we came up with a foolproof plan.

And we did. It was simply put. Pitcher Howie Rabbit was told to count to two *and* toss the ball to third base. Surely, Joey would be caught in a rundown and that would be that. Brilliant!

As the mound huddle ended, I turned and whispered to Howie Rabbit, just in case: "Remember: Count to two, and throw to third." Foolproof. Worst case, DiNapoli would make it back to second. The problem would be solved.

Normally, Howie Rabbit was a smart fellow; he got good grades and likely would wind up where the smartest kids do, at Brooklyn Tech. But at this moment, Rabbit would only get a scholarship to Dumb and Dumber University.

He counted to three and threw to second!

DiNapoli waltzed home while the entire Junior Dodgers team got a collective case of lockjaw. We were down 1-0 with three innings to go.

It stayed one-zip until the bottom of the eighth. With two out, Neil Brown, batting lefty, too easily put one over the right field chain link fence, and now we trailed by two.

Finally, we're down to our last at bat. I was up, looking one more time at that centerfield fence, disbelieving that I still haven't put one over.

Here came the pitch. *Crack!*

It was up, up and away. Uh-oh! It's down, down, *plop!*

Game over.

I shook hands with Brownie, who killed us with that lefty home run, and then I delivered the traditional and mournful Brooklyn warning: "Wait 'til next year!"

As it happened, there would be many softball "next years" in my life. Not to mention lots more ox-blood-colored bats.

But, sadly, none of them could reproduce my slugging summer of 1943.

That is, until that fateful morning at Taaffe Park, when Howie Rabbit forgot that second base wasn't third base and my burgundy bat turned yellow.

Hey, it happens. I guess, when all's said and done, you could safely say that Roy Hobbs I was not!

Taaffe Park under construction, 1930s

CRUSADING FOR THE JOE MEDWICK GLOVE

It started off as an ordinary early-summer Sunday in Brooklyn, circa 1941, and ended with a son vs. father battle over an oxblood-colored Joe Medwick glove autographed by Ducky himself.

In an ironic way, I have to blame dad for the traumatic saga, which began one evening in the spring of 1941 at Ebbets Field, home of our beloved Brooklyn Dodgers. Pop loved baseball, and on this night our Brooks were playing the New York Giants. (BOO!)

We got good seats, three rows back in the left field grandstand, which was all a nine-year-old sports nut like me could ask for -- give or take a new set of Lionel electric trains, with accessories. Better still, we were sitting in a place where I could look down at my idol, left-fielder Joe "Ducky" Medwick, so close I felt I could almost touch his bright blue cap with the "B" adorning the front.

Camped in the green pasture, Medwick already was my idol, and for all the right reasons:

1. He was Hungarian and I was half-Hunky.

2. He had a nickname, "Ducky," and I had a nickname, "Clock."

3. He had been one of the best players for the past five years, and I had been -- so I thought -- his biggest fan.

So far, it was a good night. Our Bums were ahead, 2-1, and the Giants had a man on first with two outs in the top of the ninth. Manager Leo Durocher's best reliever, Hugh Casey, had the situation well in hand. The count was 2-2. In came the pitch.

CRACK!

The Giant batter got really good wood on the ball. A hard line drive headed to left; there was no way my man, Ducky, could get it on the fly. It looked like a sure Giants run.

But, wait – what was Joe trying to do? Was he nuts? He was charging a ball that he'd never catch on the fly. No way. Except, Ducky's body language seemed to disagree. The horsehide was diving fast, but so was Medwick.

It was not like a headfirst dive, but, rather, a cleat-firster, with Joe sliding along the grass on his *tush*. PLOP! The ball landed in his mitt. Unreal. Couldn't believe what I saw. I still can't!

Never mind that Brooklyn won; this was beyond any doubt, *the greatest catch I had ever seen in my young life.*

I still was musing over it two weeks later. The Dodgers were on the road now, so Dad and I took in a Bushwicks double-header at Dexter Park, a neat ball yard on the border between Cypress Hills, Brooklyn and Woodhaven, Queens.

The semi-pro all-white Bushwicks played the best black teams in the Negro National League. On this sunny Sunday, they were up against the vaunted Homestead Grays out of Pittsburgh.

The Grays were loaded with such legends as catcher Josh Gibson and pitcher Satchel Paige, all-stars in their own right before Jackie Robinson broke Major League Baseball's color barrier. Homestead won both games, as Satch went the route each time.

Following the game, Dad and I completed our Sunday ritual with a ride on the old Myrtle Avenue elevated train -- second oldest in the borough -- to downtown Brooklyn and a solid, inexpensive dinner at the Automat on Fulton Street. The creamed spinach, mashed potatoes and a side of baked beans (with a slab of bacon) in a jar were over and done with, and it was time to head home.

But, wait.

As we turned left on Fulton, heading toward the Hoyt-Schermerhorn subway station, I stopped in my tracks. How could I have missed it after so many Sunday dinners at the Automat?

Shoulder to shoulder with the cafeteria, neatly squeezed in almost out of view, sat a tiny sporting goods store. This being a Sunday, it was closed and its windows were partly protected by a see-through gate. But there was plenty to see -- catcher's mitts, official National League baseballs, the works.

As Dad began tugging me toward the subway, I did a double-take. Was I seeing what I thought I saw in the window display?

"Wait, Dad," I pleaded.

There it was, all right: an ox-blood-colored outfielder's glove. I crouched forward and riveted my eyes on the lettering. It was autographed by Joe Medwick.

"Dad, Dad, look at that glove in the window. Joe Medwick even autographed it," I said.

I paused and then pleaded: "Could you buy that for me? I want to be as good as Joe Medwick."

Pop crouched for a good look at the price tag and shook his head. "No, you can't have it. I can't afford six bucks for a glove, even if it was signed by Babe Ruth."

Yeah, six bucks was a ton of dough in those Great Depression days. I wasn't that stupid. Both Mom and Dad were working, and Pop didn't have the most glorious job as a laborer in a paint and putty factory.

"Time to head home," he said.

Although his words were uttered with fatherly finality, I wasn't finished with my crusade. I went to bed wondering what scheme could get

Dad to change his mind. Bingo! Talking to myself, I had it all figured out. I'd use the away-at-camp ploy.

Every summer, my folks sent me to a free Jewish charity camp. That summer, it would be three weeks at the Pythian Camp in upstate New York. I would rely on the old bromide: Absence makes the heart grow fonder.

I figured that after a week had elapsed, Pop would be missing me. His harsh anti-Medwick stance would soften and I'd move in with the pitch letter. So in due course, I wrote:

"Hey, Dad, remember that Joe Medwick glove? I really need it for softball. Can I have it?"

Dad replied by mailing me a bunch of baseball clippings from *The Daily News,* which, by the way, I loved receiving, but he said nothing about that nifty oxblood-colored mitt. A week or so was left of camp. By now, he must be yearning for his only child. No? No!

My last written plea went something like this: "I really, really want that Joe Medwick glove. Please, can I?"

Ben Fischler was a terrific letter-answerer. As usual, he included clippings of the week's best baseball stories, neatly stuffed in with his letter, which answered the ox-blood-colored glove question: NO!

I had two strikes against me, but also one more at-bat: Homecoming Day, when we returned from camp. Parents melted with joy, finding their kids still alive and even sunburned. That's when I popped the question to catch him in his weakest moment.

With the other campers, I bounced off the train, into Mom and Dad's waiting embrace. I told Pop that I had my best days ever at the plate, loved softball, made something neat in arts and crafts and won the relay race.

Having exhausted my camp play-by-play and seeing both folks in a soft, warm, loving -- maybe even amenable --mood, I swung the bat.

"Dad, remember that Joe Medwick glove?"

No need to finish. I struck out. "Six dollars, Stanley. If I've told you once, I've told you a thousand times, it's too expensive! But tomorrow, I'll take you to Jay's and you can get something." (Something? Who needs a something?)

Next day, we took the Nostrand Avenue trolley, got off at Bergen and made a short walk to Jay's Stationery Store, which also had a sports department. I looked at the big window display.

"See if there's anything you like," Dad offered. "Anything up to three dollars."

Three bucks, half of the cost of the Joe Medwick glove. Finally, I found a lousy three-dollar offering. Yuck! It was bright yellow, with Globe written across the palm. It looked like crap, but I was stuck. That's it.

Dad made the purchase, and when I got home, I tried very hard to like my yellow Globe mitt, but who was I kidding? It had no autograph, no nothing. It wasn't even ox-blood-colored like any self-respecting glove should be.

That should be the end of the story, but it wasn't. I made the best of my dopey Globe glove. I even took it one Saturday on the Franklin Avenue trolley to Park Circle for a ballgame with my buddies. I only wore the yellow glove out of necessity, like a kid who's forced to put on a scarf when he knows darned well it was not that cold out but Mom said, "Do it."

Our game ended and we took a short cut to the trolley station. It meant a bit of a hike through the dense, tree-filled part of Prospect Park, but that was the fun of our "hiking" in a Brooklyn forest.

Except, there was no fun that day. Just as we reached the hill's crest, heading down toward the trolley station, a gang of kids a bit older and bigger than us emerged from behind the trees. Trouble. No doubt about it: We were getting mugged, and that's that.

One big guy in the gang saw my still-new, yellow, shiny Globe fielder's glove. He yanked it out of my hand and must have been surprised at my lack of resistance. Others grabbed our bats, balls and a couple of other things and disappeared over the hill.

Thinking about the episode on the trolley ride home, I was upset, of course. I'd never been mugged before and it was downright depressing. But, then, I suddenly looked out of the trolley window and found a sunny side of Nostrand Avenue. I chuckled to myself, a grin breaking across my mug.

I actually had two reasons to smile:

1. I hated the Globe glove. Let the poor sucker suffer with it.

2. Imagine if Dad had given in to me and the big guy had taken that six-dollar, ox-blood-colored, autographed Joe Medwick mitt. OY VEY!

It was the one time in my lengthy life that a mugging turned out to be a mitzvah!

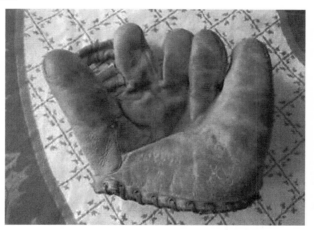

Vintage Ducky Medwick glove

EBBETS FIELD -- THE FIELD OF SORROW AND JOY

On the day my mother first took me to Ebbets Field, I became a baseball fan.

I also became a fan of our home team, the Brooklyn Dodgers.

This was in the spring of 1937, a momentous time in my young life. Within a week, I saw my first Major League Baseball game and graduated from kindergarten at P.S. 54.

The Dodgers played at a wonderfully cozy stadium named after the club's original owner, Charlie Ebbets. If you sat in the first row of the centerfield bleachers, you felt as if you were peering over the pitcher's shoulders, making him nervous.

But Mom was a big spender on this day. For a buck and a half (I was the half) she got a pair of grandstand seats on the third base side.

I can't tell you much more about the game against the Pittsburgh Pirates, because I was fixated on solving a puzzle that perplexed me ever since the seventh-inning stretch: Why were the ball park hot dogs boiled and not grilled?

In time, I would become more enthralled by what was happening on the field rather than the concession stand. By 1939, I could tell you some very important information about that ball team, occasionally called "Dem Bums."

For example, 20-game-winner Luke Hamlin was nicknamed "Hot Potato," while our third baseman Harry Lavagetto's handle was "Cookie." Catcher Ernest Gordon Phelps was labeled "Babe" and manager Leo Durocher was "The Lip."

The club had a utility infielder named Frenchy Bordagary, who came up with the best pun in baseball history. Called out on an attempted steal of second, Frenchy complained to the umpire and accidentally spat on the ump's jacket.

Bordegary was ejected and then fined $50 and suspended for a game. The next day, reporters asked Frenchy about the stiff penalty for an accidental spit, to which he replied: "That's more than I expectorated."

Then there was pitcher "Subway" Sam Nahem, a rare Jewish player for the Brooks. One time Sam made the mistake of showing up at the clubhouse much too early. Durocher had a female with him and didn't appreciate Sam's intrusion. Durocher got even by reducing Nahem's appearances on the mound. Finally, one day, a reporter asked Subway Sam how things were going with him and the manager.

Sam's grin turned to a frown.

"I'm so low on Leo's totem pole," Nahem shot back, "that I'm now pitching batting practice to the batting practice pitchers!"

It didn't matter to me that the Brooks had not won a pennant since 1920, or that those pinstriped snobs in the Bronx had a mortgage on the World Series.

I also knew that there was a team somewhere in Manhattan that played in a stadium called the Polo Grounds that actually was a football field. They were called the Giants and were to be avoided like roaches and water bugs.

Following baseball was great fun because my dad brought home the *World-Telegram* newspaper every evening. Baseball reporters Dan Daniel and Bill Roeder became my literary idols. I devoured every story, every night.

But most of my early baseball education was gleaned from Al and Shirley's candy store at the corner of Nostrand and Vernon, a block from my house (582 Marcy).

Al and Shirley's sold an item that in Brooklynese was called "pitcha cards." In other parts of the city, they were described as "picture cards" or -- for the sophisticates -- collectibles.

For one penny, a pitcha card contained a photo of a ball player on one side and a detailed description of him on the back. An added attraction was a slab of pink bubble gum the size of the card.

To Al and Shirley's regulars, the bubble gum slab was of no interest and immediately was deposited in the nearest trashcan. Only the card mattered – more specifically, the player with the bat on his shoulder.

As any candy store baseball card curator would tell you, there were "hard" cards and "easy" cards. A "hard" card would be one that had not been seen at Al and Shirley's for a good three weeks or more.

Exhibit A was Alex Kampouris, an otherwise undistinguished Dodgers infielder who became famous on Vernon Avenue because none of our gang possessed his pitcha card. Alex didn't know this, but his card was *really* hard to obtain.

After a Kampouris-less month, we dispatched Irving "Gotz" Gottlieb by trolley car to faraway Crown Street, where we had been tipped off about a candy store next to the Talmud Torah that sold the hard card that was Kampouris.

Gottlieb returned an hour later, grinning from ear to the Myrtle Avenue el. He had not one but six Alex Kampouris cards.

But Gotz's smile disappeared when Gillie Birnbaum informed Gottlieb that while he was gone, two Kampourises were unearthed at Al and Shirley's. *Quelle dommage!*

By 1940, our Brooks had become a contending ball club and I had favorites with and without nicknames. Our version of Joltin' Joe DiMaggio was Fred "Dixie" Walker, otherwise known as "The People's Cherce."

For a guy who hit home runs onto Bedford Avenue, there was Dolph Camilli, a lefty first baseman, while a not-so-small shortstop named Harold "Pee Wee" Reese looked like the rookie of the year.

Managing the Brooks was Leo "The Lip" Durocher. For those of us in Kings County, a more Brooklyn character could not have been found, even though Leo hailed from Springfield, Massachusetts.

In addition to being as smart a baseball man as you'll find, Leo doubled as a gambler, pal to Hollywood stars -- especially George Raft -- womanizer extraordinaire and, of course, loud-mouth, hence "The Lip."

By 1941, our Brooks finished atop the National League and appeared capable of doing something never accomplished in franchise history: winning a World Series. Only the elitist snobs from the Bronx stood in our way.

What happened to Leo and his team was pure Brooklyn tragedy. In the ninth inning of Game 4, the Dodgers were leading and appeared ready to tie the Series. Durocher's best reliever, Hugh Casey, got two out and had two strikes on Tommy Henrich.

Then Casey tossed a curve and Henrich struck out. Game over. Right? Three strikes and you're out, three outs in the last inning, so game over, right? No. This time, wrong!

Alas, our catcher, Mickey Owen, neglected to catch the ball -- allegedly a spitter -- and by the time he mined it well behind home plate, Henrich had reached first.

You must know the rest. It's a tragedy Shakespeare couldn't match on the best tragedy day The Bard ever had.

Next up was Joe DiMaggio, who killed Casey's slider for a hit. By the time the rally was over, the hated Bronx nine had won. The Yankees went on to capture the '41 Series, and all two million Brooklynites went into mourning.

That abject defeat negatively affected me more than any sporting event -- not counting punchball on Vernon Avenue -- up until that point in my life. I truly felt that I needed some baseball therapy, and I found it all by myself.

I quit rooting for the Brooks and switched to the St. Louis Cardinals. I just couldn't take another trauma like the Mickey Owen passed ball, and, besides, there was a lot to like about the Cards, especially the bird that sat on its bat on the team's logo.

They had a guy with the same name as mine, Stan Musial, and he wore my favorite number, six. In time he even would have a sweet nickname, Stan The Man.

Unlike yours truly, my best friend, Howie Sparer, remained true to the Brooks. That set up a bragging-rights contest between us on a summer day in 1942. The Cards were coming to Ebbets and so were Howie and me.

We met at noon at the Bedford Avenue bleachers entrance, where the big sign said, Pavilion (same thing as bleachers) 50 Cents. Getting there good and early meant that we nabbed a pair of first-row seats and then compared notes.

How wonderful to have the two best National League pitchers going up against each other, a pair of 20-game winners: Whitlow Wyatt for Brooklyn and Mort Cooper for the Cards. You just couldn't beat that combo.

True to form, they staged a nonpareil pitcher's battle to end all pitcher's battles: zip-zip going into the ninth inning. Wyatt, strong over eight innings, retired the first two Cardinals, leaving third baseman George "Whitey" Kurowski next up.

Whitey took a ball and a strike and then swung on Wyatt's third pitch, a big curve. You could tell by the crack of the bat that this would be good for extra bases ... except that the ball didn't come down for a bit.

It sailed over left fielder Ducky Medwick's head before bouncing into the seventh row of the left field stands. Ecstatic as I was, I knew that Cooper still had to take care of business in Brooklyn's half of the inning.

And that he did: one, two, three. The Cards won, 1-0, Stan (both me and Musial) won and Howie, being a good sport, took it well. No need to rib my buddy; I just kept musing about Musial.

For me, that day in Flatbush was matched for sheer joy on only one other occasion. The year was 1955. and by now I was a sports columnist for Hearst's evening broadsheet, the *New York Journal-American*.

Brooklyn was facing the Yanks yet again in the World Series, with the Bombers leading, two games to one. Game Four, October 1, 1955, was at Ebbets on a sunny-perfect autumn day, weather-wise and Dodgers-wise.

I had the good fortune -- thanks to Bums press agent Irving Rudd -- to have a box seat, a Spalding's throw from third base.

Oh, yeah, I forgot to tell you that I was back rooting for the Dodgers again, and had been for five years, while my hatred for the Bronx team had hit a peak.

It magnified when the Yanks took a 3-1 lead into the bottom of the fifth. The next five minutes ranked among my most glorious as ball fan and writer. I thank Duke Snider, in my opinion the best centerfielder in either league, for that.

The Duke -- alias Edwin -- had such a perfectly powerful-yet-lyrical swing that even when he struck out it was a work of art. But on this day, the ball came in like a fat mango and Snider sent it to baseball heaven.

I still can see the hunk of horsehide sailing over the right field score-board and onto Bedford Avenue. The two men on base preceded Duke to home plate and my Dodgers went on to victory, eventually winning the first and only World Series in the Brooks' history.

If that was my high point, the subterranean depth was plumbed a few years later, when owner Walter O'Malley conspired to move Dem Beloved Bums to Los Angeles, otherwise and correctly known as five suburbs in search of a city.

Books have since been written assigning blame for the dastardly act. Many blame the avaricious "Oom" (as in O'Malley), while others have targeted the supreme New York power broker, Robert Moses.

No matter; they left us high and dry with an empty ball yard called Ebbets Field and a decision never to root for the Mets nor the rich guys in

The Bronx. These days my baseball joy comes from reading the Oakland Athletics website.

Strange, I know. I became an Oakland A's fan back in the late 1990s. I went to a late season game at Yankee Stadium when the Bombers were at their best. Being one who always rooted for the underdog, I cheered for the A's, and especially for an unknown pitcher with a neat name who'd just been called up from the minors. Well, whaddya know, Gil Heredia shut out the Bombers, 2-0, and I became a dual fan: Heredia and the A's.

Of course, the A's website is an unreasonable facsimile for that centerfield bleacher seat at our bandbox ballpark and for Duke leading us to the World Series and that gorgeous Whitey Kurowski day, enhanced by Mort Cooper's one-zip mound masterpiece.

Yeah, I still dream about Subway Sam pitching batting practice to the batting practice pitchers, only to be one-upped by Frenchy's punishing lament; "That was more than I expectorated!"

For me, Ebbets Field still is alive and well, stashed up front in Stosh's memory bank!

Aerial view of Ebbets Field

GOING TO DEXTER PARK
TO SEE THE BUSHWICKS

One of the most fun aspects of my young life took place on summer Sundays when the Brooklyn Dodgers were on the road.

That's when my dad would take me to Dexter Park to see the Bushwicks play their unique brand of baseball: the white guys against the black guys, all in good fun.

The white guys were the Bushwicks, generally regarded as the longest running, best semi-pro baseball team in America. They began play in 1930, two years before I was born.

The black guys were represented by teams from the Negro National League as well as the Negro American League.

Outfits such as the Baltimore Elite Giants – whose starring catcher was Roy Campanella -- and the Homestead Grays, led by immortal catcher Josh Gibson, were frequent foes of the Bushwicks.

It meant that in 1944 I got to see such diamond legends as Satchel Paige, Jackie Robinson and Cool Papa Bell among the many African-American aces who visited the Bushwicks at good, old Dexter Park.

I watched Paige pitch both ends of a double-header and win them both. Gibson hit the longest home run I ever saw, and I've seen plenty.

The Bushwicks were the poor man's version of the Brooklyn Dodgers, yet they oozed class. That's because cigar magnate-team owner Max Rosner would not have it any other way.

Slapsie Maxie was a true visionary. For example, he installed lights at Dexter Park before any of the major league teams got the idea.

Rosner was marketing his team before the term even was invented. He'd sign former big-league stars, such as Dazzy Vance and Dizzy Dean, and after the World Series would import Babe Ruth and Lou Gehrig.

Granted that the Yankees' future Hall of Famers were barnstorming at the time, but who cared? Importing The Sultan of Swat and The Ironman was roughly equivalent to England's king and queen throwing out the first balls.

Although they were called the "Brooklyn" Bushwicks, that was a geographic misnomer. Dexter Park sat right smack on the border of Queens (the neighborhood of Woodhaven) and Brooklyn (Cypress Hills).

On the Brooklyn side was Franklin K. Lane High School, then brand-new, and on the other a beer garden that also served as the center-field "fence." Dexter Park held about 13,000 spectators – or, 23,000 when Babe dropped in.

For father and son Fischler, getting to a Bushwicks game was an adventure in and of itself. Two very contrasting forms of rapid transit were involved, starting with the Myrtle Avenue El.

The el -- just a half block from our house -- operated rolling stock dating back to the early 1900s. Open-ended at both ends, the cars had no doors, just iron gates, each manually operated by three conductors.

In those pre-insurance-worry days, at least six riders could cram on to the open ends. Riding that way was about as much fun as sitting in a roller coaster. After three stops, we'd change for Brooklyn's Broadway el. The contrast was keen but no less fun because the Broadway Line featured all-steel BMT Standard cars.

The big deal for kids like me was that the Standards all had front windows that opened enough for a lad to stick his head out and play motorman.

And what an adventure that was, click-clacking over the neighborhoods of Bed-Stuy, then Bushwick and, finally, Cypress Hills before reaching our station, Elderts Lane, the last stop in Brooklyn.

There was nothing fancy about Dexter Park. You sat on wood planks with a grin-and-bear-it attitude. You were secure in the knowledge that for a measly buck per ticket, this was the best baseball bargain in America.

Sociologists would have had a field day surveying the crowd. All of the East New York white folks -- including my Uncle Julius and Cousin Judd -- sat on the first base side. There were no ifs, ands or buts about that.

All the black fans and the whites not from East New York -- including me and my dad -- sat in the third base pews. There were no thoughts of of segregation or stuff like that; we just enjoyed the baseball.

(Editor's Note: Only once did Dad and I sit with Uncle Jules and Judd on the first base side. But in the end, I was punished. I got the biggest splinter in my life that day.)

Whether it was left grandstands or right, the baseball was the best with heroes on both teams. By far, one of the greatest was Josh Gibson, the Babe Ruth of black baseball.

One Gibson special four-bagger sailed over the 30-foot high wall behind the 418-foot-deep left-centerfield bleachers. It was one of the longest drives I'd seen anywhere.

Then there was my favorite, The Topper. Gibson blasted this one over the centerfield embankment, where it landed somewhere in the distant beer garden.

Instead of clearing the bases for a sure home run, Gibson stopped at second and sat on the bag, his work complete.

"Why did he do that, Pop?" I asked my dad. "Why didn't he keep running?"

"Because, son," my father explained, "he's tired. Besides, that's Mister Gibson's way of telling us that he has nothing more to prove."

A billboard adjacent to Dexter Park's right field foul line unfailingly got a giggle. It read: DON'T KILL THE UMPIRE -- MAYBE IT'S YOUR EYES: SEE GOLDBERG, THE OPTICIAN.

Max Rosner ensured that his Bushwicks stayed competitive by signing such former big-leaguers as the brothers Al and Tony Cuccinello as well as former Yankee pitcher Bots Nekola, a huge favorite.

During World War II, some big-leaguers serving in the Navy were stationed at the nearby Floyd Bennett Field Naval Base.

One was ex-Dodgers outfielder-turned-sailor Gene Hermanski, who managed to get leave every Sunday. Rosner tried to conceal his identity re-naming him Gene Walsh. The ruse usually fooled about one half of one percent of the fans.

Recruiting competent ball players during the war was a challenge. The worst also was the most hilarious. This nameless third baseman simply could not field a ground ball, so he'd make like a hockey goalie. He'd block the horsehide, then retrieve it and make the toss to first. That, too, was an adventure, since half his pegs wound up in the first base grandstands.

It was easy to rub shoulders with the stars, because the Dexter dressing rooms were next to the hot dog stand under the grandstand. I speak first-hand, since on one occasion Dad and I were on the hot dog line between games.

Suddenly, I felt a slight push from someone, but knew not who. It was a visiting ballplayer who looked down, said, "Excuse me," and walked into the visitors' dressing room.

"Who was that, Dad?" I asked. My father checked his scorecard. "He's Baltimore's catcher, Roy Campanella."

After the game, Dad and I would ride the els all the way to downtown Brooklyn, where our ritual ended at the huge Automat on Fulton Street. Our grand dinner consisted of creamed spinach, mashed potatoes and baked beans-and-bacon in a hot brown jar. It was a superior finish to any summer Sunday.

Bushwicks baseball thrived until Jackie Robinson broke the color barrier, and soon the best of the Negro National and American League players filtered into the formerly all-white majors.

Eventually, Max Rosner folded his Bushwicks and -- like the Dodgers' own Ebbets Field -- Dexter Park gave way to a middle-income housing development.

But the memories of former stars who played there, such as Dazzy Vance, Joe DiMaggio and Joe Medwick, linger. Their visits to the neat ball yard merely added luster to Dexter's field of dreams.

When the Bushwicks' alumni convened for an annual reunion, they'd start with a toast to Max Rosner and then weave stories about their exploits on the border of Brooklyn and Queens. And, invariably, ex-Bushwicks pitcher Subway Sam Nahem (who even had a stint with the Dodgers) showed up, always ready to repeat his favorite line:

"People speak of me in the same breath as Sandy Koufax," he would say, then pause. "The breath usually is, 'Sam Nahem is no Sandy Koufax!'"

The Bushwicks at Dexter Park

STREET GAMES, OR
LIVING DANGEROUSLY ON
VERNON AVENUE

Vernon Avenue, between Marcy and Nostrand, never was meant to be a "play street," but in 1943 we made it into one.

This was easy because Vernon is a long block finishing at Nostrand in a dead end. During the World War II days, the street -- virtually bereft of vehicles -- became our playground.

The number of games we played was endless, but punchball was the going-away favorite. We played punchball endlessly from April through September. Once the punchball season ended, other games were sure to leave us with ripped knees and, in the case of neighbor Raymond Seligson, a broken ankle.

October meant the start of our association-football season, closely followed by two-hand touch, ring-a-levio and, by Christmas -- weather permitting -- sled-belly-whopping, which directly led to gala snowball fights.

Nobody on Vernon knew who decided when, for example, the marble season began and ended; it seemed to happen automatically, and the season's start was universally accepted even by the ever-querulous Gillie Birnbaum. Within hours of the season's start, just about everyone on Vernon was playing a variation on skellies or in the box.

There also were seasons for boxball, stoopball, triangle, hide-and-seek, Johnny on the pony and the ever-popular cowboys and Indians.

Since neither the *Daily News*, *Post* or *Journal-American* ever ran a story about these major sporting developments on Vernon Avenue, I thought you should know what I personally experienced at age 11.

Association Football

Every Sunday morning, I showed up along with my best pal, Howie Sparer, in front of 4 Vernon with my personal pigskin. We were waiting for another two guys our age to start a game.

To our surprise -- and distinct dismay -- two "big guys" arrived on the scene. On Vernon, a "big guy" was defined as anyone two years or more older than Howie or yours truly. Some were intimidating because they were just big.

This pair of "big guys" happened to be Abe Yurkofsky and his side-kick, Richie Mishkin. They instantly challenged Howie and me to a game of association football, and we – with no way out -- reluctantly agreed to play them.

They gave us first dibs. Abe tossed the ball to Howie, and I was supposed to head out for his pass. I don't know why, but I decided not to go out and instead ran to Howie, who handed me the ball.

Utterly confused, Abe and Richie couldn't deduce our accidental but clever "reverse play," so I ran for a touchdown. We absolutely believed that we invented that play on the spot, thereby setting national football history!

Next time we got the ball, I did the same move. I ran to Howie and he handed me the ball -- almost. Instead, he kept it.

Meanwhile, Abe and Richie mistakenly went after me, while Howie ran for the touchdown. Again, we made gridiron history with the very clever invention of the fake reverse.

Naturally, the two "big guys" wanted revenge, but it was out of their grasp. By this time, a bunch of our gang showed up and immediately demanded we switch to two-hand touch, and that was that.

Still, Howie and I figured that had the *Journal-American*'s football writer, Jesse Eisenberg, been watching from the sidewalk, the next day's headline would have read: "BROOKLYN LADS INVENT NEW FOOTBALL PLAYS."

Stoopball

This was played off an apartment house wall. The "batter" tossed a tennis ball off a crevasse in the wall, while an "infielder" in the middle of the street and an "outfielder" behind him tried to catch the ball before it hit the ground.

On an otherwise crisp, sunny fall day, Raymond Seligson drifted back to snare a fly ball. Alas, poor Raymond neglected to remember that Vernon Avenue had what was commonly known as a curb.

Raymond's right ankle found out about the curb the hard way. The crack of Raymond's bone against the curb, and the subsequent Seligson shriek of pain, could have been heard in distant Prospect Park.

As a result, poor Raymond was rushed to Beth Moses Hospital and stoopball was banned on Vernon Avenue until the next morning.

Ring-a-levio

This was actually a nasty version of hide-and-seek in which the pursuer grabbed the pursued and held on while screaming "COR-COR-RING-A-LEEVIO, 1,2,3." The call of "Cor, Cor" meant "Caught, Caught."

It was dusk in August 1943 when I chased Stewie Karger along the sidewalk in front of 7 Vernon. I was about three yards away when Stewie made a sharp left and ran across Vernon to the north side.

At least that was his intent. As young Karger got a quarter way across Vernon, a 1935 Cadillac with a front bumper the size of China's Great Wall engaged Stewie. I'd guess that the old Caddie was doing no more than 10 m.p.h.

No matter. Like a football halfback fighting off a tackle with a straight-arm, Stewie challenged the Caddie. But the bumper won, and Stewie went airborne like a perfect field goal and landed on his side some 25 feet away.

That was the bad news. The good news was that Stewie was still alive. Better yet, he returned from the hospital a week later, and who should be there to greet him -- quite happily, I might add -- but the driver of the Caddie.

To my amazement, they shook hands, and Grace Karger, Stewie's mother, served coffee. We all were happy; the ring-A-levio loser, Stewie, actually was the winner by being alive!

Stupid Football

One Sunday morning, I got the bright idea that tackle football -- NFL-style -- could work on non-grassy Vernon Avenue. So we gave it a shot. Nobody got hurt for the first five minutes, but we didn't have enough guys to round out two teams.

Just then, some of the bigger "big guys" -- at least two years older than us -- showed up. We invited them to play, and they agreed. One of the biggest "big guys" was Gershy Sparer, older brother of my best friend, Howie.

In less than two minutes, Gershy tackled me, and for the first time in my life I "saw stars." No kidding, I could count at least ten stars. When I awakened from my stupor, I learned two things:

Gershy Sparer -- unlike his kid brother -- was not my best friend, or a friend at all.

1. Tackle football on a macadam surface was redefining dumb and dumber!

Boxball

I have yet another disaster to relate. Just as I whacked a ball tossed -- on a bounce -- by Norman Karger, this mildly attractive Italian lady foolishly walked across the court. What would have been a clean single for me turned into a broken right lens of the Italian lady's glasses. When her swarthy husband learned that I was the culprit, he showed up at 582 Marcy.

Damages cost my father $10. The boxball season was cancelled until the next day.

Cowboys and Indians

This merely was a milder version of ring-a-levio and only was played after we had seen a good Western on Saturday afternoon at the Kismet Theater.

As it happened, *Badlands of the Dakotas*, starring our Hollywood hero, Randolph Scott, happened to be playing. Among the many viewers that day was my P.S. 54 classmate, Harvey Mandel, and his two brothers.

After the movie, the Mandel kids returned home and excitedly talked their mother, Natalie, into playing cowboys and Indians with them in front of their house on Vernon near Marcy. Very reluctantly, Mrs. Mandel dropped her broom and played.

As Natalie told it, one of her boys "shot" her and shouted, "Bang! You're dead, Mom." Natalie fell down after being "shot." Their next-door neighbor, Sam Epstein, happened to be watching.

When Natalie Mandel didn't get up, Epstein -- quite worried -- ran over to see if she had been badly hurt.

When Sam bent over Mrs. Mandel, she opened one eye and whispered to Epstein: "Shhhh, Sam. Please don't give me away. It's the only chance I've had to rest all day."

Thus ended the cowboys and Indians season on Vernon Avenue until the next Randolph Scott Western!

The street was our playground

SNOW WHITE IS MY HOCKEY COACH

"How did you get so nuts about hockey?" is a question I'm often asked.

"Put the blame on Snow White," is my standard reply, "and you can throw in the Seven Dwarfs while you're at it."

Yeah, I know that sounds like the start of a joke, but it's not. I'll prove it by flashing back to the year 1939. The following is the truth, the whole truth and nothing but the Snow White truth.

If you were seven years old -- as I was in 1939 - there were two priorities in life, especially for this kid in Williamsburg, Brooklyn.

One was praying for our beloved Dodgers to win the National League pennant. Dem Bums had suffered through 19 years without a National League title.

The other was to see the new kids movie, *Snow White And The Seven Dwarfs*. It was a Walt Disney full-length cartoon, the first of its kind.

The Dodgers could wait.

For *Snow White*, there was no waiting. It had just opened at the Globe Theatre on Manhattan's Broadway, and every kid worth his weight in Popsicles just *had to* see it. Like right now, or yesterday.

My father, Ben Fischler, clearly understood the Snow White necessity and wasted no time with the good news. "We go on Sunday," he said.

Those four little words produced cartwheels of joy. Even though this was only Friday, I already envisioned the subway ride to see what I presumed to be the greatest movie in the history of movies.

At precisely noon on Sunday, we entered the Myrtle-Willoughby subway station, took the GG to the Hoyt-Schermerhorn station, the A Express to 42nd Street and, finally, the E Local to 50th.

The Globe was in Times Square at 47th Street. It was a five-block walk from the 50th Street station, no big deal under normal meteorological conditions.

But this was far from a normal Sunday. When we left Brooklyn, the sun was shining. When we exited at 50th and Eighth, the weather was crazier than radio humorist Henry Morgan's notorious report: "High winds, followed by flying skirts -- followed by me!"

The winds were high and accompanied by rain like you wouldn't believe. Since Dad didn't have an umbrella, he pulled me into the Davega sporting goods store on the corner of 50th and momentarily studied the scene.

He looked up and -- Eureka! -- right there, shoulder to shoulder with Davega was a place I had never heard of before, Madison Square Garden, which, by the way, was neither square nor a garden.

But what MSG did have was a large marquee. dating back to its opening night in 1925. These were the words posted that day: HOCKEY DOUBLE-HEADER STARTING AT 1:30 P.M.

Ben Fischler looked at his watch, looked back at the marquee, then stared at me before uttering the deathless words: "We're not going to see *Snow White*. We're going to a hockey game."

The wind and the rain suddenly were accompanied by a lad who didn't know whether to cry havoc or take my case to Children's Court. All I could blurt was "But, Dad ... " Alas, there were no *buts* today.

Ben Fischler dragged his stunned son straight to the Garden's box office. He purchased two hockey tickets and then tugged me like a sled in mud into the enormous building.

All I had in mind was my lost *Snow White* because of some hockey nonsense that would deprive me of seven little men warbling "Hi-ho, hi ho, it's off to work we go."

After landing in our seats, I began checking out the surroundings. Suddenly, overhead lights flashed, followed by stirring organ music being piped throughout the vast arena.

As if on cue with Gladys Goodding at the organ console, men in brightly-colored uniforms skated onto the brownish (not white in those days) ice surface. I was intrigued – riveted, if you really want to know. Kind of excited.

A game was about to begin. Men in stripes -- Dad instructed me that they were the "ice police" -- skated out between the players. The organist played our National Anthem and the contest began.

Right away, I could tell that Dad really was into the game and rooting for the guys in red. They happened to be the New York Rovers, a New York Rangers farm team in the Eastern Amateur Hockey League.

On the other side, in white jerseys, were the Washington Eagles, replete with a big bird on the front of their uniforms. I liked the looks of them and figured they might help me get even with my father's betrayal of Ms. Snow White.

Bingo! The brainstorm hit me: If Ben Fischler was going to root for the guys in red, Stanley Irwin Fischler was going to cheer like mad for the visitors. And so I did.

Soon, good things began to happen. For starters, I now had completely forgotten about Snow White. For another thing, I fixated on a special Washington player who would become my instant hero.

His name was Normie Burns, who -- although I didn't know it at the time -- was the Eagles' leading scorer. But that didn't matter so much.

What *really* mattered was that he had blond hair and reminded me of my second favorite cowboy of all-time, The Lone Ranger. In that moment, I converted The Lone Ranger -- my radio hero -- into a real hockey player.

Normie Burns was all over the ice. When the game was over, he had scored a three-goal hat trick. Most important, my father's team had lost. Yay, me! Yay, Normie Burns!

The very next day I showed up at P.S. 54 on Nostrand and Hart still thinking about the hockey game. Meanwhile, my third grade teacher, Mrs. Gould, announced that we would do our weekly Show and Tell.

Fixing her bright green eyes on me, Mrs. Gould said, "Stanley, do you have something to show us and, perhaps, tell us about?"

Instantly, the hockey game came to mind, but not Normie Burns' hat trick. I also had been fascinated by the guy in front of the net, wearing big pads and stopping shots. They called him the goaltender.

"Yes, Mrs. Gould, "I'm going to show you what I saw yesterday at a hockey game in Madison Square Garden."

"Please do," she replied.

Inspired by the puck-stoppers on both teams, I executed a number of "saves." I also tried to do a perfect split and, finally, flagged down a few imaginary pucks while supplying a rather amateurish play-by-play.

My classmates were more than mildly interested and Mrs. Gould went completely ga-ga, She closed my Show and Tell by announcing that I had earned an A for my hockey production.

Proudly, I returned to my seat thinking, "Hey, this hockey thing ain't too bad, after all. On Sunday, my father's team gets soundly beaten by the skating Lone Ranger and now I get an A for pretending to be a goalie."

Of course, Ben Fischler knew nothing about my scholastic escapade, but that night he delivered on the Sunday rain check. "We go to see Snow White next Saturday and, just in case, I'll bring an umbrella," he said.

And so he did, and so my wish to see Ms. White and her coterie with funny names, like Dopey and Sneezy, was fulfilled. This time, there was no build-up to a letdown. I gave the film *Snow White* five out of five stars.

I was pleased, Dad was pleased and we contentedly took our seats on the A train to go home. As the express pulled out of 42d Street, almost unconsciously, I turned to Dad and stunned him with a simple request.

"Dad," I said with a rare blend of angst, embarrassment and enthusiasm, "can you take me to another hockey game? Like tomorrow afternoon, maybe?"

Dad thoughtfully stopped chewing on his unlit cigar. "Sure, sure, Stanley," he said. "You mean you liked the game last Sunday?"

Visions of Norman Burns as The Lone Ranger popped into my head, then the score: Washington 5, Rovers 2. Then the A from Mrs. Gould.

"Yeah, Dad, I really like hockey," I responded.

We returned to the Garden on Sunday. This time, we got there early, caught the Met League game, and then the amateur singing contest held by Gladys Goodding (an early version of karaoke, sports arena-style). Larry Shildkret won it warbling "Apple Blossom Time."

And then the main event: the Rovers against Baltimore. The visiting Orioles were wearing the most magnificent brownish, tannish, whitish uniforms you'd ever want to see.

There was no skating Lone Ranger, no Show and Tell the next day with Mrs. Gould at P.S. 54 -- just memories of another wonderfully thrilling afternoon at Madison Square Garden.

It is a fact of life that after that doubleheader, I never stopped going to hockey games. I had become a certified puck nut for life.

In all fairness and with the utmost sincerity, I must say, "Thank you, Snow White, wherever you are!"

New York Ranger Lou Fontinato with Molly and Ben Fischler

UNDERGROUND AND OVER-CARPET HOCKEY

There's no way of proving this, but I'm pretty sure that by October 1942 I was the craziest hockey fan in the borough of Brooklyn.

Maybe the whole of New York City, discounting Staten Island.

This meant a lot of things, but mostly to satisfy my insatiable thirst for hockey, I had to do silly -- my parents thought, unwise -- things.

There were the choke-filled moments playing hockey in our dimly-lit, dust-filled, unfinished cellar at 582 Marcy Avenue. The Underground Hockey League lasted a half-week, since neither I nor my foe, Larry Shildkret, owned gas masks to serve as goalie masks.

Each of these and other Play Hockey Anywhere episodes were very important to me because, out of a 24-hour day, I figured about 23 of those hours should be devoted to some kind of hockey.

The first time I came to this conclusion was after I witnessed my first hockey game in person. I was seven years old in 1939, old enough -- at least my father thought -- to be taken to Madison Square Garden.

In those days of the Great Depression, a father could take his kid to The Garden to see a hockey game for 75 cents. A ticket cost a half-buck for the old man -- he wasn't that old -- and a quarter for the kid.

Since I was too young to stay up late for Rangers games -- they didn't start until 8:30 p.m. -- the Sunday afternoon amateur doubleheaders at

MSG were just as much fun to watch. The challenge was what to do after the Garden.

That was a vexing and perplexing question, since I couldn't bear the thought of waiting a whole week before dad took me to the Garden for another dose of ice.

I solved the equation like any self-respecting only-child would; I made up my own living-room hockey game. It was easy; all I needed were a couple of shoe boxes from the closet, a marble from my toy chest and two pencils.

With a pair of scissors, I cut openings on each box. Bingo! Those were nets for the goal. The marble became the puck, pencils were the sticks and the ice was the living room carpet.

One goal was at one end of the carpet at the foot of my dad's favorite chair, and the other was at the opposite end, next to the living room door. The Carpet Hockey League only had two teams, my right hand vs. the left.

Unfortunately, the games didn't last very long, mostly because -- two floors down below -- my beloved grandmother, Etel Friedman, was not much of a carpet hockey fan.

Gram -- that's what I called her -- possessed super-sharp hearing. As my knees churned back and forth along the carpet, it sounded to her like the thundering hoofbeats of the great horse, Silver. Nix to the Lone Ranger!

Thus, The Carpet Hockey League folded after a resounding announcement from The Commish below: "Stop with the noise up there. You're giving me a headache!"

A few years later, the WHA* of carpet hockey enjoyed a brief run. It featured two metallic hockey players, remnants of a broken Gotham hockey game that included a steel ball that was whacked back and forth until a goal was scored.

*World Hockey Association; a failed league from the 1970s

The springs of the Gotham game had a lifespan of five thunderous minutes, and that was that. No problem; I removed the two players and moved the game to the floor, at the foot of my father's living room chair.

For a goal, I used two legs on our dining room table. With my right hand, I shot the ball-as-puck with the metal player, and with my left I controlled the other metal player to try to keep the ball from going into the net through the opening between the two table legs.

While it required very little movement on the carpet – and hence no beefs from Gram -- my mother was dismayed because the steel ball often would ricochet off one of the table legs, causing chips of wood to peel off like snowflakes.

My dad wasn't too crazy about it, either, because the ball often would bounce off his well-polished Florsheim shoes, leaving an unseemly mark, while also disrupting his contented puffs on a Phillies cigar. (Another nix to carpet hockey.)

Rather than getting pissed off, my dad built me a different kind of game that once again pitted my left hand against my right. It was roughly equivalent to a contemporary Foosball game, only with a lot fewer rods to make the players work.

This version had three rods. A middle rod could be used by either player, depending on where the puck (in this case, a ping pong ball) bounced. The middle rod had players on both sides, while the last rod included two defensemen and a goalie.

In my humble, objective opinion, the result of Dad's carpentry work was one of the great inventions of all time, better even than a pinball machine. The Ben Fischler version could be played solo (left hand vs. right hand) or with one of my friends.

As for the wooden box containing the players and rink, it was indestructible. In fact, it lasted through two cousins and eventually reverted back to me for my kids. It was a lot healthier than the ill-fated Cellar Hockey League.

My grandma, alas, was aroused by that ridiculous hockey brainstorm, taking hockey underground. The Cellar Hockey League (CHL) was based on a premise that some in-house hockey had to be played on cold winter nights.

Our 582 Marcy cellar was not to be confused with a finished basement. It was dank, dark (only one tiny light bulb) and had a floor that was uneven and comprised of dirt and possibly hardened lava from a prehistoric Marcy volcano.

The CHL was born one night when nobody in the family was looking. My pal, Larry Shildkret, and I tiptoed down to the cellar with hockey sticks and an old tennis ball. We alternated as shooter and goalie in a rather thin "rink."

It was loads of fun for about ten minutes. By that time, we had churned up the dirt-lava floor so that it looked as if an Oklahoma dust storm had hit Marcy Avenue. Within fifteen minutes, we hardly could see each other.

By the twenty-minute mark, we were saved from our choking by grandma's high-decibel yell, "WHAT'S GOING ON DOWN THERE?" And that's how The Cellar Hockey League began and ended in one night.

Still, the quest for alternate hockey continued, and in 1948, the family of my best friend, Howie Sparer, moved to a big home on East 28th Street in Flatbush, across from James Madison High School.

The best part of the Sparers' new residence was that it actually had a finished basement – or should I say unfinished, since the Sparer family still awaited a furniture delivery.

This meant that there was plenty of empty basement room, which also meant that we now had yet another indoor "rink." And this one proved to be a beauty, although a short-lived one.

Howie and I loved it because we could play in a well-lit, spanking-new basement featuring brand new linoleum (the "ice"), with nobody to bother us – or so we thought.

Howie and I launched our Flatbush League season with a lively match, delighted that we could breathe easy, see the puck (tennis ball) and be secure in the knowledge that my grandma was not downstairs in her living room.

Ah, but what we didn't bargain for was Howie's big sister, Norma, who happened to drop over to Chez Sparer for a well-deserved nap just as our second period was coming to a close.

Matter of fact, the period ended when Howie lustily checked me into the basement's left "boards." Fortunately, the boards didn't crumble, although I do think Norma buckled more than a bit, thinking it was an earthquake.

Unfortunately, the reverberations were felt all the way up to the second floor, where Norma was enjoying a nap. Was -- but no more.

While Howie's body check went unpenalized, the fallout from Norma's awakening did result in league-misconduct punishment of another kind.

Flitting downstairs, two steps at a time, Norma dissolved the most promising, linoleum-floored underground hockey league before it could conclude its first game.

Tragic as the Flatbush League's folding was at the time, it did inspire yet another way to play hockey in a normal house without any interference or a need for a new linoleum floor.

Despite overwhelming odds against it, The Toilet Arena Hockey League (TAHL) was born and, in fact, survived for several seasons in an atmosphere of joy and heightened sensitivity of the olfactory nerves.

The TAHL was born while I was sitting on the crapper poring through an NHL guide and wondering if any hockey player had come from Dysart, Saskatchewan, other than Fernie Flaman of the Boston Bruins.

Since hockey already was on my mind, it was perfectly natural that I should think about another left hand vs. right hand game, this one in the compact Fischler bathroom.

While comfortably sitting on the can, I leaned forward and found that a game was possible while simultaneously doing my daily duty to kidneys and hockey.

First, I contrived a goal net by placing my left thumb on the tiled bathroom floor, while my left middle finger became the other side of the net.

My left index finger -- very moveable -- became the goalie. For a puck, I used a nickel. I would shoot it with my right index finger. The goalie (my left index finger) either made the save or was beaten by the nickel.

In contrast to the many other indoor hockey games, the Toilet Arena Hockey League was both foolproof and crowd-proof. There was no cellar dust, no thundering knees on the carpet, no Grandma and no Norma to call off the game.

What's more, no game lasted more than the time it took to take one good dump as the bowels declared.

I actually was thinking of promoting NTAHL as a wonderful double-fix. With just three fingers and one nickel, you could have some fast hockey fun -- while also curing constipation!

Howie, Norma and Gershy Sparer, 1938

HUNGARIAN JEW AND IRISH CATHOLIC BECOME LIFETIME BUDDIES AT MSG

In the fall of 1947 -- when first they met -- Jim Hernon and Stan Fischler were as different as a space ship and the Staten Island ferry.

Hernon was an Irish-Catholic kid from Woodside, Queens, whose father was a city cop. His mom was a housewife.

Fischler was a Hungarian-Jewish kid from Williamsburg, Brooklyn, whose father worked in a putty factory. So did his mom.

Neither Jim nor Stan knew each other until Lester Patrick Night at Madison Square Garden in November 1947. The Rangers were playing the Toronto Maple Leafs and that's why the two intense teenagers wound up there.

The odds of their sitting in adjoining seats were not very good. The Garden held 15,925 seats, and 15,923 were occupied by Rangers fans. That included Section 333, Row E of MSG's end balcony.

There were ten seats in Row E, and somehow Hernon occupied Seat 5 and Fischler had Seat 6. Those two neighboring pews were the first things they had in common. More would come.

Neither talked to the other before Miss Gladys Goodding played the National Anthem on the Garden's organ console. Nor did they exchange words after Gladys concluded The Star Spangled Banner.

Then, referee Bill Chadwick dropped the puck and the clash began -- New York's favorite hockey team against Canada's favorite hockey team.

Stan -- that's me -- noticed something different about next-seat-neighbor Hernon. Unlike the other 15,923 spectators, James did not leap from his seat in glee when Tony Leswick scored the game's first goal for New York.

Matter of fact, Neighbor James was as glum as the 15-year-old sitting next to him, meaning me. To the two of us, a Rangers goal -- *any* Rangers goal -- was cause for deep mourning.

Hernon's abject silence amid the roaring crowd got me wondering. Perhaps this MSG neighbor of mine just happened to be a quiet guy who couldn't care less who won or lost. More study was necessary.

Then, it happened. Syl Apps scored for Toronto and by actual count, two out of the 15,925 leaped from their chairs: Fischler and Hernon.

"Holy crap!" I said, turning to my neighbor. "Are you really a Leafs fan?"

"Yeah," he said in perfect Woodside-ese. In the first intermission, we got to talking about all things Leafs. Then, after a brief pause, Jim delivered a surprise announcement that would change my life.

He very casually mentioned that he played roller hockey – for a team, no less. I was terribly impressed because one of my life's ambitions at age 15 was to actually play for a hockey team, even on roller skates.

Young Hernon, being a modest sort, didn't tell me that he was captain and best player on the Queens-based Woodside Whippets. He only allowed that the Whippets skated in the Long Island City YMCA Roller Hockey League. That was it.

"How would you like to play on the Whippets?" Hernon offhandedly asked.

Not very offhandedly, and not too calmly, I said, "Sure would." My new pal then gave me the details:

"Show up at Woodside Park, a few blocks from the IND's Roosevelt Avenue subway station next Saturday morning at 11:00. Bring a stick and skates and you'll be in business," he said. Just like that. I couldn't believe my ears.

Well, that -- "You're in business" -- was easy for Jim to say, and he said it. I gleefully digested the three words and then we got back to the important business of rooting for Toronto.

All I remember was that the Leafs won, we shook hands with a "See ya next Saturday" and I spent the next six days wondering just what I had gotten myself into. More importantly, how could I get out of it?

Couldn't.

This much was certain: I had never played for a hockey team before, I didn't know any of my prospective teammates and -- as I had already surmised -- I'd be the one and only Jew on the Woodside Whippets.

Scary, at least to me.

I didn't sleep much on the eve of my momentous debut as a Whippet; I just kept thinking about what I had to do and what I couldn't do. My conclusion was that I had no idea on either count.

At about 6:00 on Saturday morning, as dawn was breaking, it dawned on me that the one hockey thing I could not do was lift the puck. I knew that you couldn't score if you couldn't lift the puck.

With that in mind, I got on the GG (Brooklyn-Queens Crosstown) subway an hour early, and when I arrived at the Roosevelt Avenue station, I found a quiet corner of the mezzanine and began one full hour of attempted puck-lifting.

One out of every five shots managed to lift an inch or maybe an inch and a half off the ground. I said to myself, "This will never do -- plus, I don't know what to do about it!"

But time had run out on my puck-lifting practice and I nervously made my way to the designated Woodside playground.

Sure enough, there were two goal nets and three guys on roller skates knocking a roll of black electrician's tape around the rink.

None of them looked like the Jim Hernon I had met at The Garden, and that made me more nervous. Was this Hernon guy playing a trick on me?

I was thinking this and other discouraging words when who should suddenly emerge from the sidewalk, skating into the playground, but Hernon himself.

The first thing I noticed was that he was wearing a neat white sweater -- some call them jerseys -- with little red letters working at an angle from right down to left, spelling out W-H-I-P-P-E-T-S.

"Hey, Stan, you made it after all," Jim said by way of welcome. "I'm gonna introduce you to the guys and tell you what you have to do."

To a man, they welcomed me: Artie Kane, Roderick McKenzie, Gabby Cheroux, Joe Giaimo, Bob Schanz, Harry Schanz, Fred Meier and the goalie, Frank Pagello, smoking a cigarette, no less.

I was impressed, but nervous; there was not a Jewish name in the lot. I wondered what Hernon told them about me. But there was no time for thinking. Jimmy pulled me aside and said I'd play defense alongside Meier.

"Now," Hernon intoned very seriously, "just *pay attention!*"

Sorry, but I hadn't the faintest idea what Jim meant by "pay attention." That never was my specialty.

My brand-new defense mate, Fred Meier, was more reassuring. "We'll be just fine," Freddie promised. "I'll cover for you in case things don't work out."

I guess things worked out, although I don't remember much about the game other than Hernon's deathless words, "pay attention!" And that we beat the Sunnyside Americans, 3-2.

Oh, yeah, one other thing: As I unclamped my Chicago-brand roller skates, Hernon sat next to me on the park bench. I fully expected a feeble "Thanks but no thanks" for showing up, and a farewell to the Whippets.

I was about to reply, something like "It was fun while it lasted," when Jim broke into a smile. "You made the team, Stan. But you're gonna need a Whippets sweater. It costs two bucks and gimme a number for the back."

With a half-grin and a half-stammer, I said I'd take a "6" if nobody had that uniform number; nobody did. For the rest of 1947-48, I was the left defenseman on the Woodside Whippets with Freddie Meier covering for me on the right.

Every week with every game, I kept wondering what these *goyim* thought of the only Jew on the Woodside Whippets. Then, one day while we were riding the bus to a game in Sunnyside, Joe Giaimo popped the question.

"Hey, Fischler, what are you?"

The question was too broad for a quick answer so I timidly shot back a "Whaddya mean?" half wondering what his next question might be.

"I mean," Joe asserted, "are you Catholic like me or some other religion? What are you?"

For half-a-second, I considered bullshitting my way out of this nerve-wracking third degree. But with the other half-second, I figured that the consequences of lying would be worse.

"I'm Jewish," I shot back trembling inside over what reaction my admission would bring.

Giaimo: "No kidding."

To my amazement -- and relief, I might add -- that was that. Accepted, with no further comment necessary. I was one of the boys.

I knew it for sure when -- at the end of the season -- they invited me to Lost Battalion Hall on Queens Boulevard. The Long Island City YMCA had an awards night and the Whippets actually won a trophy.

After the event, Gentleman Jim pulled out a tiny black Kodak camera and asked me to pose with Artie Kane -- holding the tiny trophy -- and himself. It was a very proud moment in my hockey life. (I still have the picture.)

Thanks to teammate Meier, who was true to his word and covered for me, I finished the season a true Whippet. I had paid attention as Jim instructed. As for Fred, he turned out to be an eternal pal.

Actually I was more than just a friend to Hernon, and the vice was versa. We attended every Leafs-Rangers game, rooting very hard for Syl Apps, Wild Bill Ezinicki, Turk Broda and the other Toronto guys.

We skated regularly at the Brooklyn Ice Palace, and when the Palace closed for the summer, we stayed in touch. One day, I startled Hernon when I said I'd ride my Roadmaster two-wheeler bike to his house.

I knew it was a crazy gamble. I'd have to pedal through Williamsburg and Greenpoint and find the bridge into Queens and hope it had a walkway where I could ride my bike.

Then, when I got to the other side, I'd have to find my way to Woodside without the help of the IND GG subway line.

But motivation was mighty. First, I wanted Jim to know that I regarded him as a friend among friends. Second, that I was better on a bike than I was on skates. Third, I wondered what life was like among the *goyim*.

In a word, it was *different*. No sign of a kosher deli in Woodside. No sign of a *shul*. Nothing at all Jewish like Williamsburg. But was it ever friendly.

Jimmy took me to his apartment on the second floor of a four-story building. I met his very Irish mom and his dad, a large New York cop who made me think of Bing Crosby doing a chorus of "Galway Bay."

Still, I was nervous when I saw the crucifix on the wall. Not sure exactly why, but it bothered me a great deal. I yearned for a Star of David instead.

Finally, Jim took me down to his local park, where he introduced me to guys I'd never seen before. They were ready for a game of stickball, but I was not.

Stickball was not a game we played on Vernon Avenue, but this was 66th Street and I couldn't nix a game, not in front of Pal Jim. It would turn into one of the single most embarrassing moments in my young life.

I must have set a Queens borough record for consecutive strikeouts. I expected to be humbled, humiliated and the butt of 66th Street Woodside stickball jokes for at least a century.

Nothing doing. If this had happened on my home Vernon Avenue turf, I would have been run out of the neighborhood, all the way to Lafayette Avenue.

But the *goyim* were sympathetic, empathetic and tried every which way to help. However, I had the solution. Looking at my watch, I yelled, "Hey guys, it's almost four. Gotta get on my bike back to Brooklyn."

What really mattered is that Jim Hernon appreciated my pedaling all the way from another borough to pay him and his 66th Street chums a visit.

We became lifelong friends. I was invited to Jimmy's marriage to Sheila and we continued going to Leafs games until Hernon left for the Army in mid-1950s.

By that time, I had gotten rid of my *goyim* concerns and found more strong pals among the ex-Whippets, especially my defense buddy, Fred Meier, and Joe Giaimo, who eventually became a biggie in Queens politics.

* * *

A hockey high point for me came more than a decade ago by way of NHL Commissioner Gary Bettman. He phoned to report that I was a winner of the Lester Patrick Award for service to hockey in the U.S.A.

For the formal ceremony at the New York Hilton, I invited family but -- no less important -- my two favorite Whippets teammates, Jim Hernon and Fred Meier.

I couldn't believe how their respective personalities had held up over the years. Fred still was droll and cool, while Jim displayed the same intensity he had the first time he told me to pay attention.

I brought them over to fellow Patrick winner Brian Leetch's table. I told the Rangers' Hall Fame defenseman that Hernon as a Whippet was like Rangers captain Mark Messier was to Brian on the Blueshirts.

"What about this guy?" said Leetch, pulling Fred a foot closer to the table.

"Just like you," I told Brian, "Freddie wore number two. And just like you on the Rangers, he was our best defenseman."

Brian rose from his seat and gave Freddie a hug and Jim a great big handshake. Altogether, it was one of the best scenes of my life.

After the ceremony was over, Jim returned to his home on Long Island and Freddie to Greenwood Lake. I grabbed the subway back to my apartment at 110th Street and Broadway.

All the while, I kept thinking about what a lifetime bummer it would have been had Jimmy not invited me to skate with the *goyim* from Woodside on a team with the unlikely name, Whippets.

Also, I recalled that I finally had confessed to Jimmy that I never really solved my big weakness.

"What are you talking about?" he insisted.

"I'm still trying to figure out how to "pay attention!"

P.S.: Jim Hernon died in 2015, a day after Freddie and I visited him at a Queens hospital. To our tight little roller hockey gang, it was like we lost our Babe Ruth.

Still living in Greenwood Lake, Meier regularly writes to me in exquisite longhand. I reply, also in long hand, but a bit less legibly.

Every one of our letters closes with the eternal theme:

"Whippets forever!"

The Meier-Fischler hockey ties continue now that Fred's son, Andy, does some hockey work with me. Andy keeps in touch via email and passes my messages on to Fred, now electronically; but the theme is still the same:

"Whippets forever!"

Woodside Whippets Fred Meier and Jim Hernon at Niagara Falls

PART FIVE
Radio, Movies And The Theater

ADVENTURES OF TOM MIX
AND THE BROKEN TOOTH

As cowboys went, Tom Mix was my radio hero. At age nine, in 1941, I could take or leave Roy Rogers or those other giddyap Wild West guys, tall in their saddles.

I loved Tom Mix. He was my superhero long before the advent of superheroes.

Superman, Batman, Captain Marvel, The Human Torch and Submariner: take them all; put 'em in a box, wrap 'em with a ribbon into one fifteen-minute radio broadcast and I'd still like Tom Mix over everybody.

The real Mix had been a genuine, spurs-and-all cowboy but also a silent film star who later did some talkies. All told, he starred in tons of flicks, and I didn't know or care about a single one.

All I cared about was Tom Mix on the radio, Monday through Friday, 5:45 p.m., WOR, 710 on the dial.

In my childhood fantasy, Tom Mix never died.

To me, the radio Tom was the real Mix. As a result, I lived every weekday for Tom's adventures with his trusty horse, Tony, and his amusing, always reliable sidekick, known as The Wrangler.

Not that I needed any added attractions, but for years Mix was sponsored by the Ralston-Purina Company, which, among other things, produced a Ralston cereal roughly equivalent to Cream of Wheat or Wheatena.

I wasn't crazy about hot Ralston, but I admired the company's generosity. Every month, Tom would give away a prize, and not a phony one like Little Orphan Annie's "secret decoder," which was just a prop for promoting Ovaltine.

With two Ralston box tops mailed to Checkerboard Square in St. Louis, I got really good, no-kidding-around stuff. That included a monthly Tom Mix comic book, which was better than anything I could purchase at the candy store.

Once, I obtained a magnificent Tom Mix ivory folding knife. It was so good that I nearly cut my finger off closing it at the 1940 World's Fair. Fortunately, my Aunt Lucie got me first aid just in time.

Another month, Tom mailed me a certificate reaffirming that I was a Ralston Straight Shooter. That honor was not to be taken lightly.

Other give-away gems included Tom's miniature silver spurs as well as a genuine decoder that offered solid clues about Mix's latest chapter. I consider the decoder his best ever, no-finger-cutting giveaway.

On any Brooklyn afternoon -- before tuning in to Tom -- I might be playing a game of ring-a-levio on Vernon Avenue with the boys or perhaps some silly school thing like going to the Children's Museum.

But, on this particular afternoon, I was spending time at a very important neighborhood landmark, the Tompkins Park Library. It was a square, one-story edifice directly in the middle of the swings, monkey bars and assorted slides.

While I never could confirm it, I guessed that the little library must have had several secret basements -- maybe seven -- because the one and only main floor could not possibly contain so many books that I always wanted and got.

I mean, it had Red Dutton's book, *Hockey*; a swell transportation history, *Fares, Please*; and my favorite for that particular month, a literary baseball classic, *The Kid from Tomkinsville*, by John R. Tunis.

I had heard a lot about Tunis being a terrific writer of sports books, and since I happened to be a baseball nut, I eagerly pulled *The Kid from*

Tomkinsville off the shelf, found an empty table and chair and opened the opus.

Once I started poring through it, I couldn't stop. Not that I was any kind of critic -- I sure wasn't -- but this Tunis guy really could write. The proof was that I had devoured a good, three chapters when I finally was shocked into grim reality.

I looked up at the clock hanging over Miss Librarian's desk and darned near fainted at the sight, even had to look a second time.

Egad! It was 5:30 p.m. Holy crap!

Tom Mix would come on in fifteen minutes. This is insane, I thought. I never missed a Mix opening in my young life and I certainly didn't plan to end my streak that night.

Breaking all records, I checked out *The Kid from Tomkinsville* from the librarian and bolted from the building. I tried very hard to calculate -- in terms of minutes and city blocks to cover -- whether I could make the Mix opener or not.

I had a dozen minutes left and getting from the library to Marcy Avenue already wasted half a minute. As soon as I cleared the park, I was at the corner of Marcy and Lafayette Avenues. Lafayette was a big, two-way thoroughfare. Trouble.

It was busy with cars, plus the red traffic light was against me. To save a few seconds, I crossed Marcy on my side of the street and then went into high gear when the green light flashed.

The next block was smallish Kosciuszko Street with no light, no traffic. DeKalb was next -- a biggie like Lafayette -- and the red light went against me again. I didn't have the option of crossing Marcy anymore.

When a green light came on at DeKalb, I sped past the S&L Kosher Deli, the hat cleaners, the dry cleaners and then came Pulaski Street and Hart – just two more blocks to go and I could almost see 582 Marcy, my haven for Tom.

The next-to-last block was Willoughby, one-way but busy, with a string of cars and even a truck. I was running in place and trying to think of what Mix would do in my shoes. At last, the truck passed and there was an opening.

Off and running, I had only Vernon Avenue to cross and I'd be home. *Then, it happened!*

Right in front of Jack's fruit and vegetable store, my right shoe hit a crack in the sidewalk. I plunged forward like a linebacker making a tackle, only I wasn't wearing a face guard. All I had on my shoulders was my very bare head.

It was an imperfect one-point landing, the point being my mouth or -- more specifically -- my front tooth on concrete. Pushing away all thoughts, I pulled myself up, ran like heck across Vernon and grasped the downstairs door key.

I opened the steel gate, pounced through the vestibule -- not even saying "Hello" to Grandma Etel -- and mounted the stairs, two at a time. I went up one flight and then the second, made a left turn down the hall and went into the living room.

Our old, brown-paneled, upright RCA Victor radio was turned off, meaning more seconds wasted. I flicked the toggle switch and moved the orange dial to 710 and prayed that I missed not one single second of Mix's adventure.

The sound came on slowly -- too darn slowly -- on the old Victor, but now it was clear, softly at first and then louder. I couldn't believe that I was hearing the show's standard opening tune, "When It's Round Up Time In Texas."

I had made it, after all.

Not only did I miss nothing of Tom's adventure -- with trusty Wrangler and the great horse, Tony -- but I even beat the opening Ralston commercial and then listened intently as Mix rounded up the rustlers on the dusty trail.

I wish I could recall more details, but I can't. Looking backward, I guess that my headfirst kissing of the Marcy Avenue sidewalk gave me a concussion, only that word hadn't been invented at the time.

In any event, my mom was so busy cooking in the kitchen that she didn't say a thing to me until the Mix episode was over.

But now, it was 6 p.m. and the all-clear signal went off in her motherly head. She walked into the living room and did a double take, somewhat shaken by what her eyes beheld.

"Stanley, what happened to you? Your lips are bleeding," she said. Then came a second double-take. "And look at your tooth."

"What tooth, Mom?"

"Stanley, you broke your front tooth. How in the world did that happen?"

For a moment, I was totally tongue-tied. The incident in front of Jack's fruit and vegetable store by now was a blur in my mind. But I had to explain the fact that my mouth was bleeding.

I did the best I could, but admittedly, as the only witness for the defense, I was not likely to win any trial by jury. "Mom, the sidewalk came up - in front of Jack's. It came up -- and tripped me," I responded.

By this time, Mom had little interest in my alibi. She had to fix her wounded son. Out came the bottle of alcohol, cotton swabs, iodine, Band-Aids and whatever else stopped lips from bleeding.

The wound was treated. Cool Hand Mom sipped her unfinished coffee. Except for a missing minuscule piece of chipped front tooth, all seemed right with the world. To show Mom that my lips had bled for good purpose, I pulled out my library book.

"Guess what, Mom," I chirped, showing her *The Kid from Tomkinsville*. "I got this from the Tompkins Park library and I'm gonna write a book report."

Then, contentedly whispering to myself, I got to the big headline, the only one that really mattered: "I made it home for the Tom Mix show -- by seconds only!"

Tom Mix

A THEATER NAMED KISMET AND THE AIRPLANE STORE

I have two religions.

First and foremost, I'm Jewish, but you knew that already.

Back in 1942, at age 10, I joined a second religion.

It didn't really have a name other than Going-To-The-Movies. The cathedral was a theater called Kismet whose oversized marquee had a "C'mon a my house" kind of look to it.

For ten cents a double-feature, I came -- at 1 p.m. every Saturday.

The Kismet was one third of Brooklyn's Interboro cinema chain, the others being the Sumner (on Sumner Avenue) and the State (on DeKalb and Bedford). My beloved Kismet was located on DeKalb Avenue, just off Tompkins.

In a sort of neighborhood pecking order, the Sumner got the flicks first, then the Kismet and, finally, the State. In my nabe, we wouldn't even think of crossing the borders to go either to the Sumner or State despite their enticing marquees.

It was in the Kismet that I worshiped such silver screen deities as the lovely Ella Raines, the lovelier Joan Leslie, scary Brian Donlevy, heroic Joel McRae, not to mention the absolutely riotous Bud Abbott and Lou Costello.

Since I was a leg man almost since birth, I would have to add Betty Grable to my list, but with an asterisk. (I liked Betty best from the waist down.)

The first movie I ever saw was *Coconut Grove*, starring Fred McMurray. This was in 1938 and I was six. It was a funny musical but I loved it because of the choo-choo train sequences. (If railroads were in it, the movie got five stars.)

Coconut Grove was followed by *Union Pacific*, which I *kvelled* over for the same reason: trains. That, plus leggy Barbara Stanwyck who -- though I was then only seven -- I wanted to marry, the sooner the better. (Maybe tonight!)

I actually found out about the Kismet Theater even before I could read. It happened when I was three years old and standing around the corner from our 582 Marcy brownstone.

I noticed two billboards side by side, on the wall outside Jack's fruit and vegetable store. One billboard had a big picture of baked beans, and the other had writing that I couldn't understand 'cause I couldn't read.

But doing a three-year-old's deductive reasoning, I figured that the writing told everything you wanted to know about the adjoining baked beans and asked my mom if that was true.

"No," she replied, "what you see on the right is a list of all the movies this month at the Kismet. When you learn to read, then you can go to the movies."

Thanks to Mrs. Gould at P.S. 54, I eventually learned to read. That enabled me to understand the billboard, and now I could differentiate between the Kismet's double-features and Heinz baked beans.

But movie-going wasn't the only exciting thing about Saturday afternoon. Walking was an adventure in itself, starting at Goodman's deli, where the sign in the window urged, SEND A SALAMI TO YOUR BOY IN THE ARMY.

Onward I marched along Tompkins Avenue when I finally approached my all-time favorite establishment in the nabe. The sign in front said it all, CUTLER'S HOBBIES. Or did it say it all? Not really, not when you got inside the tiny place.

To me and my pals, Cutler's Hobbies was better known as the "airplane store." It had flying models, solid models, fighters, bombers and that artfully well-disguised aphrodisiac: Testor's Airplane Glue! (Fortunately, by the ton!)

Ah, but model planes and Testor's airplane glue could wait. It was on to DeKalb Avenue. A left turn and there it was, the magnificent Kismet, with its generous marquee listing the feature picture, *A Yank In The RAF*.

Underneath was a banner in cool blue and white surrounded by large, painted icicles: HEALTHFULLY AIR COOLED. In July 1942, this was some kind of meteorological miracle.

Sure enough, the Kismet lobby was air-cooled -- but the cool stopped cold, right there at the ticket-taker's chair. Any similarity between air-cooled in the lobby and air-cooled in the theater itself was purely coincidental.

Who cared? Not I, sir. A double-feature loomed, plus what we called "a chapter" (from a 13-part serial) plus a cartoon and -- best of all -- the races. Put 'em all together and it means you'd better have a "matron" handy.

A matron was a middle-aged woman armed with flashlight. She patrolled the theater's two aisles like a warden on Riker's Island. The matron had a simple rule: One false move and you're out of there.

No sane kid would break that rule because it meant he'd miss the races. And if you had the winning ticket, you'd get a prize. (Usually an eighth of the crowd had winning tickets.)

Once the race began, it was like the Kentucky Derby times 100: roar upon roar until the finish, when the winners went completely nuts, cashing in their winning tickets when the double-feature was over.

Not that the prizes were anything out of the F.A.O. Schwarz toy store. But who could argue with a free rabbit's foot or a copy of Action Comics or, at worst, a key ring. Hey, the fun was in the winning: no more, no less.

On the way home, I made my obligatory stop at The Airplane Store. This time I bought a solid -- as opposed to flying -- model of an RAF Spitfire (as in the movie) and two tubes of Testor's airplane glue.

That night, while my folks were listening to radio's *Your Hit Parade*, I began gluing my Spitfire together while listening to the most famous world-war tune of the month, "Coming In On A Wing And A Prayer."

The more I glued, the more I felt as if I, in fact, was flying high and then coming in on a wing and a prayer. Except that I merely landed unscathed on the living room table.

Once in a while, Dad would glance over at me, admiring my almost-finished Spitfire, oblivious to the fact that my nose was virtually coupled to the tube of Testor's airplane glue.

As for my mind, it already was somewhere in the 582 Marcy stratosphere. Eventually, my body glided to the bedroom and as I hit the sack, I managed to forget about Betty Grable's gorgeous gams in *A Yank In The RAF*.

A truly brilliant -- and very practical -- thought came to mind. Matter of fact, I actually smiled myself to sleep -- Testor's will do that -- with a can't-miss marketing idea.

At the earliest opportunity, I would re-visit Tompkins Avenue and suggest to Mr. and Mrs. Cutler that their sign should be more to the point and certainly more appealing. Like this: THE AIRPLANE GLUE STORE!

The Kismet Theater, 1930s

THE DAY THE
MARX BROTHERS
WEREN'T FUNNY

Howie Sparer was my best friend, and that meant that we did a lot of things together. It was 1945 -- we were both 13-years-old -- and we loved the movies.

Every Saturday, for three straight weeks, we'd walk up to DeKalb and Tompkins Avenues and visit our local cinema, the Kismet, for the afternoon double-feature plus a cowboy chapter, a Looney Tunes cartoon and a newsreel.

That was a very big deal, but an even bigger flick favorite was our monthly trek down to Fulton Street -- Brooklyn's Times Square -- where there were theaters galore, mostly big, flagship movie houses.

What a selection: RKO Albee, Brooklyn Paramount (the largest theater in the city), Loews Metropolitan, Fabian Fox, the Strand and, a notch below, the Majestic, the only place in town where you could watch a *triple-feature.*

We'd get on the DeKalb Avenue trolley, at the corner of Nostrand and DeKalb, and get off where DeKalb met Fulton Street in front of the classic, white-domed Dime Savings Bank. That put us amidst the cavalcade of cinemas. We were pumped.

Yikes! For the first time in our young lives, on this particular, woe-begone Saturday, there wasn't an enticing flick among the host of theaters. Not one. What to do?

Well, we couldn't go home; that would be an insult to our adventure. We had to find a movie house that would take our buck and give us a good time.

"Let's go back and check the Loews Met just to be sure," said Howie. "Got nothing to lose."

No good. Some stupid love story. Not a chance.

We were near where Fulton meets Court Street. Never in our young lives had we drifted beyond Court. We never had to, since there were no movie houses we knew of past Fulton. Plus, the nabe got tough heading south on Court.

"Look," I said, "if we go down Court we just might find something. So what if it ain't first-run?"

That prompted Howie's favorite flavored comment of the year: "Yeah, I always told you, 'What's life without a little adventure?' so let's go."

With that, we turned left on Court and started looking for a theater. The more we walked, the more we left the business district and entered foreign turf. We had never seen the seamier side of Court before, and it excited us.

But the more we walked, the more we worried, because Red Hook was just ahead. In 1945, Red Hook was regarded as one of the toughest, scariest neighborhoods in the city, home of the notorious Redskin Rumba gang.

Finally, one block from Atlantic Avenue, we noticed a movie theater marquee. It was the Para-Court.

"This might be it," I said hopefully. Well, yeah, it was a cinema all right, but the double-bill was right out of the Staten Island landfill.

"N. G." said Howie. "No good!" Now what? We paused and mused. We were at a crossroads, literally and figuratively, at Court and Atlantic. Where to go?

"Should we cross Atlantic?" I asked Howie; hoping he'd say negative. He grinned. "What's life without a little adventure?"

And so we did. Eureka! There was another theater ahead, -- the Lido -- and it sat on our side of the street. We checked the marquee: THE MARX BROTHERS IN *HORSE FEATHERS*; LAWRENCE TIERNEY IN *DILLINGER*.

We both had heard about the Marx Brothers, but neither of us had seen them in action. On the other hand, everybody had heard about Dillinger. No questions asked, we plunked down our quarters, walked in and there were the Marx Brothers.

Horse Feathers was only a quarter of the way through, and by the time it ended, we unanimously agreed to see it again later that day at the Lido. Nothing against *Dillinger*, but we couldn't wait for more Chico, Harpo, Groucho and Zeppo.

The second viewing was funnier than the first. Out we went: a right turn on Court, walk to Fulton and then find the DeKalb Avenue trolley station. As we approached it, we could see the DeKalb streetcar pulling away two stops ahead.

"Let's walk," I said, "and when the next trolley comes, we'll get on."

It gradually was getting darker as we sauntered past Brooklyn Technical High School and Fort Greene Park, but we hardly noticed. We also forgot about the trolley. All we did -- minute by minute -- was recount the hilarious Marx scenes.

"Y'know what?" Howie declared with finality. "The heck with the trolley, let's go walk all the way home."

And so we did. We laughed our heads off over the classroom scene; we regaled each other recalling Harpo "telling" the "swordfish" punch line outside the speakeasy. One scene after another, guffaws, until it was dark.

Conveniently, we had forgotten that Howie's parents, Sally and Sidney Sparer, both were working at a factory, Spare-Way Food Products, and Howie was supervised by his big sister, Norma, a guardian, but not an angel.

Since neither of us wore watches, we had no idea of the hour. The only time we had was time to tell more funny lines from Groucho and laugh about Chico's piano-foolery. We were having so much fun we had forgotten about Norma.

Big, big -- call it gigantic -- mistake.

As 20-year-olds went at that time, Norma was one of the two most beautiful women in the nabe, with the other being her close gal-pal, Mickey. But along with Norma's great legs and other sweet features, she had a temper.

Oy vey, did she have a temper; Vesuvius would have blushed in envy.

Of course, with the Brothers Marx on our minds, who could think about Norma? On the other hand, Norma was thinking about us. They were not sweet things, not even sweet and sour. Howie's guardian had let her guard down.

The dinner she had cooked had gone cold; she had no idea where we were and no one carried a phone around in those days. To say that Norma was worried and furious would be the understatement of the half-century.

After all, she was in charge of her baby brother. As far as she was concerned, Howie had disappeared, maybe gotten kidnapped. Hey, it hap-pened to a Lindbergh; it could happen to a Sparer.

Meanwhile, we two miscreants had giggled our way to 1 Vernon Avenue. After having so many laughs, I decided to go upstairs to the Sparer apartment for ten more minutes of exchanging Marx routines with my best friend, Howie. Why not?

Big mistake, young fella. Very big error. Should have gone straight home.

Norma must have heard us laughing up the stairway because when we got to the top she greeted us like a tornado-cyclone-hurricane blend. Norma's high-decibel assault blew me down the staircase and back onto Vernon Avenue.

Stunned to the very core, I traipsed the block home trying to recall what Norma had said to me during her tirade. Finally, I remembered something about Stanley being the one who caused her anxiety attack and that I should get the hell home.

Just as I arrived in our living room, my mom hung up the phone. Norma had been on the other end of the line, explaining to Molly Fischler what a schmuck her son had been, something about being a bad influence on darling Howie.

To her everlasting credit, Molly Fischler was not intimidated by Norma Sparer. Mom brushed off the blast and, instead, wanted to know all about our adventure.

"So," she asked, "what did you fellas see?"

"The Marx Brothers in *Horse Feathers*," I replied.

Mom -- she loved movies -- was curious. "So, how did you like them? I bet you did."

I thought for a moment and then told the truth and nothing but the truth.

"Mom, they were as funny as could be. But when we got to Howie's apartment, the Marx Brothers weren't funny anymore!"

The Lido Theater, 1930s

DOING THE TIMES SQUARE TROT

Broadway beckoned and Molly Fischler obliged. Meanwhile, I held her hand and shivered.

It was late 1940, and the lines around the Paramount Theater were so long they extended around Broadway and onto 44th street, seeming to stretch all the way to West New York, New Jersey.

Mother Molly and son, Stanley, age eight, stood on the Paramount line, waiting to see Benny, as in Jack, as in the brand, new movie, *Buck Benny Rides Again.*

"Mom," I implored in my finest Brooklynese, "it's freezin' cold out here."

"Patience," she shot back. "You'll never regret the wait once you see what's inside."

As usual, Mother Fischler was right. It had been in the family genes that when Jack Benny performed -- on radio or in movies -- we laughed. On this day, we would guffaw a lot more because, well, *Buck Benny Rides Again.*

The cast included Jack along with his radio troupe, featuring Rochester, Mary Livingston and Phil Harris. Even Jack's pet polar bear, Carmichael, would get into the act. I mean, how do you top having a polar bear in a cowboy flick?

"You'll see, Stanley," Mother Fischler chirped as the line moved onto Broadway with the box office at last in sight. "They also have a stage show here at the Paramount."

"What's a stage show?" I wondered, never having been to a first-run Broadway movie house in my young life.

Mom said, "There'll also be a live band -- happens that Gene Krupa's Orchestra is playing -- and some funny guys called Borrah Minnevitch And His Harmonica Rascals."

Sounded good to me, so I shut my mouth and followed Mom into the theater. As we took our seats, I was momentarily stunned when a mammoth organ suddenly slid out of a large wall crevice above us on the left.

If that wasn't magical enough, next came the magnificent strains of "Begin The Beguine," thanks to Dick Liebert at the console, and at no extra cost.

Soon, Liebert finished his set, whereupon he and the organ disappeared into the wall and the house lights dimmed. Within the next hour, we laughed it up as Benny played cowboy and won the heart of the ever-beauteous Ellen Drew.

When "The End" flashed across the silver screen, another loud development erupted from below. It was live music. Piercing the Paramount air were pungent sounds of trumpets, woodwinds and, heart-pounding drums.

Rising out of the Paramount underground, the Gene Krupa Band surfaced. Yow! There was the drummer man, himself, Krupa, armed with his tom-toms, crushing his high hat and tinkling a cowbell to the rhythms of "Drum Boogie."

For a lad who'd never seen a Broadway stage show at a first-run theater like the Paramount, this was a deluxe thrill. And that didn't even include Krupa's warbling duet of Anita O'Day and Roy Eldridge doing "Let Me Off Uptown."

Mom didn't know it at the time, but she had introduced me to a form of entertainment -- stage show and movie -- that would become my show biz staple for years.

The choices were endless. Up Broadway from the Paramount was the Strand, Warner's flagship theater. Universal's Capitol was across from the Strand. A few blocks away, shoulder to shoulder, sat Loew's State and Criterion.

But the jewel of them all was in Rockefeller Center -- Radio City Music Hall on Sixth and 50th. Radio City, as we simply called it, was fancy-schmancy, which meant it was off limits to us -- too expensive -- except for special occasions.

Radio City's style was Art Deco, and it featured a house band, not to mention a very sophisticated stage show, starring the extra-leggy Rockettes with gams like you wouldn't believe, even from the last row, balcony.

I have to confess that we militantly boycotted Radio City, unless Aunt Hattie was coming in from Albany and she was buying the costly ducats.

Somewhere in between high-class Radio City and the earthy Paramount was a unique movie palace, the Roxy, right next to the brand-new Sixth Avenue subway station. As first-run movie places went, the, Roxy was an aberration.

Almost as big as Radio City and almost as fancy, the Roxy showed first-run flicks, but it almost never featured a stage show, unless it was one of those *ne plus ultra* acts, starring a legend such as Marlene Dietrich or Mae West.

My favorite stage show of all time happened to take place at the Roxy. It starred Jack Benny and his radio pals. For me it was a lifetime event, like watching the Islanders play in Game Seven of a Stanley Cup Final, something they never have.

My buddy, Lewis Klotz, who met me at the Roxy, did what I did: He brought lunch because we knew we'd do the unthinkable and stay over for a second show. All things considered, we guessed right.

As for Benny's act, the audience loved Jack so much that endless applause demanded encore after *encore*. It was so overwhelming that pal Lewis finally turned to me and asked the question that also had stirred my mind.

"How are they gonna manage to get Benny off the stage?"

Then, it happened, a stroke of stage-managing genius that finally produced an easy exit for show-stopping Jack.

First, Benny made a wisecrack about his "arch-enemy," comedian Fred Allen. That, in and of itself, meant automatic laughs.

But instead of actually mentioning Allen by name, Jack suddenly stopped cold. At that instant, the theater blacked out and a gigantic picture of Fred Allen flashed on the big screen.

By the time everyone stopped laughing in the darkened Roxy, Benny had conducted an orderly retreat off stage. It was the most brilliant bit of stage-managing I'd ever seen.

As predicted, Lewis and I were not the only Benny fans who hung out for the second show; there were many. We downed our sandwiches and then savored the second Benny-go-round. It had some fresh, laugh-roaring material and the same Allen-related exit.

Unlike the Roxy, Loews State accompanied every one of its first-run flicks with a stage show, but it was a cut below the others. It was more like old-time vaudeville and always featured a stand-up comic.

It could be Milton Berle, Joey Adams or Myron Cohen, although my favorite -- by far -- was Henny Youngman, known as King of the One-Liners. For my two bits, the Brooklyn funnyman had an advantage over his rivals: his face.

Something about Henny's moony mug made you smile before he even opened his mouth. Then, he'd pull out his trusty violin, do a chorus of "When The Gypsy Made His Violin Cry" and toss a quickie:

"A fellow walked up to me and said, 'Do you see a cop around here?' I said, 'No.' He said, 'Stick 'em up!'"

Or:

"I was so ugly when I was born that the doctor slapped my mother!"

Decades later, I had the thrill of my life. As a *New York Journal-American* feature writer, I was assigned to write a piece about Henny, since he had launched a clever phone gimmick called "Dial A Joke."

For me, it was a blast. Henny and I sat on a Central Park bench and did the interview. But whenever a passer-by recognized Youngman, Henny stopped our chat, signed an autograph and then, very naturally, told another one-liner.

"I haven't spoken to my wife in three weeks. I didn't want to interrupt her!"

It was like being at the Loew's State all over again, except that the stage shows that Mom and I loved so much were gone. None at the Paramount, the Capital or Strand for that matter.

After I closed my notebook and thanked Youngman for his time, Henny shot back, "I got one more for you, kid. Take this home with you."

"I once played Little League ball and stole second base. But I felt guilty and went back!"

I did take it home with me and never forgot Henny or that cold, windy day on West 44th Street, waiting to see Krupa on stage and "Buck Benny Rides Again!" on the big screen.

That was my movie-and-stage-show era, and I hoped it would never end. Alas, it did, and that leaves me only one thing to do.

First, I remember Benny at the Roxy, then I put on a Krupa CD -- with Anita and Roy -- and do what they were doing, "Let Me Off Uptown!"

Except, I do it in my dreams!

Molly Fischler, the secretary with the best legs in Brooklyn

PART SIX
My Love Affair
With Music

VICTOR THE VICTROLA AND ME

Sometime in the early 1920s, the Victor Company built a recording machine that would play a big part in my young life.

They called it a Victrola, and by the age of five, I regarded it as a very nice windup toy. To make it work, you had to turn a crank about a dozen times and it was off and running, playing all kinds of music.

My parents stashed it in the corner of our tiny living room. I liked it so much I gave it a name, Victor the Victrola.

It was 1936, and I made Victor my "pet" because the record player had a picture of a small dog on its top, accompanied by a slogan, "His Master's Voice."

While our more affluent neighbors played their records on electric phonographs, we low-income-ites made do with Victor the Victrola. Of course to make music, some physical work was required.

The large handle -- or crank -- that stuck out of Victor's right side had to be pumped. A dozen revolutions of the handle and Victor the Victrola was ready for action.

The next bit of business was placing a record on the turntable. That done, you had to lift the gizmo carrying a steel needle and place the needle carefully at the very edge of the record.

A switch next to the turntable was flipped and round and round went the record until it reached the end. At that point, you lifted the gizmo off the disc, placed it on its side hanger and removed the record.

Meanwhile, I learned all about important music on our radio -- also an old Victor product. On WNEW, there was disc jockey Martin Block's *Make Believe Ballroom*. If Martin played a tune, you knew it was a hit.

Block wasn't the only deejay. Fred Robbins had his *Robbins' Nest* and every Saturday night Lucky Strike Cigarettes sponsored *Your Hit Parade*, featuring Mark Warnow's orchestra with Kitty Kallen on vocals.

In 1937, Mom Fischler gave me the green light to make music with Victor. She handed me a Decca record, "Honky Tonk Train Blues," with Meade (Lux) Lewis tinkling a solo on the piano. I put it on and was hooked.

It was a good start, but I leaned toward tunes for my age. I liked Ella Fitzgerald's "A-Tisket, A-Tasket," backed by Chick Webb's band. Another favorite was "Ferdinand the Bull" from the cartoon movie of the same name.

By age seven, in 1939, I was old enough to purchase my own records. For a mere dime, I could buy a best-selling Decca at the music store two blocks away at Tompkins and Willoughby.

My first purchase almost featured Judy Garland singing "Over The Rainbow," since I had just seen *The Wizard of Oz*. But even then, whiny Judy turned me off. I had another sweet, more upbeat singing lady in mind.

I was crazy about Wee Bonnie Baker. You would have been, too, if you had heard her warbling "Oh, Johnny, Oh." I didn't know what sex was at the time, but I instinctively knew that Wee Bonnie Baker was sexy.

Bonnie's sizzling hit proved to be one of the subtlest, near-X-rated tunes of all-time. No wonder I played it on Victor about 100 times, so many times that Mom had to intervene to save Vic from exhaustion.

"You see those silver lines on the record?" Molly Fischler sagely intoned. "Those silver lines mean something. They mean that you're play-ing Bonnie Baker too much. Get it?"

"So, what am I supposed to do, Mom?" I innocently inquired.

"Here's a dime. Get yourself another record."

It was 1939. The Nazis had invaded Poland and World War II was underway. There was only one record to purchase, Kate Smith's "God Bless America." I played it once, and it almost made me cry. Still does.

Meanwhile, a new source of music entered my life, via Hollywood. All of 10 years-old in 1942, I headed for the Kismet Theater on DeKalb and Tompkins to see beauteous Ann Rutherford starring in *Orchestra Wives*.

Neither Ann nor her love opposite, George Montgomery nor the assorted Orchestra Wives were the target of my affection. Not even close. It was the Glenn Miller Orchestra with his own assortment of stars.

They included gorgeous vocalist Marian Hutton, sax man and mighty singer, Tex Beneke, and an aces group called The Modernaires. Together, they knocked off some of the top tunes of the Big Band era.

Beneke was outstanding as he belted out "(I've Got A Gal in) Kalamazoo." Hutton was first up with "At Last," while "Serenade In Blue" gave me goose pimples. Meanwhile, "Mister Miller" put me "In The Mood."

Kay Kyser's "Playmates" and Tommy Dorsey's "Chicago" were among my other favorite "straight" tunes. But there was an in-between category -- call it "Novelty" -- that I adored. Novelty songs were either intentionally funny or were about a topic (like war or the Depression) that had the country's attention; "Dry Bones" and "Der Fuhrer's Face" were two popular examples in the '40s.

Jack Benny's radio bandleader, Phil Harris, played the novelties best, and best of them all was "That's What I Like About The South."

I played it so often that the black vinyl -- as Mom had forecast -- turned to silver and threatened to break the record in half every time I put it on the turntable.

Around that time, certain personal scenes automatically brought tunes to mind, and still do to this day. The first time it happened was during a winter evening in 1944. I was 12 and working on a model airplane.

While I was toying with the Ryan trainer, sweet sounds of Dinah Shore were wafting out of Victor. It was a tune, "You'd Be So Nice To Come Home To," and a time that I fondly remember to this day.

Another time, I was returning from a hike in New Jersey with my Aunt Helen. We had trudged through a heavy rain and, finally, wound up on Main Street in Millburn. It might have seemed unmemorable, yet it's fixed in my mind.

The sun had burst through the clouds as we ambled past a record store. Over its loudspeaker was Glenn Miller's group doing "Idaho." The scene -- the sun and the song -- have been with me forever.

By far, the capper of my Big Band love affair arrived in 1945. I had become enamored with Tommy Dorsey's superior trombone play-ing on "Song of India," and my folks knew I was infatuated with the tune and Dorsey.

For my bar mitzvah *present,* Mom and Dad took me to the 400 Club at 400 Fifth Avenue, where Tommy's band was the headliner.

What I'll never forget is that at the end of the band's second set, I summoned all the nerve at my command, walked over to The Great Man and timidly asked for his autograph.

"Here you are, son," Mr. Dorsey said, gently resting his trombone on its holster. "I hope you're enjoying our music."

I'm sure I said something like, "Yes, Mister Dorsey, I sure do like your music," but I stumbled back to our table thinking I was somewhere to the left of Dreamland.

In order to ensure that I'll never forget that evening at the 400 Club, I play Dorsey's "Marie" or "I'm Getting Sentimental Over You" on a regular basis. But not on Victor anymore.

Sometime after World War II, our beloved Victrola broke down, I guess from old age. Wasting no time, my folks sprung for a brand-new electric, Zenith radio-phonograph. I have to say it was a beauty in every which way.

It not only made the records sound better but was built so you actu-ally could stack a few disks on top of each other and have it play music for a good half-hour.

"Such a mechanism," said my astonished mother.

Yeah, the shiny new Zenith was a big winner, no question about that. But I must confess that I missed that old Victrola that had comfortably sat in the living room corner delivering beautiful music for so long.

Man, oh, man, how I'd like to wind up Victor just once more!

Victor the Victrola

THE DRUM LESSON,
STARRING BETTY SABIN'S
PERFUMED NEGLIGEE

Music has been a part of my life since I was knee-high to a grasshopper. Tunes permeated our little third-floor apartment at 582 Marcy Avenue in many ways and times, starting with breakfast.

Without fail, my mom and dad tuned our old, brown Victor stand-on-its-own-four-feet radio to station WOR, 710 on the dial, at 7:00 a.m. every weekday for the *John Gambling Show*.

In between Gambling's merry chatter, he featured a live, three-piece band that played all kinds of good songs. They'd even reach out for Gilbert and Sullivan's *HMS Pinafore* or Rodgers and Hart's "Blue Moon."

In the corner of our living room sat another Victor product, a wind-up Victrola phonograph that played only a one-speed, 78 rpm record. For that, my parents gifted me with my first disc, Kay Kyser's rendition of "Playmates."

This was rapidly followed by Bob Crosby's "The Little Red Fox" and "Oh Johnny, Oh," with Little Bonnie Baker doing the very sexy vocal while fronting for Orrin Tucker's band.

By the time I entered Eastern District High School at age 14, my basic musical education consisted of DJ-listening. The radio programs *Milkman's*

Matinee, Martin Block's *Make Believe Ballroom* and Fred Robbins's *Robbin's Nest* were my faves.

Most of the best disc jockeys were on WNEW, 1130 on the dial. Put 'em all together, and their records inspired me to be a drummer, preferably like the one and only Gene Krupa, give or take Buddy Rich.

But to be a drummer, one needed a drum teacher and, maybe later, a real set -- including snare drum, bass drum, high-hat, cymbals, wood block and cowbell.

Fortunately, E.D. High featured an instrument class. Freshmen could sign up with the band leader, Mr. Al Scheer. He would assign us to an instrument. Naturally, I was hoping he'd put me on drums.

"What instrument would you like?" the mustached Mr. Scheer asked me.

"Drums," I eagerly replied.

A frown crossed Scheer's face. "Sorry, kid, but I teach instruments -- not drums. I'm gonna put you on trombone."

He did, and I never regretted it.

That said, my passion for percussion wouldn't go away. It was confirmed at the first assembly, when our freshman class was ushered into the high school's theater while crisp, inspiring, martial music graced our ears.

The Gold and White Band was enthusiastically playing Sousa's "On Parade." Pounding away on his snare drum was a wiry fellow who obviously was having a ball. So, was I, just listening and admiring his stick work -- fast and furious.

After the assembly, I hustled over to the drummer man, who was packing away his Gretsch snare. Before he could utter a phrase, I told him I loved the way he did his rolls and paradiddles, and how I wished I could do that.

"You could," he shot back, "if you want to take lessons from me."

Larry Subin was his name. He lived in Bed-Stuy on Lafayette Avenue near Sumner, just a 15-minute walk from my house, five minutes by bike.

Larry, wisely, didn't put me on real drums right away. Instead, he taught percussion two ways: using the legendary Harry M. Bauer instruction book, with ancient Harry's mug plastered on the 1910's cover; and then, what I learned from Uncle Harry's fine lessons was practiced under the Argus eye of Larry. He insisted that I do my pounding on what's known in the biz as a "drum pad."

The pad consisted of a thick, rubber slab attached to an angled base. From my Harry M. Bauer book, I learned how to play a flam, double paradiddle, and even a flam-and-stroke, among other tricks of the stick trade. I was music-happy.

But after six months, I became less happy. After one successful lesson, Larry said he'd give me an A for my drumming. Then he dropped the bomb and announced that he had just enlisted in the U.S. Navy!

Ah, but there was a sweet use for that bit of adversity. Larry kept me in the drumming family. He passed me on to his father, the eminent Phil Sabin, a pro's pro. (Yes, father and son had differently-spelled surnames.) Phil drummed in Meyer Davis's society band.

"You'll like my father," consoled Larry. "My Dad even plays jobs like the Presidential Ball. He's the best."

Under Phil Sabin's tutelage, my drum-learning didn't miss a beat. Same time (Saturday morning at eleven), same station (on Lafayette), same book (Harry M. Bauer, Volume 2).

Phil Sabin looked like Larry Subin plus 25 years: lithe and handsome. The only difference -- which I never could figure out – was the discrepancy in the spelling of their last names.

Ah, but there was an extra, added attraction offered by "The Sabin Follies," Phil's crazy-gorgeous wife, Betty.

By sheer coincidence, I encountered the fetching Betty for the first time on the very same week I had viewed the movie, *Orchestra Wives*, down the block at the Kismet Theater.

The 20th-Century Fox flick starred the Glenn Miller Orchestra along with those curiously alluring beauties -- Anne Rutherford, Lynn Bari and Carole Landis.

Put that trio altogether, then multiply by ten, and you get Betty Sabin. On my pal Howie's unofficial -- yet oft-reliable -- Brooklyn rating scale of one to ten, Betty climbed to a twelve, aspiring for twenty!

In terms of my Saturday morning motivation, the equation was 30 percent for Phil teaching me the tom-toms and the rest to get a gander at the drum teacher's wife. (Hubba-hubba was the name of the game.)

Betty helped spur my motivation in several ways; mostly just by being within telescope distance. But there were other seductive Betty sidebars.

One of my favorites was her habit of leaving a bottle of expensive perfume on my drum table. Occasionally, she'd visit for a drop of Chanel No. 5. Meanwhile, I would deeply inhale the dual aromas: from Chanel and Betty's body beautiful.

Meanwhile, Phiery Phil pushed me to a point on drums where I was ready to buy the traps set -- second-hand, of course -- from Manny's, on 47th Street. My dad accompanied me to carry the modest percussion collection home.

Granted, the bass drum was too big and the cymbals too cheap, but Phil steered me through all the challenges. In time, I got to like my percussion collection and couldn't wait to play for real dough -- with a group, of course.

A couple of weeks before I "graduated" from Sabin's School of Drumming, I had two rather exciting encounters with the sizzling Mrs. Sabin. The first neatly fit the tune, "Give Me Something To Remember You By."

It went this way: One morning, Betty bumped into my practice pad bridge table that was shared by her perfume and my Harry M. Bauer book. Betty's "bump" sent Chanel No. 5 spilling all over Harry's mug on the cover, plus a few paradiddle pages to boot.

That magical Chanel No. 5 aroma never would disappear. On days when I wouldn't feel like practicing, I'd open my Harry M. Bauer, take a big Chanel sniff and momentarily daydream about Mrs. S. Then, I'd hit the pad.

But that was small potatoes compared to our confrontation a few weeks later. It was a sweet Saturday morning in spring, the kind that must have inspired Rodgers and Hammerstein to compose, "June Is Bustin' Out All Over."

I busted out my red Roadmaster bike, packed my Harry M Bauer and pedaled south to Lafayette Avenue. The vibrant sun had me mesmerized as I wheeled off Marcy and onto Lafayette. I was totally oblivious to the minute or hour.

At the brownstone, I leaned my bike -- no locks in 1949 -- against the metal gate. Still daydreaming, I raced up the stoop-staircase to the second-floor door.

I rang the bell and did my usual wait. This time, it took a bit longer than usual but no big deal. I was about to ring again when I heard noises from the hallway inside the house.

Suddenly, Betty Sabin opened the inside door and then the outside door. To say the least, she did not look happy. To say the most, she was ravishing-to-the-power-of-50. A strong whiff of Chanel radiated off her almost-covered body.

I gasped. The raven-haired beauty was adorned -- well, almost! -- in a negligee that one could see through all the way to the borough of Queens.

Betty: "What are you doing here?"

Me: "I have a drum lesson with Phil."

Betty: "Your drum lesson is at 11. Do you know what time it is now? It's only 10:45. Those 15 minutes mean a lot to Phil."

She turned around, and this time I could see through her negligee all the way to Staten Island. The door closed behind her, leaving me nothing better to do than walk around the block and convince myself of the vision I had just encountered.

When I returned, Phil welcomed me, gave his lesson and then sat me down for a bit of adult-to-kid advice.

"Stanley," he said, "I'm sorry if Betty was harsh with you. Someday you'll understand what she meant by those '15 minutes meaning a lot' to me. In the meantime, I'm going to tell you a story to make my point."

Phil pulled out a pack of Chesterfields, slowly opened the top and picked out the cigarette that looked like a good opener for his tale. He lit up, puffed a few times and then went on with his fable.

It was about the legendary Rip Van Winkle, who slept for twenty years straight at his Catskill abode. Rip's wife, Sheila Van Winkle, kept waiting for her husband to awaken. Finally, after twenty years, she got fed up with waiting for Rip to rise.

Phil took another puff on his Chesterfield, blew some well-contoured smoke rings and continued with his story.

"Rip's wife decided to wake him. So, she walked down to the stream and filled three buckets with cold stream water. Then she returned and poured the first bucketful on Rip, but got no reaction," he said.

"Then, she did likewise with the second bucket. Still no reaction. Finally, in utter frustration, she poured the third bucket and screamed: 'RIP, RIP, FOR CHRIST'S SAKE, GET UP ALREADY; IT'S TWENTY YEARS THAT YOU'VE BEEN ASLEEP.'

"Rip finally opened his left eye, turned to his wife and blurted, 'Just five more minutes!' "

Phil paused, took one more puff on his Chesterfield, and said, "Get the point, kid?"

I did, and after that had just two more lessons slated with Phil. After the second lesson, he told me that this was the end of our run.

"I'm leaving on the road with Meyer Davis," he said. "It will be a long road trip. This is it for you and me."

Phil then pronounced me ready to play drums for dollars. We shook hands. Then the magnificent Betty -- this time fully dressed -- walked over, gave me a hug and a kiss and I took off for the world of music.

That was the last time I saw Phil Sabin, and I do believe he would have been proud of me. I eventually got paid for playing drums in assorted small bands. We played summer Catskill Hotels in 1950, 1951 and 1952.

My favorite was the first, Greenfield Manor in Greenfield Park, N.Y., a short hop from Ellenville. Our group included Ivan Margolin on piano, Bernie Rappaport on trombone and Irwin Tuchfeld doubling on both clarinet and saxophone.

At the start, we argued about the importance of naming our quartet. Margolin pushed for The Blue Notes. Rappy said that it should be a more catchy name, and backed it up with one we all liked.

Our band herewith was known as Joe Banana And His Bunch -- Music With Appeal!

We got paid ten bucks a week, plus free room and board at Greenfield Manor. Our Mondays were totally free. At most, we played three hours per night. A set included a fox trot, then something Latin, a jump tune and occasionally a waltz.

Of course, every night we all prayed that young, single women would come up with their parents, but, sadly, it never happened. The closest was red-headed Paulette, the bookkeeper's daughter. Alas, she was 14, too young.

Every once in a while, I'd think about Phil Sabin. I'd wonder where he was playing drums with Meyer Davis and his orchestra. Occasionally, my mind would drift back to the Sabins' brownstone on Lafayette.

Amazingly, for many years after my last visit to the Sabin abode, every time I sniffed Chanel No. 5, one and only one tune came to mind: "Something To Remember You By." And any time I wanted to daydream about Phil's wife – preferably, in her negligee – I merely opened my Harry M. Bauer book and took a good long sniff of Betty No. 5!

Stan practicing at home

DRUMMING IN THE BORSCHT BELT, 1950

L ike Gene Krupa, I wanted to be a drummer.

Krupa was a drummer, and I faked it.

This was the spring of 1950 and I had finished four years of rim-shotting at the combined Phil Sabin and Son Drum School.

Didn't matter that it was in the Sabin living room on Lafayette Avenue across from brand-new P.S. 25.

Between Phil and his son, Lou, I was deemed ready to purchase a used set of traps at Manny's music store on West 47th Street. That was my high school and drum school graduation gift. That and a set of brushes for soft fox trots and a cowbell for I don't know what.

All I needed was a band that wanted a drummer who could distinguish between the rhythms of a fox trot, rhumba, Lindy Hop, mambo and a *frailach* or two. Maybe even *My Yiddishe Mama*.

Then along came yours truly, Irwin Tuchfeld, Bernie Rappaport and Ivan Margolin, and a dance band was born. We called ourselves The Blue Notes, although Rappy preferred Joe Banana And His Bunch -- Music With Appeal.

Tuch played the clarinet and sax very well, Rappy did likewise on trombone and Margolin earned the nickname "Ivan The Terrible Piano Player."

On drums, I did my best to keep up with the lads because I never knew whether Ivan would play a rhumba fast and think it was a mambo. With Tuch and Rappy, no problem. Both were legit musicians.

Don't ask me how, but Tuch -- a smallish fellow with glasses -- got us a gig at a place called Greenfield Manor in Greenfield Park, New York – the Catskills or the Borscht Belt. The music job just seemed to emerge from thin air.

At the time, I didn't know much about the 500-odd hotels in The Belt except that the Concord in Kiamesha Lake earned five out of five stars, as did its keen competitor, Grossinger's (The G), in Ferndale.

As for Greenfield Manor, on further review, it would earn a minus-3 rating if such stars existed. But, really, it didn't matter because we had a gig for a big ten bucks a week.

No sweat. Why should we complain? Room and board were free. We had a whole day off, and we played music for a couple of hours a day and prayed that *maidlachs* would show up with their mommas and poppas. (Sadly, few did.)

Okay, okay, so The Manor wasn't exactly perfect, and that's the world's understatement of understatements. Still, I loved many quirky things about it, including the brothers who owned it -- Mandelawitz and Mandel. (Don't ask me where Mandel's "witz" disappeared to, but it likely was submerged in the *smetena,* alias sour cream.)

And if you're still wondering why Greenfield Manor was not a five-star hotel, here are some clues:

- Where a swimming pool should have been, there was a grassy knoll.

- Where the tennis court was, nobody could play on it because the grass was higher than in Africa's Serengeti. (Rappy swore that he once saw a lion moseying along through the tennis court grass.)

- The handball court was invisible to the naked eye -- because there was none -- and plans for a softball tournament were abandoned because the softball diamond was as visible as the handball court.

Ah, but there was a building to covet: the casino. Replete with standup piano, table and a dance floor, this was our home court. It was where the paying customers came to hear Tuchfeld & Company reign supreme. "Blue Moon" and "Besame Mucho" were our favorite tunes. We played requests. My dad once requested that we play "Far Away." Then, he'd add, "As far away as possible!"

Our Little Irwin Tuchfeld was a clarinet prodigy. His specialty was a medley of Yiddish favorites, including a *frailich*, "Russian Sher" and a tear-jerker called "Mine Shteitela Belz." (For encores, "Shain Vie De Le Vounu.")

Although Tuchfeld had memorized every tune in his medley, there were two fascinating music books to go with them that every Borscht Belt band had to have in order to survive.

They were known to one and all as *Kammen International Dance Folio*, numbers 1 and 9. (Nobody ever discovered what ever happened to the other seven *Kammens*.) Between the two Kammens, we had every Yiddish tune ever composed by Sholom Secunda.

On clarinet, Tuch was like a miniature Benny Goodman and the guests loved him; Rappy, too. Me? Eh. Ivan? They didn't call him The Terrible for nothing.

A week or so before we arrived, Rappaport, our trombonist, learned about a cut-rate sale of dance tunes. They became part of our repertoire. Rappy meant well, but the collection could have been titled, "Tunes Nobody Ever Heard Of and Never Will, and You'll Soon Know the Reason Why."

As far as I can remember, we wound up playing just one of the cut-rate songs, a foxtrot with the catchy title of "Penguin At The Waldorf." We gave it a couple of tries and then dropped it in the round file. The penguins should have followed.

Our round of dance music began soon after dinner and lasted for as long as there were guests on the dance floor, usually until 10 p.m. We then were done for the night.

You'd think that that would have allowed us a couple of hours to cavort in the various hip villages, such as South Fallsberg, Ferndale or Kiamesha Lake. But none of us had a car, and the only available vehicle belonged to Sol, the handyman, one of the curious characters who peopled The Manor.

Sol's vehicle was a well-kept, light-blue 1934 Plymouth convertible with a rumble seat. That meant that two of us could squeeze alongside Sol, and the other pair would breeze along with the breeze in the rumble seat.

Sol made some extra bucks with his Plymouth jitney mostly because The Manor lacked the most important feature: a swimming pool. But our clever hotel owners, Mandelawitz and Mandel, made a deal with a bunga-low colony down the road that featured -- ha! -- an artificial lake.

Actually it was more like a pond that had a ratio of 60 percent water and 40 percent mud. Which meant that anyone who emerged from a "swim" in the artificial lake looked like he or she had climbed out of an oil spill.

Sol would ferry The Manor's customers a mile or so up the road to the artificial lake. As far as I could tell, his other job as handyman was to screw the voluptuous -- an understatement -- Eva, a former displaced person from the war in Europe who ran the day camp when enough kids showed up with their mommas.

We band members once held a closed contest to describe Eva's sub-tropical body, but the best we could come up with was to say that she was "built like a brick shithouse." Runner-up was Ivan's brilliant insight: "She's some piece of ass!"

Without transportation, we were limited to either walking to wher-ever we wanted to go or hitchhiking. Greenfield Park was about a mile down the road. It was a pleasant walk, mostly because we strolled past Beerkill Lodge, which was a "real" hotel. It had a swimming pool, even a genuine, no-mud lake and a sprinkling of *nofkes*, alias girls.

To us, Beerkill simply was a symbol of what we yearned for when we matured as musicians. For now, Beerkill was an off-limits paradise. Ditto for Tamarack Lodge, a four-star joint a half-mile past Beerkill.

As for Greenfield Park itself, the hamlet consisted of Kass's Corner, a general store -- with soda fountain -- where you could buy just about anything short of a rugby ball and best of all, it boasted an impossible-to-beat pinball machine.

Being a pinball addict, I can assure you that Kass's pinball machine had the toughest terrain of any I had ever tried. Even the usually reliable flippers were against you. And I know no one who ever beat it for a free game.

The rest of Greenfield Park consisted of a post office and a movie theater, but that's being too kind. The theater was attached to the general store and consisted of two dozen benches, a screen and projector. The beauty part was that it featured good flicks, including Joan Crawford in *Mildred Pierce*.

I should have mentioned that there was a second Sol at The Manor: Sol Mandel, son of the non-witz owner. Sol was a tall, skinny guy who was studying hotel management at Brooklyn's Kingsboro Community College. Sol Mandel took his job very seriously, except when he was taking his job very humorously. Sometimes -- as you shall see -- we couldn't tell the difference.

Sol's job -- among other things -- was supervising the band and handling calls that came over the one phone in The Manor. So, if a Mrs. Ginsburg in Brooklyn wanted to speak to her sister, Tilly, who was vacationing at The Manor, she had to phone the hotel.

Sol would answer. Then, he'd get on the hotel's public address system and boom: "TELEPHONE CALL FOR TILLY GINSBERG; TILLY GINSBERG IS WANTED ON THE TELEPHONE."

Wherever she may have been, Tilly would hustle over to Sol's desk and take her call.

I should mention that Sol -- pretty much a pal of the band -- was a self-styled comedian. When he'd finish paging the guest for the phone call, he'd always ad-lib something ridiculous.

One of his favorite lines was from a radio show about the Royal Canadian Mounted Police called *Renfrew of the Royal Mounted*. Renfrew had a trusty dog named King.

So after paging Tilly Ginsberg, Sol would close with, "Go get 'em, King!" and we'd unfailingly crack up. Which proves that we didn't have much else to do except take outdoor showers in a hut next to the main house, although The Manor was the only house.

When we arrived at The Manor a few days short of the July 4th weekend holiday, we were shown to our quarters; which were neither *deluxe, luxe* or even *de.*

It was an attic alcove above the third floor that featured nothing more than four cots, a window and nothing resembling a bathroom. Washing, peeing or crapping had to be done one floor down in what amounted to a communal toilet with a washbasin.

What we soon would learn is that our room had wild temperature swings. At night, it felt like the Arctic Circle and by day it could pass for Equatorial Africa.

Up until that point, the band had its own table in the dining room. But on July 5th, Sol Mandel casually informed us that hereafter our meals would be taken in the children's dining room, otherwise known as Bedlam, Inc.

"Bullshit," roared Tuch. "Let's invite Sol up to our room after dinner and find out why we can't eat with the guests. We'll go nuts eating with those crazy kids."

As far as I can remember, this was the first labor dispute of my young life and that of the three other guys. Sure enough, Sol accepted our invitation and arrived promptly at 11 p.m., shortly after we had completed our night's worth of music.

I could tell that Rappy, Ivan and Tuch were as nervous as I was and puzzled over what rationale Sol would produce to support our confinement to the children's-dining-room lunacy.

The four of us sat on the edge of our beds while Sol wasted no time getting to the point.

"Boys," he intoned with the utmost seriousness, "there are three reasons why you have to eat with the kids."

There was a pregnant pause as we studied the possibilities in our heads. Sol continued: "A -- you're adorable."

At that point, our high-level conference had ended because the four of us were on the floor laughing and could not stop. You have to understand that "A You're Adorable" was number one on the hit parade, and Sol just disarmed us with a neat knuckler.

Sol led the cast of characters, of which there were many. One of our favorites was a 60-year-old car salesman named Sheldon Greenblatt. He loved hanging around the bandstand schmoozing with us during our breaks. Occasionally, he'd take us for a ride in his 1940 brown, four-door DeSoto sedan.

What we loved about Greenblatt was a running gag he pulled every day and that we eagerly anticipated. He would do it at breakfast, lunch or dinner, wherever he happened to be within earshot of The Manor's loudspeaker.

It went like this: Someone would phone a guest, and Sol Mandel would take the name, turn on the loudspeaker and broadcast: "Telephone call for Abe Friedman. Abe Friedman is wanted on the telephone."

If Greenblatt happened to be in the dining room, he'd leap out of his chair, take five steps, apply the brakes and say, "My name isn't Friedman" and return to his chair.

For some strange reason, we thought it was the best running gag of the summer.

What wasn't funny was the dearth of guests at Greenfield Manor around the first week of August. The situation got so serious that there were nights when we'd be thrilled if four couples made it to the dance floor.

Both Mandelowitz and Mandel finally concluded that they didn't need a dance band if there were no dancers. Another high-level conference was held and this time Sol Mandel was serious. He was granting us a two-week furlough without pay and then we'd return a week before Labor Day and finish the season.

That seemed fair enough. We accepted Handyman Sol's offer to drive us to Manhattan in his '34 Plymouth convertible. Sol and two guys sat in front and the other pair in the rumble seat.

We drew straws, and Rappy and I "won" the rumble seat. Ordinarily, a rumble seat ride could be as much fun as Coney Island's Cyclone. Except that it rained all the way from Ellenville to Williamsburg, and there never was a rumble seat designed that had its own umbrella.

According to plan, we returned for the big Labor Day weekend and, thankfully, Greenfield Manor was packed with guests.

The *smetena* flowed like wine and the *gribbines* were so good that Greenblatt even forgot to do his "I'm not Friedman" gag.

It was such a glorious weekend that we band members figured that our band's baby-sitter, Sol, would soften his heart and give us a going-away present, a kind of nutritional gift, allowing us just one dinner in the dining room, away from the snotty, screaming kids.

"There's one reason why you can't eat in the main dining room," Sol explained in a no-joke manner this time. "We're packed. There's no room!"

The four of us pissed and moaned about it for about two minutes until Ivan the Terrible Piano Player offered the perfect squelch.

"Who cares? Going away from Greenfield Manor is a going-away present enough!"

Ben and Molly Fischler in the Catskills

Editor's Note: The following monograph is dedicated to the memory of Rich Conaty. For many years, Rich provided musical pleasure with his weekly Big Broadcast *on WFUV-FM.*

MUSIC, PLACES AND
LOVELY PEOPLE

"These Foolish Things (Remind Me of You)"

That's the title of a Golden Oldie. Words by Holt Marvell, with music via Jack Strachey and Harry Link.

It became a hit in 1935. I was three at the time.

It could have been the first song I ever heard on our big, brown RCA Victor radio that dominated our tiny living room at 582 Marcy in Williamsburg.

To this day, I still find the words to "These Foolish Things" both haunting and meaningful.

> *A cigarette that bears a lipstick's traces.*
> *An airline ticket to romantic places.*
> *And still my heart has wings.*
> *These foolish things remind me of you.*

Foolish things as reminders? You bet. Play a song, and it'll remind me of something. In my head, there's a song about practically everything in this world.

When I was four years old in 1936, I began absorbing popular tunes on the radio. In no time at all, I became enthralled with the Big Band music of Benny Goodman, Artie Shaw and Paul Whiteman, just to name a few.

Over the years, I realized that certain songs reminded me of specific things I was doing at that moment, whether it was in the living room, hockey rink or at P.S. 54. The tunes still open my memory bank.

Here's a for-instance: When I play Dinah Shore's version of "You'd Be So Nice to Come Home To," I'm reminded of the early 1940s and my passion for building model war planes. One night, Dinah sang "You'd Be So Nice" while I was finishing a flying model of the Army's Ryan Trainer. When I hear Dinah, I visualize that almost-completed aircraft.

Any time I hear Peggy Lee warbling "Somebody Else Is Taking My Place," the 1942 St. Louis Cardinals come to mind. In August of that year, the Cards trailed first-place Brooklyn by eight games. St. Lou seemed dead. But the Dodgers faded. The Cards caught them and won the National League pennant. At that moment, I made a slight change in the tune. My amended title was, "Somebody Else Is Taking First Place."

How about Bing Crosby and Connie Boswell pumping out "An Apple for the Teacher"? When I hear their duet, Poof!, just like that, P.S. 54 comes to mind along with a lovely teacher, Mrs. Frances Hochberg, who inspired me to write.

Eddie Condon's rendition of that evergreen, "Sugar," reminds me of our neighborhood record shop on Tompkins and Willoughby. You could buy a 78 rpm disk in 1940 for a dime or, at most, a quarter.

Here are some samples and the year I originally heard them:

1936: "I'm an Old Cowhand": At four years old, I was too young to know that Johnny Mercer wrote this ditty as a cowboy spoof. Now I know better, as evidenced by his ironic lines:

> *I'm an old cowhand from the Rio Grande*
> *But my legs ain't bowed and my cheeks ain't tan.*
> *I'm a cowboy who never saw a cow,*

Never roped a steer 'cause I don't know how

Sure ain't a fixing to start in now

Oh, yippee yi yo kayah,

1937: "Bei Mir Biest Du Schon": By age five, I had a pretty good idea that I was Jewish. The Andrews Sisters' half-Yiddish version of "Bei Mir" resonated with me for months. It became my Jewish anthem and, while "Bei Mir" was at it, also made stars out of the not-so-Jewish Andrews Sisters.

1941: "The Things I Love": World War II had ravaged Europe for three years when Jan Savitt's band recorded one of the sweetest tunes this side of Heaven. Alan DeWitt's voice is long forgotten, but not the opening lyrics:

The glow of sunset in the summer skies,

The golden flicker of the fireflies.

The gleam of love light in your lovely eyes,

These are the things I love.

I was nine years old when it topped the hit parade. Don't get miffed when I confess that my first vision upon hearing "The Things I Love" always is a chocolate ice cream soda (no whipped cream) at Al and Shirley's candy store on Nostrand and Vernon.

1943: "I Thought About You": This is another Johnny Mercer gem penned while he was riding the New York Central's 20th Century Limited to Chicago. Here's how it opens:

I took a trip on the train and I thought about you.

I passed a shadowy lane and I thought about you.

It calls to mind my '43 trip to Albany on the Central's brand-new Empire State Express. I was heading for a week's visit with my Aunt Hattie, Uncle Paul and kid-cousin Ira Sheier. When I hear Mercer emote his tune, visions of the Central's streamlined Empire State steam locomotive still dance in my head.

Unknown Year: "My Buddy": This standard always stirs sentimental thoughts about two pals who died way too soon. The first, Howie Sparer, is someone I mention throughout this book. I'll say it again: He was my best friend. He was so since kindergarten and he remained so throughout our lives.

I'd see him every Wednesday in 1962-63 at Rangers games in the old Garden. His mezzanine seat was right behind the press box. But he was missing on one Wednesday night in January '63.

This was unusual; Howie never missed a home game on Wednesday nights. (I was told he had a bad cold.) That Friday, I went to Baltimore and then Hershey for a couple of minor league games.

I never saw Howie again. He died that Saturday night of complications too complicated for me to understand. He was just 31. I never fully recovered from the passing of my pal Howie.

My other lost chum was Paul Ringe, who I knew from Brooklyn College and later as a professional drummer. Paul and I socialized at hockey games, parties and elsewhere. About 20 or so years ago, I was stunned to learn that Paul had died of a heart attack.

Many musician buddies attended Paul's funeral at Riverside Chapel on the Upper West Side. During one eulogy, a saxophonist powerfully played that sweet tune from yesteryear, "My Buddy."

Nights are long since you went away,

I think about you all through the day.

My buddy, my buddy,

Nobody quite so true.

One fun musical memory involved the wedding of Alice Perlmutter and Barry Cohen on April 12, 1992, at Sailor's Snug Harbor on Staten Island. That afternoon, Paul's band swung like the Brighton Express in B-flat major.

And there was The Ringe Man, himself -- Handsome Paul -- pounding out "Drum Boogie" on his Slingerland tom-toms with a few pulsating stick whacks on the Zildjian cymbals.

Howie was quite a music man as well. One Sunday in August 1953, he invaded the Brickman Hotel lobby in South Fallsburg, hellbent for the 88 keys on the lounge upright.

The Sparer posse witnessing this event included Jack Goldstein and yours truly. A gal horde crowded around Howie as he banged out his favorite of all favorites, "It Had to Be You."

Ah, memories. On that same trip, we traveled via Moe Goldstein's new, green, Hudson Hornet automobile. (Moe being Jack's dad.) Plowing through a downpour on Route 17, the Hud inexplicably skidded across the four-lane highway.

That should have killed us three times over, but, miraculously, the Hudson came to a halt just inches from a ditch. I kid you not. Two seconds after the car stopped moving, Jack's radio generously played "May The Good Lord Bless and Keep You."

For best pals like Howie and Paul, the music stopped -- but the melody lingers on -- sweetly, lovingly. Sort of like this, another verse from "These Foolish Things":

A tinkling piano in the next apartment,

Those stumblin' words that told you what my heart meant,

A fairgrounds' painted swings

These foolish things remind me of you!

All of you.

Howie Sparer, 1950s

About the Author

Stan Fischler, known as The Hockey Maven, is a December 2021 inductee to the U.S. Hockey Hall of Fame. He has won eight New York Emmy awards and the Lester Patrick Award for his contributions to ice hockey in the United States. He has covered hockey in print, broadcast or online for over 50 years.

In other realms -- particularly the underground -- he's known as The Subway Maven. Stan's book, *Uptown, Downtown*, was the original history of the New York subway system. He wrote a sequel, *The Subway*, and he's also written histories of the metropolitan-area commuter railroads as well as books on subways and transit systems around the world. A semi-auto-biographical book, *Confessions of a Trolley Dodger from Brooklyn*, sold out.

During the 1970s, Stan and his wife, Shirley, ran the New York bureau of the *Toronto Daily Star*. Stan interviewed such celebrities as New York Mayor John Lindsay, actress Carol Channing and actor Jerry Stiller. He covered major events such as the New York City and Newark race riots and major sporting events such as the World Series and the American debut of international soccer star Pele. When the Rolling Stones visited New York for a concert, he interviewed them as well as early film stars such as Ruby Keeler and Mae West.

Fischler has written for many publications, including *The New York Times*, *Sports Illustrated*, *Sport*, *Newsweek*, *Hockey Digest* and *The Hockey News*. Fischler has authored or co-authored more than 100 books; in addition to the titles mentioned above, he has written extensively on both hockey and baseball.

For television, Fischler co-produced an award-winning documentary, *Little Rink*, about table hockey, and produced, wrote and emceed a Metro Channel series, *Subway Series*, which won several awards. Stan has also appeared on many NHL documentaries over the years.

Whenever he had the time, Stan did stand-up comedy in Manhattan and Long Island. As a historian, he gave tours sponsored by the 92d Street Y, including walks through Williamsburg, Brooklyn and the Catskills (the Borscht Belt), where he once played drums in a dance band.

In January 1999, Mayor Rudolph Giuliani designated Fischler a Centennial Historian of the City of New York.

Today, Fischler does weekly historic features for NHL.com as well as for the New York Islanders (the column is called "Maven's Memories") and the New Jersey Devils ("Sundays with Stan"). His hockey newsletter, *The Fischler Report*, is the only 52-weeks-a-year publication of its kind and is in its 29th year. It now appears online along with Stan's new online hockey segment, "Java Jive."

Fischler holds a master's degree in education from Long Island University and has taught news and feature writing at Queens College, Columbia University and Fordham University. Dozens of interns he has mentored over the years are now in prominent TV, print-media, or NHL-related roles.

Stan now lives in Israel with his youngest son, Simon, his daughter-in-law, Lilach, three grandchildren, and an assortment of dogs.